Published by
Edward Elgar Publishing Limited
Gower House
Croft Road
Aldershot
Hants GU11 3HR
England

Gower Publishing Company
Old Post Road
Brookfield
Vermont 05036
USA

British Library Cataloguing in Publication Data

The structure of modern ideology: critical
  perspectives on social and political theory
  1. ideology. Sociological perspectives
  I. O'Sullivan, Noel
  306'.42

ISBN 1 85278 036 3

Printed and bound in Great Britain by
Biddles Ltd, Guildford and King's Lynn

The Structure of Modern Ideology

Critical Perspectives on Social and Political Theory

Edited by
Noel O'Sullivan
Reader in Politics, University of Hull

EDWARD ELGAR

Contents

Contributors

Margaret Canovan is Senior Lecturer at the University of Keele

Diana Coole is Lecturer at the University of Leeds

Gordon Graham is Reader at the University of St Andrews

Harro Höpfl is Senior Lecturer at the University of Lancaster

Jorge Larrain is Reader at the University of Birmingham

David Manning is Senior Lecturer at the University of Durham

Kenneth Minogue is Professor at the London School of Economics

Noel O'Sullivan is Reader at the University of Hull

Preface

When the term 'ideology' was coined by Destutt de Tracy at the end of the eighteenth century it had a reasonably precise meaning. De Tracy belonged to a group of philosophers known as the Idéologues,[1] and he used the term to refer to their dream of bringing about a revolution in the nature of man and society by applying the principles of Newtonian science to the study of the human mind. Since de Tracy's time, the history of the concept has been one of multiple revisions on the one hand and ever-increasing ambiguity on the other. The result is that the precise value of the concept for the purpose of political analysis is a matter of intense disagreement. While the present volume makes no claim to resolve that disagreement, it aims to contribute to the contemporary debate in three related ways. The first is by identifying the kind of discourse to which ideology belongs and the principal positions adopted within it. It is with this theme that the first three essays are concerned. The second is by considering in some detail the various revisions of the concept of ideology made by the schools of philosophy which have exercised most influence upon recent discussion. This is the concern of the three essays in the second part. Finally, two concluding essays consider in what sense it is possible to have non-ideological politics.

So far as the debate at large is concerned, it seems wise to begin on a note of salutary scepticism. In an essay on 'Isms and Ideology', Harro Höpfl situates some of the most familiar and influential ways of thinking about ideology within a type of discourse about politics whose novelty is not always appreciated. The main characteristic of this discourse is the fact that 'historians, sociologists, political scientists, philosophers and students of litera-ture, as well as politicians and journalists, have come to depend for their livelihood upon their ability to constitute and structure

identities and fields of study for themselves by means of -isms'. This might be harmless enough, were it not for the fact that it has fostered a deeply ingrained tendency in the modern mind to reify '-isms', so that the social sciences, for example, are populated by a vast range of mysterious entities – variously conceived of as 'systems', 'historical forces', 'movements', 'structures', 'mechanisms', and 'principles' – which are believed to mould and shape human affairs. In the course of a subtle piece of intellectual history, Höpfl traces the origins of this almost demonological type of discourse back as far as the early seventeenth century, and examines the way it eventually became possible for statements like 'fascism is a form/consequence/outgrowth of capitalism', to be accepted without any sense of their problematic nature.

Within the framework of the debate itself, two opposed schools of thought can be distinguished, one of which may be termed the 'restrictive' school, and the other (following Martin Seliger)[2] the 'inclusive'. For the restrictive school, only a limited range of political positions are ideological; those outside that range are non-ideological. In the present volume, Kenneth Minogue's analysis of what he terms 'the ideological project' provides an eloquent illustration of the restrictive position. This project is rooted in one of the fundamental features of much Western political thought, which is the quest for a totally objective vantage point from which to judge the political arena. What might at first sight seem to be merely a recondite issue in the theory of knowledge turns out in practice, Minogue maintains, to encourage a highly destructive style of politics. It does this because thinkers who believe that they occupy the Archimedian point are inclined to conclude that the whole existing order of civilization is an unnatural and alienating mask which prevents the 'real' or 'true' human being from adequately expressing himself. Notoriously, defenders of the ideological project pose as liberators and benefactors, but the consequences of their attempts to tear away the mask of civilization are uniformly oppressive. Elsewhere,[3] Minogue has subjected the Marxist version of this project to extended criticism. Here, however, he illustrates the nature of the ideological project by reference to a thinker whose significance for the theory of ideology has suffered from relative neglect, despite the fact that he has some claims – as Minogue shows – to be regarded as at once the most extreme and most suggestive representative of that project.

Noble as Nietzsche's attack on what he regarded as the slave morality of the Western world may sound, Minogue rejects it on the three grounds upon which he rejects every other version of the ideological project: intellectual dogmatism; travesty of the existing order at large; and a systematic caricature of the nature of the state in particular.

While Minogue writes from a restrictive standpoint, David Manning defends an unreservedly inclusive position. For defenders of this position there is no question of identifying a specific ideological project, since every political position is intrinsically ideological. In Manning's view, ideology is inescapable because it is rooted in the unavoidably different ways of life attendant upon the human condition. In a political perspective, it is what gives group identity and practical inspiration to those who share a way of life, enabling them to sustain their own identity in political competition with other lifestyles. From this perspective, it is naive to believe that politics can ever be about truth, reason, impartiality, or justice, unless those terms mean whatever each ideology defines them to mean. On this view, then, all ideologies have the same objective, which is to win power by persuading as many as possible to subscribe to them.

To some, such a position will appear unduly sceptical. To others, it will appear refreshingly realistic. In either case, however, it has the merit of compelling a return to first principles. The three essays in Part II are intended to facilitate that return, through a review of the kind of philosophic considerations that have contributed to recent theorizing about ideology.

In the course of a comprehensive survey of recent developments in Marxist theory, Jorge Larrain argues that a mistaken impression of novelty has frequently been created by the idea that there is a single, unified conception of ideology within Marxism. In an essay which enriches the original doctrine of Marx and Engels, Larrain dismisses this oversimplified view. Above all, Larrain stresses the continuing relevance of the original doctrine, on the ground that the key polarities which he identifies within it continue to define the principal philosophic issues presented by the concept of ideology.

Although the school of philosophy known as phenomenology has equivocal implications for politics, Diana Coole uses the writings of Merleau-Ponty to illustrate how its doctrines may support

what she terms a theory of 'existential ideology'. What that means emerges from Merleau-Ponty's critique of the Marxist theory of ideology, on the ground that it ultimately derives from an uncritical acceptance of the Cartesian view of the world. For Merleau-Ponty, the principal objection to Cartesianism is that it encourages a 'rationalist' theory of ideology which mistakenly assumes that it is possible to rise above all particular social perspectives and reach a non-ideological definition of the nature of man. An existential theory, by contrast, accepts that there is no escape from ideology. Not the least interesting aspect of the essay is the light that it sheds on themes already touched upon by Minogue, Manning and Larrain. Diana Coole, however, adds a new dimension to the debate in the course of exploring Merleau-Ponty's belief that a thorough-going relativism is not the inevitable concomitant of an existential theory of ideology.

One of the most influential theories of ideology to have emerged in the post-war era is that of Hannah Arendt. Certain vital aspects of Arendt's theory, however, have never been very clear. Amongst these, the precise role assigned by her to ideology in totalitarianism has been the subject of conflicting interpretations. In particular, it has always been uncertain whether or not Arendt believed that the leaders of totalitarian regimes took their ideologies seriously. Drawing on new material in Arendt's unpublished papers, Margaret Canovan provides a systematic reinterpretation of this controversial aspect of Arendt's work.

The book concludes with two essays which explore, from very different standpoints, the possibility of escaping from ideological commitment. For Gordon Graham, the possibility of so doing turns upon the question of whether a purely pragmatic type of politics is conceivable. His essay argues that it is, and explores the logical implications of the idea of pure political pragmatism in some depth. Approaching the same problem from a different perspective, Noel O'Sullivan argues that ideology always entails what he terms a programmatic conception of politics and that, in the absence of programmatic politics, the concept of ideology ceases to be intelligible. To the extent that it is possible to identify a formal or non-programmatic kind of politics, therefore, the charge of being ideological would not be so much false as absurd.

NOTES

1. See A. Picovet, *Les Idéologues* (1891).
2. See M. Seliger, *Ideology and Politics* (London: Allen & Unwin, 1976).
3. K. Minogue, *Alien Powers* (London: Weidenfeld & Nicolson, 1985).

PART I
The Structure of Ideology

1.   Isms and Ideology[1]

Harro Höpfl

In the conversation of scholars in the humanities and social sciences, as well as in common political speech, it has long been an unquestioned habit to use -isms, particularly when the subject under consideration is ideology or ideologies. Thus, it is commonly understood that the subject matter of discussions on ideology is 'all those isms' and generalizations and speculations are made, assertions are validated or invalidated, and inferences drawn on the basis of things already identified as -isms as the agreed referent. Conversely, the conventional wisdom of writers about 'feminism', for example, is that we must first distinguish 'liberal feminism', 'socialist (or Marxist) feminism', 'radical feminism', 'anarcha-feminism' and so on. Equally, however, '-isms' regularly denote things of much more general, and even more problematic, identity than ideology or ideologies.

In short, it seems as if historians, sociologists, political scientists, philosophers and students of literature, as well as politicians and journalists, depend for their livelihoods upon their ability to constitute and structure identities and fields of study for themselves by means of -isms. But the nature of the entities thus labelled or identified is far from clear. An investigation of how this habit established itself might shed some light on the obscurities and confusions generated by the use of this suffix. Those who have little taste for history may rapidly harvest the results of this necessarily labour-intensive enquiry from the summary provided on pp. 14–15. And even they may find something to interest them in the reflections that it has occasioned. Equally however, the account of -isms that is offered here explains why any challenge to the habit of using them is likely to be ignored.

We may begin, obviously enough, with some etymology. The derivation of the suffix is from the Greek *-ismos* or *-isma*,

3

employed to form nouns of action, generally but by no means always from verbs. This linguistic habit was assimilated by the Romans, who latinized the masculine form of the suffix as *-ismus*, and from them it passed directly or indirectly[2] into all European languages. The employment of the suffix until the sixteenth century was in the Greek and Roman manner, to indicate an action, a course or habit of acting, or the result of an action.

However, the use of the suffix remained rather rare, and was confined to formal language. What is more important for our purposes is that there seems not to have been a single instance before the sixteenth century when the suffix was used to denote a body of doctrine, or the complex constituted by a body of doctrine and its partisans. The linguistic habit of using '-isms' in these senses seems to be exclusively early modern in origin. What is more, it is little noticed and almost entirely unexplained, so much so that it appears to be mere chance whether a particular etymological dictionary registers the existence of -ism formations at all.[3] And yet the invention of even a single word which passes into common speech is something of interest to the historian of ideas. For changes in the world are much more usually disguised and obscured by insensible transformations in the meanings of old words,[4] than signalled by new words. And when a whole flood of neologisms[5] passes into common usage, we have good reason for suspecting some remarkable transformation in the perceived world of the community which finds the neologisms serviceable.

The difficulty is not of course that of explaining the survival and fecundity of the -ism habit once it had become established, but of explaining how it established itself in the first place. An historically satisfactory account would consist (a) of an identification of the time and milieu in which -isms first proliferated; and (b) ideally, of an exhibition of the continuum of initiatives and responses of language-users, between the earliest uses and the time at which the habit can be regarded as established. Most satisfactory of all would be to find someone with sensitivity to language who remarked on the occurrence at the time. I am able to satisfy these ideal requirements only to a very limited degree, and offer my conclusions along with an invitation to the better-informed to do better. The tentative character of my observations is inescapable, given that there is no alternative here to inductive generalization from such random instances as have come to one's

notice. And although there must necessarily be a first user or coiner of every neologism, no-one can ever be certain that their own identification of the first user is correct. On the other hand, the appearance of a whole spate of neologisms allows a greater confidence about the generalization that the spate in fact occurred, and that it occurred about that time, than about the dating of any individual first use.

These caveats being presupposed, two periods in European thought appear to have been particularly productive of -isms. The later, and infinitely the more fertile, is the first half of the nineteenth century, of which I shall speak shortly. The earlier was the later sixteenth and early seventeenth century. What is significant about the earlier period is that the use of -isms to designate doctrines seems to have originated then, and it is with this period I now concern myself.

The context in which -isms make their appearance in this new sense is religio-political controversies – and more precisely the fragmentation of Christian orthodoxy into confessions ('heresies' from their opponents' point of view). This was in any case a time fertile in various kinds of linguistic innovations, and also the time at which vernaculars began to vie with Latin as vehicles for scholarly communication. And it seems to be in the vitriolic and highly standardized exchanges of polemic between 'papists' and 'the new religion', 'the so-called reformed religion', or 'the Fifth Gospel' (to designate the parties to these exchanges by some of the names they called each other) that this new use of the -ism suffix first emerged. The use of the term to designate philosophical schools, usually in a derogatory manner, seems to be contemporaneous,[6] and the fact did not go altogether unremarked. As early as 1570, the compiler of an early *Manipulus Vocabulorum: A Dictionarie of Englishe and Latine Words*,[7] perhaps sensitized to -isms by the fact that his work was arranged according to syllables, noted three sorts of -ism. The first he described as of 'common speech' (he meant the common speech of scholars, not plebeians), and gave as examples 'Sc[h]isme, Baptisme, Sophisme, Exorcisme' and 'divers others'. These are merely words in the strict Greco-Roman etymological tradition to which we have already referred. 'The second be taken of a countrey or language, as of latine *latinisme* . . .; Greek *Graecisme*; . . . Barbarie, *Barbarism*; . . . Laconie, *laconisme*; Attic, *Atticisme*; Britannie, *Britanisme*; Scotte, *Scotisme* . . .

and many others'.[8] But most interesting of all is Levins' third category, which he did not however identify as a contemporary innovation:

> The third is of sectes and factions, whom we cal after the masters and beginners of opinions and doctrines, as of pape, *papisme*; Luther, *Lutheranisme*; Ariane, *Arianisme*; Calvine, *Calvinisme*; Plato, *Platonisme* and such other sects, the followers whereof do end in -*ist*, as . . . Baptiste, . . . *sophiste* . . .; *latiniste* . . . *laconiste* . . . and such other, as many or mo[re] as ende in isme: for commonly they have both one primitive [i.e. original, root]: the first, signifying the sect itself, tongue or manner of people, and the latter betokening him, that eyther is good and cunning [knowledgeable], or else is studious and earnest in the same.

From about the middle of the sixteenth century, then, the -ism suffix was not infrequently employed in French, English and Latin in a new way to refer to theological or religious positions considered heretical, and also to refer to the doctrines of various philosophical schools.[9] At any rate, the Jesuit Emond Auger in his *Pedagogue d'Armes* of 1568 referred to his opponents' 'sale et vilain Calvinisme'; Cardinal William Allen in 1581 found 'Paganisme, Arianisme, Pelagianisme, Zwinglianisme' to be characteristic of his opponents, and the Jesuit Antonio Possevino in his various writings of the 1580s and 1590s found occasion to accuse his opponents of (*inter alia*) *Mahometismus, Saracenismus, Atheismus* (for which he had a particular fondness; he even used it in one of his book-titles), *Arianismus, Judaismus, Calvinismus, Anabaptismus, Lutheranismus, Picardismus*, the last six plus some others being produced as a single list to designate the contents of the doctrines of the Polish Confederation.[10]

Now neither disputes between philosophical schools nor the relentless war between orthodoxy and heresy, schism and unbelief are peculiar to the sixteenth century. And yet neither Greek, Roman, nor medieval writers seem ever to have felt the need to go beyond the personal suffix -*istes*, -*ista*, -*(i)anus*, -*eius*, or any of the related European ways of forming a personal noun to denote the adherent of some person or doctrine, to the grammatically-related abstract substantive -*ismus* or -*isma* in these contexts.[11] There is no end of examples of the personal suffix -*ista* or -*(i)anus* in Roman, medieval and early modern writings.[12] It may be noted

in passing, that these suffixes were frequently (but by no means universally) derogatory.[13] But to designate what an *-ista, -(i)anus*, etc., does or believes, writers were perfectly content to use expressions like 'the doctrine/teachings of –', or 'these men/*-ists/* fanatics/schismatics/heretics hold that –'. Where -ism formations were generated, these did not refer to a body of doctrine. The only exceptions to this which I have been able to find prove on inspection to be more apparent than real: *Judaismos (-mus)*, which is Hellenistic Greek and appears in the Greek Old Testament,[14] *Christianismos (-mus)*, which first appears in the writings of Ignatius (martyred 107 or 117 AD)[15] and has a continuous history thereafter, though *Christianitas* appears to have been much more common, and *Paganismus*, which Du Cange traces to the pronouncements of a Church Council in 744 AD. *Christianismus* appears to have been suggested by, and formed on, the analogy of *Judaismus* (in Ignatius, the context in which it is used is an express contrast between the two); the latter in turn, according to the Oxford English Dictionary,[16] seems to have been modelled on the Greeks. The emphasis in all these words is therefore on acting, on a manner or habit of conduct, and not on an intellectual system or doctrine. These words closely parallel other Greek words with the -ism suffix, in which there is no suggestion at all of a doctrinal content: barbarism, solecism, sophism.[17]

The early modern innovation, then, is to find people accused of Anabaptism, Lutheranism, Calvinism, Romanism or papism, separatism, sectarianism, Arminianism and so forth. Perhaps little more was generally involved than the addition to the vocabulary of abuse[18] (an art assiduously cultivated on all sides) of a convenient way of forming substantives to designate a body of false belief. And certainly there are few examples of the practice (which in the nineteenth century becomes prevalent) of using -isms to denote an agent or agency of some kind: -isms were used as object, not as subject, and the personal *-ist* or *-(i)an* was reserved for the latter. But it is worth remarking that right from the establishment of the linguistic habit, -isms have tended to shed any determinate referent, and to become vague and derogatory synonyms for heresy and for pernicious doctrines and practices in general.[19] As I hope to show later, it is of some significance that -isms have never referred unambiguously to something as

(relatively) determinate as a doctrine or a body of doctrine, even when their form has suggested such a referent.

In sum, the habit of using -isms arose in the later sixteenth and seventeenth century in the context of doctrinal conflict. It must be said, however, that even in the later sixteenth century -ism terms remain comparatively uncommon; it was far more usual to designate one's opponents in the traditional manner by means of the personal suffixes *-ist*, *-(i)an*[20] or any of the other cognate European ways of forming a personal substantive to designate the adherent of some individual doctrine, cause,[21] opinion or sect. Sixteenth-century German appears not to have contracted the -ism habit at all. Most dictionaries of the time do not note either the innovation or instances. And although -isms became fairly common thereafter, the alternative suffixes *-cy* or *-ty* (or their European equivalents) were better established, and remained pre-ferred ways of constituting abstract substantives, especially in German.[22] Where -isms were invented, especially in English and French, the existence of a group of people, a 'heretical' sect, seems to have been a prerequisite for their invention. And many -ism terms which succeeded in passing into common usage did not retain any clear doctrinal referent, or never had one in the first place: those who attacked 'separatisme', 'puritanisme', 'Jesui-tisme', 'Machiavell(ian)isme', 'Arminianisme', 'Cavalierisme', or 'Normanisme'[23] did not conceive their target to be primarily a doctrine, if indeed they thought of it as a doctrine at all. And all this suggests that the main reason for the spread of the -ism habit is to be found precisely in the original Greco-Roman function of the suffix, which designated not a doctrine but rather a way of life (*Christianismos*, *Judaismos*, *Hellenismos*, *Paganismus*), or a peculiarity or habit of conduct. The 'confessions', 'sects', 'heresies' designated in -ism were not merely a matter of assent to some abstract proposition. The fact that the primary connotation of the -ism suffix today is taken to be that of 'doctrine' thus seems to derive from the sixteenth- and seventeenth-century use of the suffix (in the traditional Greco-Roman manner) to designate cer-tain ways of life, of whose character heretical doctrine was deemed to be constitutive.

For the rest of the seventeenth and much of the eighteenth century, there appear not to have been many new coinages of -isms.[24] The *Encyclopédie ou Dictionnaire Raisonné des Sciences*,

des Arts et des Metiers, the war-machine of the *philosophes* but also an attempt to abridge the sum of extant knowledge at about mid-century, used the suffix quite freely in its titles for articles on the history of philosophy as a technical term for philosophies or doctrines, the format being, for example, '*Hobbisme, ou Philosophie de Hobbes*'.[25] This is a straightforward continuation and extension of previous practice, except in so far as the suffix in this context was no longer necessarily abusive; the article '*Eclectisme*', for example, is by no means hostile, whereas the article '*Jésuite*' (not '*Jésuitisme*') is unredeemedly so. There were of course favourite -isms in common use amongst *philosophes* which have both the abusiveness of the earlier, and the indeterminacy and spurious air of technicality and precision of the later, use of the suffix: 'fanaticism', 'enthusiasm', 'barbarism', 'despotism'.[26] Apart from these, Scottish writers (the flower of the British Enlightenment) such as Hume, Robertson, Smith, Ferguson, seem to have found little or no use for -isms. And the authors of *The Federalist*, for example, in fact appear never to have spoken of 'federalism', 'constitutionalism' or 'republicanism' (unlike any book ever written about them), even though the latter word was extant, as were analogous formations like 'feudalism', which they did not use either, and 'despotism', which was sanctified by its usage in *L'Esprit des Lois*. It is not until the end of the eighteenth century that we come upon a positive spate of neologisms, whereupon the habit entrenches itself to such a degree as to become universal and unshakeable.[27]

The early nineteenth century was a time of unparalleled fertility in linguistic innovation in Europe. -Isms constitute only a fraction, albeit a crucial one, of the flood of nineteenth-century neologisms,[28] a time which witnessed the arrival, or the turning to new uses, of such terms as industry, industrialist, class, masses, intellectual, crank, doctrinaire, ideology, organization, bureaucracy, sociology, nationality. This, however, is also the time which begat: individualism, collectivism, socialism, communism, conservatism, absolutism, constitutionalism, commercialism, medievalism, egalitarianism, humanism, liberalism, utilitarianism, capitalism, primitivism, classicism, romanticism, nationalism, to name but a representative selection from a whole plethora of durable -isms.

This plague of -isms did not pass unnoticed at the time. So

prevalent had the practice become by the 1830s, and in all the major European languages ('liberalism' was apparently invented in Spain, 'conservatism' in England, 'individualism', 'socialism' and 'communism' in France, all these terms travelling speedily to Germany) that 'Ism' (as a noun), 'ismatic' and 'ismatize' (as adjective and verb respectively) were devised to reprehend the phenomenon.[28]

The first striking feature of these neologisms is that they no longer automatically denigrated, as well as designated. Metternich opined that all -isms are abusive. And there is indeed often a greater urgency in polemic about having a name for a doctrine or mode of conduct of which one disapproves than for what one approves: truth and right-doing need no special label. But this does not get us very far. I asserted earlier that -isms of the first vintage designated heretics and their whole manner of conducting themselves. Something of this survives into the nineteenth-century neologisms: they designate, at least initially, the whole phenomenon of a minority conspicuous because of its heterodoxy in doctrine and singularity in conduct. But a counter -ism, with which the heterodox may describe their opponents, is an obvious next move in polemic. And once the habit of employing -isms had become established, it is common to find people inventing a name to describe their own position along with one to designate their opponents,[29] or indeed to adopt the name first applied to them by those opponents.[30] And thus the political world comes to be demarcated into -isms.

The next feature of these -isms also seems striking enough, although it has been little remarked upon. They all seem to emerge out of a rather unusual context, which might perhaps best be described as educated political polemic. This is a kind of political discourse which is by no means universal, for it is conducted not by professional politicians, nor by writers in their service, but by intellectuals. And what the discourse of intellectuals presupposes is that political activity ought to be construed as the conflict of doctrines and that the right doctrine is the key to right political conduct; in other words that the qualification for political activity is intellect. Now although that opinion bears a resemblance to Plato's, it is not one which was at all common before the Enlightenment. For example, when a man set himself to write a book *de regimine principum*, a mirror for princes, or even a

manual of statecraft in the manner of Machiavelli or his opponents, he did not do so in the belief that his superior intellect or doctrine would enable him to make a better job of ruling than existing princes and magistrates. What is presupposed in this kind of writing is a common knowledge of what is right, which has to be put into a manageable and memorable form and passed on, and (or) a knowledge of affairs of state, of the *arcana imperii*, the 'kingly mystery' or 'cabinet-counsels'.[31] And even Hobbes, who thought there were 'certain rules' (that is, sure, reliable rules) analogous to those of geometry, which if followed would make civil government into a 'science', none the less conceded, when it came to arguments about which form of government was superior in aptitude to keep the peace, that what he had to offer was merely probable reasonings.[32]

The belief that the qualification for right political conduct is a 'scientific' understanding of the world appears as a premise and implication of the thought of the *philosophes* and *économistes* (or *Physiocrates*). It generated a new form of employment (full-time, but without reliable remuneration) and this perhaps accounts for the invention of the term 'intellectual' about this time or slightly subsequently. And in the sort of writing in which -isms were most frequently coined and employed subsequently, interpretation of the world and political prescription went hand in hand. Indeed, a rationalization was offered. Comte, following in the footsteps of St-Simon (and like him a notable coiner of neologisms), made 'savoir pour prévoir' his motto. *Savoir pour prévoir* was in fact the animating belief of all the 'social physicists', 'sociologists', 'social scientists', whether reactionary, socialist, utilitarian, liberal, conservative or whatever. What was required for a correct politics, was 'the unity of theory and practice'. And since it was an occupational belief of 'social science' that there is a motor of history (history being conceived as a unilinear process from one stage or state of society to the next), and that the working of this motor is intelligible to science, it was imperative that one's prescriptions should have the character of predictions inferred from the march of history, and should be seen to be so inferred. To make 'correct' prescriptions for political conduct was therefore to offer a diagnosis of the present, and to diagnose the present it was required that one see it as a 'stage' in historical 'development', the single most indispensable concept in nineteenth-century social

thought. He who would participate in politics fully qualified, so to speak, had therefore to be a historian, a 'philosophical' historian of course, and not that species of fact-grubbing antiquarians who earned themselves the lofty contempt of Comte. In other words, what was needed was someone who did not lose himself in the *minutiae* of detailed research, but rather who contemplated the large movements, the play of historical forces, the cunning of reason, the march of mind, the laws of historical development, social dynamics, the unfolding of the positive spirit, the passage from undifferentiated homogeneity to differentiated heterogeneity, and so on and so forth.

It is here that -isms came into their own, and the characteristic meanings and functions which they acquired in the course of their employment in this context have never left them. For what was required in the political discourse of intellectuals was as follows. Intellectuals served two masters, with predictable consequences. On the one hand, theirs was an activity of the understanding: to apprehend their time (and indeed the world) in thought. But understanding was not an end in itself: it was with a view to controlling the world. And this required rhetoric, the art and skill of persuading, as well as that sophistication in analysis on which the intellectual prides himself. The scholar is not alienated by tomes, but tomes, so it was confidently believed, do not change the world; they do not persuade the actual agents or factors of historical change. To persuade *them*, something altogether more crisp and compact than a tome is required. -Isms performed both functions *à merveille*: they served in the construction of developmental histories as the name for the large forces and agencies operative in 'social change', and they served to abridge and summarize such histories for ready reference in the cut and thrust of polemic. -Isms were thus no longer simply names, even abusive names, for a body of doctrine: they could now denote agents and causes, and not merely (as hitherto) the contents of someone's beliefs.

A curiosity of the history of -isms at this time is that the connotations and semantic capacities of the idea of a 'system' and those of words in -ism became identical. 'System' has from Greek times been a specialized academic term to denote a coherent, articulated complex of any kind, and thence derivatively an orderly exposition or theory of some subject. From the seventeenth century onward

it became increasingly common to speak of both the human body
and of the cosmos as 'systems'. Now, the cosmos, the body natural
and the 'body politic' or commonwealth or state, have traditionally
been linked by correspondence or analogy; presumably the
description of cosmos and human body as systems suggested the
analogy of the state, body politic or civil society as also a system.
In the eighteenth century at any rate, 'political system' became a
commonplace,[33] as did terms like 'the feudal system', 'the mercantile system', 'the natural system'.[34] Meanwhile the older use of
'system' to denote an articulated doctrine, a philosophy, continued
unabated. Thus by the nineteenth century, 'system' might denote
either a practice, or a 'concrete system' – that is, a system deemed
to exist in the world – or phenomenon of some complexity, or a
doctrine. It had therefore precisely the same range of connotations
as -isms, and thus 'the x-ist system' and 'x-ism' came to be alternative ways of saying the same thing,[35] each participating in the
reification and equivocation of the other. It seems that in this
assimilation, the conception of a whole made up of interacting
parts (which is inherent in the idea of a mechanical system) was
communicated to -isms, just as the idea of agency or capacity of
being an agent, already implicit in the Greco-Roman use of -isms,
was communicated to the idea of a system – a kind of entity of
which it had previously been possible to predicate only existence,
functioning, possession of interacting components, and other
intransitive characteristics. Some hypotheses such as these are
necessary to account for the Marxist use of 'capitalism' (Marx
himself seems to have preferred 'the capitalist system' or some
such formulation). For 'capitalism' almost never means a doctrine
or set of beliefs; indeed theorists of 'capitalism' commonly emphasize that doctrines are an epiphenomenon of capitalism which
can either dispense with them or alternatively generate them *ad
libitum*. Equally 'capitalism' almost never has as its focal meaning
'conduct characteristic of capitalists' or the 'manner of living of
capitalists'; it means precisely the 'system' within which capitalists
operate, and which determines their conduct.

A final point deserves emphasis. It has been noted earlier that
right from the inception of the habit of employing them, -isms
have tended to mean more (and not infrequently less) than *simply*
a body of beliefs or doctrines. Some remarks of Damourette and
Pichon[36] are in place here. Commenting on what they recognized

as the inadequacy of the interpretation of *-isme* as simply a 'suffixe de qualité', they argued that implicit in terms having that suffix (and also in the fact that their gender is masculine)[37] is the notion of 'quelque *force particulière*, et de quelque *principe vitale*, de quelque *volonté* tantôt obscure et rudimentaire, tantôt avouée et proclamée . . .' (my italics). They cited the natural science example of 'botulism', and they might have added 'embolism', 'organism', 'mechanism', 'magnetism' and 'aneurism', to all of which 'agency', 'power' or 'force' may readily be imputed. But even ordinary educated usage knows of a whole range of terms which illustrates the point, indirectly but instructively. Scepticism, stoicism, cynicism, optimism, pessimism, realism, idealism, hedonism, materialism, enthusiasm, dogmatism are all terms which originated in philosophical parlance. What is of interest is the change (in fact, attrition) of meaning these terms suffered as a consequence of their passage into common speech. For any doctrinal meaning such terms once had has been sloughed off (who would now associate 'optimism' with theodicy?) and they now designate merely an attitude or disposition. And, of course, attitudes or dispositions are precisely the sort of thing to which agency is imputed. They are deemed capable of prompting conduct; indeed the most usual use of the terms here cited is precisely to explain conduct by instancing motives (*force particulière*), principles (*principe vitale*), or desires (*volonté*). The change of meaning undergone here presupposes that common usage takes -ism to denote agents or agencies of an impersonal kind. It is not far-fetched to suppose that the -isms pretending to refer to phenomena which are our chief concern, ape their etymological elder brothers and paradigms, in respect of the implication of capacity for acting, the connotation of an active principle[38] or force. Hence their utility in the historiography and political prescription of those who conceive of the political world as a field of 'forces', 'factors' (in the etymological sense of 'doers') and other impersonal agencies.

The results of the investigation so far can be summarized by a tabulation of -isms according to their genealogy and according to their focal meaning. In terms of genealogy, there seem to be the following groups:

1. Nouns of action derived from, or modelled on, the Greco-Roman use of the suffix, and denoting a habit, practice, pecu-

liarity of conduct, or act, characteristic of some person or group, or simply a noun formed from a verb to designate a completed action, an act or the consequence of an act. This group does not concern us except in respect of the fact that the verbal, active connotation of this word-formation has been communicated to the -isms that do concern us.

2. -Isms generated in religious and religio-political polemic, where both context and -isms have a strongly marked doctrinal connotation, at any rate in their original use.

3. -Isms generated in politico-intellectual controversy since the early nineteenth century, a linguistic practice apparently derived by extension and analogy from (2).

4. -Isms acclimatized to scholarly use after being generated in polemic.

5. -Isms coined expressly for scholarly use.

6. -Isms which were first used by scholars but subsequently passed into common usage, usually at the expense of precision of reference.

In terms of meaning, -isms seem to denote the following broad categories:

(a) a body of related propositions, a doctrine, a philosophy in the technical or colloquial sense, an ideology; all these usually, at any rate initially, associated with a determinate body of adherents, identified as -ists;

(b) a tradition;

(c) a rhetoric – that is, a complex of terms used for their persuasive power;

(d) an attitude, disposition or general orientation;

(e) the spirit, essence, ethos, drift, flavour or tenor of a manner of thinking or acting, or both;

(f) an 'historical force', movement, agency, current, principle, system, or phenomenon of any kind.

Analysis into these categories, however, misses the crucial point that any particular example of an -ism may encompass part or all of this range of meanings, and that *use of -isms does not oblige the user to determine which meaning specifically he has in mind.* And to avoid the imputation that distinctions are here being made

for their own sake, it may be permissible to point out that the distinctions here are not fine or subtle, but rather broad and obvious. Thus no tradition consists simply of doctrines – it always implies characteristic practices, preoccupations and attitudes as well – and no tradition permits of a statement in the form of a limited and defined set of doctrines. A rhetoric, again, is neither a tradition nor a set of doctrines, in that a continuity of words and phrases habitually used in persuasion by no means indicates even as much substantive continuity or identity as is implied in a tradition.[39] An attitude or disposition, again, can and usually will, straddle several traditions or doctrines simultaneously and may be independent of doctrine altogether.[40] An ethos or spirit pretends to characterize the essence of a tradition or doctrine. And finally, any and all of these meanings may be used quite independently of the connotation of a 'historical force'.

The upshot of all this, for the benefit of those moved only by considerations of utility, is that it would be very wide of the mark for social scientists and historians to assume that in -isms they have no more than simply a convenient suffix to denote a doctrine. For -isms do not *simply* designate anything whatever. Indeed the range of possible meanings intimated by a term in -isms is enormous and undiscriminating. And whatever may be the reasons why such terms find ready, not to say universal, employment in scholarly as well as polemical speech, it is certainly not because their referents and connotations are clear and unequivocal. A no doubt libellous suggestion would be that such terms owe their popularity precisely to the fact that they do not require a decision about what it is one is talking about. A more charitable interpretation would point to the difficulty experienced in the humanities and social sciences in finding synthesizing concepts.

The case to be made here requires circumspect statement. I am not asserting that any term is forever branded with the marks of its original usage; the person who refers to 'Thursday' is not implicitly committed to the worship of Thor, or even liable to recall it to mind. And if 'individualism', for example, was originally devised as a term of abuse,[41] it does not follow that anyone now using the term will find himself willy-nilly adopting a hostile attitude to whatever it is he means to designate by that term. But the 'genetic fallacy' about words is in its way no more naive than what might be termed the 'implement' or 'Humpty Dumpty'

fallacy, the view (in other words) that words are simply 'tools' to be 'employed' in 'communication'. For the availability of words is the availability of thoughts. What can be said and what can be thought is of course not the same thing. But neither are words merely inert receptacles and implements for thought. Thoughts are the activity of a thinker, and a thinker cannot simply 'control' his words as a workman can control his tools: for to control words would be to control thoughts, and to control thoughts would be to think, and so *ad infinitum*. The question is, therefore, not (*pace* Humpty Dumpty), 'who's to be master, that's all,' for that would be true only of conventional or stipulative definitions, which are about as dependable as New Year's resolutions.

While it may be a truism to say that thought is at the mercy of the concepts it employs, the implications of that truism cannot be evaded simply by a good resolution to take care over one's organizing ideas. Any use of an -ism ought therefore to be accompanied by a pause for reflection aimed at clarifying the precise character of the referent. And in general, there seem to be only three sorts of -isms which, at least in the hands of careful users, occasion no particular difficulty. The first is when the context of usage is specific, and where those identified by an -ism themselves accept(ed) the identification. In all such cases, 'activity' or 'effects' will be ascribed to -ism only as a figure of speech. The second – and this relates particularly but not exclusively to a practice common among philosophers – is when the -ism refers to positions in a clearly defined debate, and when all the participants in the debate are operating with the same paradigmatic thinkers and works, as referents of the -ism suffix. Even here, I cannot persuade myself that the practice is free from the dangers of reification. No doubt 'Platonic realism' is unproblematic in a way in which the ascription of 'realism' to Machiavelli is certainly not, and no doubt a philosopher will know well enough what he means by 'Humean scepticism'. But can the same be said of 'positivism', 'scientism', 'histori(ci)sm' or 'rationalism'? The prudent philosopher will of course instantly clarify the referent of such terms with a definition, and is unlikely to confuse a philosophical doctrine or position with a 'historical force', but as I have already remarked, controlling one's thoughts is analogous in difficulty to jumping over one's own shadow. A final uncontentious use of -isms, already intimated in the previous comment, is when -isms are invented ad hoc as a

shorthand for some determinate doctrine already identified independently of -isms. Thus confusion or obscurity is unlikely to be occasioned by references (in context) to 'Ramism' or 'psychopannychism'.

These concessions are not intended as a life-raft to those who think (to take a couple of examples gleaned from a random perusal of a book and a publisher's catalogue) that 'liberalism, nationalism and Marxism . . . are vital factors in the contemporary world' is a meaningful proposition, or that an intelligible subject-matter can be constituted by the concepts of 'despotism, pseudo-modernist absolutism and feudalism'. For the -isms which I regard as not inherently problematic are those which have for their referent a specific doctrine, preferably in the context of a clearly defined debate. Such -isms correspond to the earliest extended usage of the suffix, before it acquired the connotations of 'system', 'force', or 'historical phenomenon of any kind whatever', and are all the more unobjectionable for having ceased to carry any automatically derogatory connotation.

Difficulties begin when the meaning of -ism is extended, as it usually is, to cover a tradition with a markedly doctrinal content. But since the concept of an intellectual tradition has of late been receiving increased attention, anyone who persists in supposing that a tradition, even an intellectual one, has an essence – as for example when 'real' or 'true' socialism is contrasted with facsimiles, perversions, deviations, distortions, etc. – has only himself to blame. A tradition is a postulated continuity of thought and practice, the ground for postulating its existence being discernible continuities and debts, of which the bearers either were, or could have been, aware. An uncontentious identification of 'ideologies' by means of -isms is also possible, for ideologies may be treated as analogous to traditions in the above sense. In neither case is there any overwhelming temptation to misconstrue -isms as the sort of thing that can *have* causes, essences or effects, or which can itself *be* the essence or cause of something else (as when it is supposed that the proposition that 'fascism is a form/consequence/ outgrowth of capitalism' could be a significant assertion). And if it should be asked what objection there is to the idea that -isms might have essences, the answer is that 'essence' means that which makes something *this* rather than *that* thing, the property without which it would be other than it is. But in the humanities and social

sciences, the problem is precisely what the identity denoted by an -ism is. To imagine that what is so designated is in some sense a 'thing out there' in the world, or the evidence, or the facts, still more to postulate essences for such things, is simply reification, mistaking theoretical constructs and stipulations for a recognition of realities.[42]

It will perhaps now be apparent why -isms with a specifically doctrinal referent are inherently less problematic than -isms purporting to refer to a phenomenon – such as fascism, imperialism, totalitarianism, racism, sexism, monetarism, capitalism, communism, colonialism, leftism, pacifism, individualism, collectivism, and so on. For -isms designating doctrines refer to self-identifications: the character of the evidence needed for, and adequate to their imputation is clear. People either did or did not derive certain of their views from Calvin, or at any rate found in Calvin an authoritative expositor of views to which they subscribed; in this sense 'Calvinism' is unproblematic, even if there may well be extreme technical difficulties about finding or evaluating the relevant evidence.

Consider, however, the referents of -isms claiming to designate historic ('social') phenomena. There is (as has been seen) nothing whatever about the past record or current usage of the suffix to suggest univocality. A common move by scholars uneasily aware of that fact is to preface discussions whose subject-matter is constituted by an -ism with a declaration of a determination to use this -ism to mean *x*, that is, to attempt to isolate or abstract one component from the indeterminate identification already implicit in current usage. But such isolation does not switch off or neutralize the other components; it merely temporarily obscures them from view. The hope that it will do so permanently is likely to remain a pious one. In so far as one component can be isolated and identified independently of the -ism, the latter is demonstrably redundant, and its retention merely a recurrent incentive to reintroduce the inclusiveness and range of connotations that established the -ism in current usage in the first place.

For current usage of such -isms does have its own sense, point, intentionality; this is not a matter of mere indeterminacy or confusion. The sense, point and intentionality implicit in -isms purporting to designate phenomena is to make a contribution to practical political discourse. The understanding of political practice implicit

in such discourse is, at its worst, a kind of demonology. At their worst, -isms designate and figure in the constitution of a world peopled by impersonal forces and agencies, sometimes benign but frequently malevolent, which sometimes 'triumph' or 'dominate', and generally lurk, skulk or lie dormant, which 'grow', 'develop', 'pervade', 'infect', have 'manifestations', 'forms' and 'symptoms', and which may be 'struggled' or 'fought' against (as Saints have wrestled with demons, and as the Church Militant fights against the Forces of Darkness), 'thwarted', 'smashed', 'undermined', 'appeased', or (changing the metaphor from military or demonic to medical) may be 'diagnosed', may be in 'crisis', may be 'dealt with', may 'decay', and so on. Blatantly demonological imagery will of course not be admitted into academic company, but the metaphor is ambiguous, and consequently there is no real difficulty about -isms attaining respectability: for 'demons' and 'disease' read 'forces', 'systems' or 'the system', 'mechanism', 'structures'. And this kingdom of spectres is not readily exorcized from one's intellectual world by the simple expedient of a prefatory declaration (an incantation) of a determination to use this -ism to mean x.

To take an example, 'racism' or 'racialism' is currently used to mean one, some, most or all of: xenophobia; a resentment (not shared by the commentator) at the actual disturbance, or the real or imagined possibility of the disturbance, of a manner of living by the arrival of some identifiable new group; a disposition to find scapegoats or lay the blame for real or imagined hardships anywhere except at one's own doorstep; an antipathy towards the conduct of some group of persons; the espousal of the doctrines of (say) Count Gobineau, Houston Stewart Chamberlain, or Alfred Rosenberg; an unwillingness to associate with, employ, or give favourable or equal treatment to persons of another ethnic group; the opinion that persons of a particular nationality, group of nationalities, cultural classification, race or colour are in some, or most, or all respects superior to those of some other group, most other groups or all other groups.

Now these are perfectly discrete and separable predicates. There is nothing whatever inconceivable about a person or group to whom one of them may be ascribed, but not the rest, even if the reference is exclusively to opinions. There is even less reason to expect a connection between opinions which a person might

avow, or assent to if prompted, on the one hand, and his conduct on the other. It is not unheard of for a person to express hostility towards, let us say, 'the Irish', and yet to fail to conduct himself in hostile fashion towards Irish persons he encounters. But the term 'racism' links all these predicates into a unity, and a unity of a very special sort: a menacing 'thing', 'force' or phenomenon, which can thereupon serve as the object for imputations of causality, agency, responsibility or blame, or which can count as an enemy to be 'fought', 'smashed' or 'struggled' against, or (to change to medical metaphors) a 'disease' to be 'diagnosed', whose 'causes' or 'roots' can be determined, so that a 'remedy', 'cure', 'antidote', 'treatment' can be devised. And there is of course nothing in the least puzzling about people availing themselves of an -ism to make their experience intelligible; on the contrary, there are as many reasons for doing so as there are reasons why the suffix established itself in common usage in the first place. In the particular instance of 'racism', the implication of impersonal agency inherent in the suffix might (for example) be entirely congruent with an individual's or group's experience of animosity, discrimination or slight, prompted (as it appears to the victim) by no personal act or attribute other than his race. None the less, take away the -ism, and the 'thing', agency or 'force' constituted by the -ism dissolves, leaving behind a whole range of distinct experiences, events and phenomena which might be rejoined or disconnected in a variety of ways, including non-demonological and non-reifying ones. Retain the -ism and the 'force' is still with you.

NOTES

1. This is a revised version of an article first published in the *British Journal of Political Science*, 13 (1983) pp. 1–17.
2. '-Isme' is the universal English orthography of the suffix until the late seventeenth century. Does this indicate that the habit (like so much else) was imported from France, that it was felt that an obeisance ought to be made to the Latin derivation, or merely that the pronunciation was -is*me* and not -is*em*, unlike modern English?
3. Thus E. Huguet's admirable *Dictionnaire de la langue française au 16ᵉ Siècle* (Paris: Didier, 1928–77) does not notice the occurrence of Anabaptisme, catechisme, Calvinisme, Machiavellisme or Judaisme, even though the last term had an idiomatic as well as an ordinary use. G. W. Lampe's *Patristic Greek Lexicon* (Oxford: Oxford University Press, 1961) ignores -ism forma-

tions, if indeed there are any to be ignored; so does the *Thesaurus Linguae Latinae*.

4. Consider the history of the terms 'revolution', 'state' and 'industry' for example.

5. This term, first found in English about 1800, the French being considerably older, mimics the oldest Greek uses of '-isms': resembling solecism, schism, exorcism, nepotism, aphorism, despotism.

6. The *Oxford English Dictionary* does not identify first uses for most of the familiar philosophical -isms before the eighteenth century, but this is, I think, merely an oversight; I cannot praise this work too highly for the most part and my debts to it will be apparent.

7. Peter Levins (or Levens), 1570; reproduced *Early English Text Society*, 1867 (reprinted New York: Greenwood Press, 1969).

8. *Britanisme* and *Scotisme* I have encountered nowhere else. Levins' etymology of *Barbarism* as derived from a place-name is erroneous. It should be noted that *Atticism* and *Barbarism* are entirely comparable to *Christianismus, Judaismus* and *Paganismus*, which are discussed below. Thus Thomas Thomas, in his *Dictionarium Linguae Latinae et Anglicanae* (1587, repr. Scolar: Menston, 1972) defines *Atticismus* as 'a manner of speaking used in Athens; the phrase or elegancie of the Athenian Tongue', *Barbarismus* as 'the corrupt form of speaking or pronouncing'; and *Laconismus* as 'a short fashion of speaking in few wordes contayning much matter'. He does not note *Latinisme* or the other country- or sect-denotatives; if Levins invented some of them himself, this would be confirmation for my dating of the spread of the habit.

9. Examples, approximate dates of appearance in brackets, from the sixteenth to the mid-seventeenth century: Lutheranisme, Lutherisme (Fr., 1554), Lutherienisme (Fr., 1570), Calvinisme (Fr., 1562, Latin, 1575), Anabaptisme (Fr., 1564), papisme (used by Calvin in 1541), Romanisme (apparently later than papisme), puritanisme (mid-1560s), Brownisme (established by 1580), separatism (established by 1600), atheisme (Fr., 1555, rare German occurrence, 1596), Muhammadanism (1584). Terms well established by 1640 include antinomianisme, Socinianisme, millenialisme, Arianisme, Donatisme, Platonisme, scholasticisme, Protestantisme, enthusiasme, libertinisme, Erastianisme, gentilisme.

10. To my knowledge, the first book sporting an -ism in its title was published in 1576 (cf. fn 23 below). Another work, *Iesuitismi pars prima* of 1582 managed to get *Pharasaismus* into the long title. Its author followed this with *Iesuitismi pars secunda* in 1584, this time adding his own coinage *Puritanopapismi, seu doctrinae Jesuiticae* (note the doctrinal reference). A belated Catholic riposte was *Calvino-Turcismus* in 1597.

11. F-F. Rosenfeld (in F. Maurer and H. Rupp (eds), *Deutsche Wortgeschichte*, vol. I (Berlin and New York: De Gruyter, 1974), p. 419) asserts that 'it appears that abstract substantives in *-ismus* [were] already common among the Church Fathers, [and that for example] Erasmus liked to employ them in his Latin polemical writing'. While Rosenfeld's other comments are generally helpful, this assertion is infuriating: I find no examples of -isms in Erasmus's polemical writings and none in the Church Fathers, although both he and they were happy enough to brand opponents as '-ists' or '-(i)ans'. Erasmus uses 'Ciceronianus' and 'Barbarus' (which had an established -ism (barbarism) in both Greek and Latin) in book-titles, but does not progress to -ism in either work. But who knows what might be found in the hundred-odd volumes of Migne's *Patrologia Latina* and *Patrologia Graeca* or in the Erasmian corpus *in toto*. Du Cange, *Glossarium Mediae et Infimae Latinitatis*,

1678 (repr. Graz: Akademische Verlagsanstalt, 1954), notes no -ism formations at all to go with the personal suffix, and neither does any other dictionary of late or medieval Latin or Greek that I have consulted.

12. The Thomason Collection, a treasure-trove of pamphlets, sermons, books,
    speeches and official statements assembled between 1640 and 1661 and run-
    ning to about 20,000 titles, lists scarcely any containing an -isme, except of
    course terms like catechisme, baptisme. A pamphlet of 1641 listed there and
    entitled 'A Discovery of twenty-nine Sects. . . .' gives all the names of the
    sects in -ists, -(i)ans, or -ites. Thomas Edwards's celebrated *Gangraena*
    (1646), describing itself as a 'Catalogue and Discovery of many of the errours,
    heresies, blasphemies and pernicious practices of the Sectaries', not
    infrequently uses -ismes like Socinianisme, antinomianisme, Arminianisme,
    Familisme (the heresy of the Family of Love), etc., but far more usually uses
    the personal -ists. And while -ismes are common in the texts of the tracts
    listed in the collection, the titles containing -isme can be counted on the
    fingers of two hands. See *The Catalogue of the pamphlets, books . . . collected
    by George Thomason 1640–1661* (London: British Museum, 1908).

13. The *Acts of the Apostles*, 11:26, records that the *Christiani* were first so
    described at Antioch; whether the title was originally merely designative or
    also derogatory is not clear.

14. *2 Machabeus*, 2:21, and elsewhere: the meaning is the religion of the Jews.
    Reference in OED, entry '-ism'.

15. The OED attributes it to Justin Martyr, c. 150 AD, which merely illustrates
    the perfectly indemonstrable nature of assertions about first appearances of
    a word. Ignatius's writings are extant in two forms in Latin and Greek each,
    but *Christianismus (-os)* appears in all versions. See *Patrum Apostolicorum
    Opera*, ed. A. R. M. Dressel (Leipzig: J. C. Hinrichs, 1857), pp. 148–9,
    166–7.

16. The OED entry for -ism ought to have served as a model for dictionaries in
    all languages, but did not. The *Trésor de la langue française*, ed. P. Imbs
    (Paris: CNRG, 1971–), which is also exemplary, will have an entry under
    -isme, but has not got there yet. The entry in Paul Robert, *Dictionnaire
    alphabetique et analogique de la langue française*, vol. 4 (Paris: Société du
    Nouveau Littré, 1965–70), and *Supplément*, is flat and rather tendentious:
    'suffixe savant' forsooth. German, Italian and Spanish dictionaries that I have
    consulted tend to have no entry for -ism at all.

17. *Sophism*, which is classical Greek and appears in all Western European
    languages via the Latin, never meant the doctrine of the Sophists, but always
    an argument or fallacy like those typical of a Sophist. *Catechism*, which
    according to von Wartburg derives from fourth-century patristic Greek, refers
    not specifically to doctrines, but to the art or product (and hence, presumably
    by analogical extension, the instrument) of *catechesis*. The medieval term
    dogmatismus, in the same way, meant the teaching of the Church.

18. This is implicit in the fact that -isms designated heresies.

19. As some of the examples given in footnote 23 below illustrate, an extension
    of -isms to designate political referents was easy, given the interdependence
    of religion and politics of the time. An additional example would be 'statism',
    attested by the OED for 1609, whose meaning is roughly the political attitude
    of *Politiques*.

20. Rosenfeld, cited in footnote 11, notes the popularity of *-ist* (plural *-isten*) in
    sixteenth-century German, to which may be added Latin, French, English.
    Ad hoc formulations in *-ist* were everyday occurrences; Rosenfeld cites
    papist, bullist, Martinist, Lutherist, Summist, Interimist, Concordists. He

asserts that this ending became popular in the medieval conflicts between Realists and Nominalists; according to Du Cange, however, the medieval terms were *reales* and *nominales*, not *realista* and *nominalista* (*Glossarium Mediae et Infimae Latinitatis*).

21. A term first used in this sense by Huguenots. See, for example, the 'Lettre de Pierre Carpentier' of 1572, reproduced in Simon Goulart, *Memoires de L'Estat de France sous Charles Neufiesme*, vol. I ('Meidelbourg', 1576), p. 357: 'ceux qui nourroisoyent les factions et conspirations qu'on apelle la Cause'.

22. Luther habitually spoke of 'das Papsttum', or 'die Romanisten'. The *Catalogue of the Thomason Collection*, cited in footnote 5, contains many illustrations of the suffix -*cy* or -*ty* being used where the modern equivalent would be or is -ism: 'episcopacy' (for 'episcopalianism'), 'malignancy' (the practice of being a 'Malignant' or royalist), 'prelacy' or 'prelaty', 'Independency' (Independentism), 'popery' or 'papistry', and even 'antinomy' (for 'antinomianism'). 'Democracy' shares the features of this use of the suffix.

23. *Anti-Cavalierisme* was the title of a pamphlet of 1642 by John Goodwin; the term does not recur in the text but it meant that 'colluvies . . . heap . . . or gathering together of the scum, the drosse, and garbage of the land . . ., Jesuits, Papists and Atheists . . . commonly known by the name of Cavaliers' (W. Haller (ed), *Tracts on Liberty in the Puritan Revolution*, vol. 2 (reprinted New York: Octagon, 1965), p. 2). Goodwin also invented 'Babylonisme' along the way (p. 32). For *Anti-Normanisme* see John Hare, *St Edward's Ghost*, or *Anti-Normanisme* (1647). *Jesuitism* seems first to have been devised by a German writing in Latin in 1576: '*Assertio veteris ac veri Christianismi adversus novum et fictum Jesuitismum, seu Societatem Jesu*'. The English translation of the pamphlet merely had 'new and counterfaicte secte of Jesuites'. Clearly the cunning, underhand and treacherous practices imputed to the Jesuits, and not their doctrines, were at issue here. '*Machiavellisme*' is late sixteenth-century (1592 according to OED), *Machiavellianisme* appears in the 1620s. The apparent reference of the term to the teachings of Machiavelli is of course entirely spurious.

24. Examples include 'theism' or 'deism', 'optimism', 'materialism', 'fatalism'.

25. The article on *Atomisme* redescribes its subject as 'doctrine des atomes'. Articles, mostly by Diderot, on -*isme* include: Epicuréisme, Héraclitisme, Hobbisme, Jansenisme, Leibnitzianisme, Scepticisme, Stoicisme, Platonisme, Phyronisme, Pythagorisme; usually (unlike modern practice) the suffix does not indicate a tradition, but rather the doctrine of one person.

26. All are freely used in the *Encyclopédie*. The article 'Jésuite' for example speaks of 'ce système de fanatisme, d'indépendance [*sc.*: of the state] et de machiavélisme' and also of 'despotisme'. For Hume's use of 'enthusiasm', 'fanaticism' see for example the (1754) *History of Great Britain*, ed. D. Forbes (Harmondsworth: Pelican, 1970), pp. 71, 72, 73, 227, 616. The 'scotticisms' which Scottish writers were anxious to eliminate from their prose were of course idioms, not doctrines. 'Despotism' seems to date from the late seventeenth century (Imbs (ed), *Trésor*), and originally meant 'toute autorité qui s'exerce de façon tyrannique'.

27. There appears to be no word or group of words incapable of sporting an -ism; I suggested 'Ismism' as the title for this paper. The OED has some choice examples of what it charmingly terms 'nonce-formations': L. S. Deism (a parody of Deism), Rule-Britanniaism, know-nothingism, to which one might add terms like hallelujahism, me-tooism, and so on.

28. Helpful observations may be found in R. Williams, *Culture and Society*

(Harmondsworth: Penguin, 1967), pp. 13–16; R. Nisbet, *The Sociological Tradition* (London: Heinemann, 1970), p. 23; and E. J. Hobsbawm, *The Age of Revolutions* (London: Weidenfeld, 1962), pp. 17 ff.

28. In 1790, William Cowper wrote: 'Let your divinity . . . be the divinity of the glorious Reformation! I mean in contradistinction to Arminianism, and all the other *isms* (sic) that were ever broached in this world of error and ignorance.' (I owe this reference to Mr Russell Price.) This use of -ism as a substantive, which is still in reference to the original extended usage of -isms in *religio-political* controversy, had been anticipated in 1680: 'Jesuitism, Puritanism, Quakerism and . . . all other Isms from Schism' (OED, *Supplement*). But in 1793 Edmund Burke wrote of the conflict 'between the rabble of systems, Fayettism, Condorcetism, Monarchism, or Democratism, or Federalism, on the one side, and the fundamental laws of France on the other' (*Policy of the Allies*, in *Works*, vol. IV (London: J. C. Nimmo, 1899), pp. 420–1.) Clearly, the reference here is exclusively to *political* 'factions' and 'systems'.

29. Thus 'socialism', 'communism', 'positivism', 'Fabianism' seem all to have been devised to designate *approved* doctrines, tenets, policies, etc.

30. I do not know why Methodism, originally an opprobrious term, was accepted by Methodists, whereas 'Quakerism' has never quite appealed to the 'Society of Friends (Quakers)', even though the original imputation of a propensity to convulsive fits is now quite lost. In the same way Roman Catholics accept 'Roman Catholicism' but never 'Romanism' or 'papism'. The derogatory connotation of the suffix, at any rate, is not quite dead: thus 'democratism' (attributed to Burke, 1793 (OED), and also found in French in the same year and occasionally subsequently (Imbs, ed., *Trésor*)) has never 'taken', and nor has Bentham's attempted neologism, 'religionism'.

31. For example, Sir Robert Filmer, *Pariarcha* (late 1630s), ed. P. Laslett (Oxford: Blackwells, 1949), p. 54: 'I have nothing to do to meddle with the mysteries of the present state. Such *arcana imperii* or cabinet councils, the vulgar may not pry into.'

32. *De Cive*, ed. S. Lamprecht (New York: Appleton-Century-Crofts, 1949), p. 17: 'that monarchy is the most commodious government [is] the one thing alone I confess in this whole book not to be demonstrated, but only probably stated.' This admission is not repeated in *Leviathan*, but *De Cive* was reissued by Hobbes in the same year.

33. This usage was anticipated by Hobbes, who in *Leviathan* (ch. 22) used 'system' to refer to 'any number of men joined in one interest, or business', and who therefore also described the commonwealth or state as a 'system', although he did not actually refer to 'political systems'. A worthy contemporary of the 'Metaphysical' poets and preachers, he was apparently pleased by this 'conceit' as a new version of the well-worn body/body politic analogy or similitude or correspondence. He soon tired of it and reverted in the rest of the chapter to talk of 'bodies'.

34. See (representatively): A Smith, *Inquiry into the Nature and Causes of the Wealth of Nations* (1776) (London: George Routledge and Sons, nd), 'Bk. IV. Systems of Political Economy'; ch. I: 'Of the Principle of the Commercial or Mercantile System'; ch. IX: 'Agricultural Systems'; in these cases the reference is to doctrines, but (Bk. IV, ch. IX), p. 540: 'All *systems* either of preference or of restraint being thus completely taken away, the obvious and simple *system* of natural liberty establishes itself of its own accord' (my italics), where the first reference implies the *philosophe* term of abuse 'esprit de système' and the second is to a set of arrangements. See also W. Robert-

son, *History of the Reign of Charles the Fifth*, ed. W. H. Prescott (London: George Routledge, 1857): 'feudal system' (pp. 6, 10), 'the vast system' of Charlemagne (p. 8); A. Ferguson, *An Essay on the History of Civil Society* (1767) (New Brunswick: Transaction, 1980): 'system of laws' (p. 121), 'happy system of policy' (p. 133), 'system of national virtues' (p. 151); J-J. Rousseau, *Du Contrat Social* (1762), Bk. I, ch. 9, 'système social'; D'Holbach, *Système de la Nature* (1770) (repr. Hildesheim: Georg Olms, 1966), where 'système' is used in neutral fashion in the title, but derogatorily ('systèmes enfantés par l'imagination', vol. I, p. i) in most of the text; e.g. vol. I, ch. 7, vol. II, ch. ii.

35. The equivalence is apparent in the quotations from Burke and Smith, footnotes 28 and 34 above.

36. J. Damourette and E. Pichon, *Des Mots à la Pensée*, vol. I (Paris: D'Artrey, 1911–27), pp. 384–5, s. 323.

37. They saw a '*sexuisemblance*' in the fact that the -ism suffix is masculine in gender in all European languages that have genders. Dutch is the sole exception. One hesitates to join them in this bear-pit.

38. The term 'principle' had already attained unparalleled confusion of meaning in the eighteenth century. The confusions are faithfully portrayed by Bentham in a footnote to his *Principles of Morals and Legislation* (ch. I, footnote 2), characteristically entitled 'a principle, what [*sc.*: what is it?]'.

39. The notion of a 'rhetoric' is perhaps unfamiliar. An example of it would be what might be called the 'rhetoric of Protestant patriotism' of seventeenth-century England. It is not a tradition except in the sense that anything having a continuous history might be called a tradition, but rather a complex of trigger-words to which Englishmen of that time were expected to respond predictably. It included terms like 'the glorious reformation', 'the example of the best reformed churches', 'our Protestant brethren [abroad]', 'the Antichrist' (*sc.* the pope and his agents), 'the machinations of Papists, popish priests, Jesuites', 'conspiracies', 'plots', 'treasons', the 'liberty of Protestant Englishmen', etc. Such language might as easily be used by Filmer (compare his link, *d'ailleurs* a familiar polemical ploy, between Jesuits and Puritans) as by Milton or the Levellers.

40. See for example the sensible distinction in N. O'Sullivan, *Conservatism* (London: J. M. Dent and Sons, 1976), p. 9, between a conservative attitude and a conservative ideology.

41. The term was invented (it seems) by de Maistre in 1820. See S. Lukes, 'The Meanings of Individualism', *Journal of the History of Ideas*, xxxii (1971), 45–66 *passim*, especially p. 46.

42. Note should also be taken of the objections to imputations of essences (the particular instance being 'socialism') offered by W. H. Greenleaf: 'Laski and British Socialism', *History of Political Thought*, II (1981), pp. 574–6.

2.   Nietzsche and the Ideological Project

Kenneth Minogue

The attempt to locate Nietzsche in terms of the idea of ideology is irresistible because he is centrally concerned with the hot pursuit of what he takes to be illusions. Indeed, he is engaged by exactly the same critical passions as the exponents of ideology. Yet he did not choose to take up the term itself, and lightness of touch in his philosophical style distinguishes him from the rather heavy-footed unmasking characteristic of what I shall call 'the ideological project'. My purpose is to explore the Nietzsche–ideology relationship by sketching the outlines of a context by which to understand it.

THE IDEOLOGICAL PROJECT

'Ideology' as a term began as the description of a practical project for the purification of thought. By a 'project' here I mean something similar to that designated 'a research programme' by philosophers of science. A possibility of intellectual and practical advance swims before the vision of intellectuals, and generation by generation they pursue, develop, and refine it, hoping (usually in vain) to bring it to fruition. Such projects are usually thrown off by philosophy, and the ideological project is no exception. The Socrates who analysed arguments in order to refine them into true knowledge by way of a conversational dialectic was engaged in philosophy. Notionally equal pursuers of truth tested the reasons for their beliefs, and discarded those beliefs which could not stand the probing. The shadow of the ideological project may only be detected in the Platonic belief that error is caused not by

bad reasoning, but by more remote, non-rational causes, such as the passions. The distinction between the reasons for a belief and the causes of one is crucial. In criticizing the reasoning of another, I treat him as an equal, for we are all liable to error. If, on the other hand, I construe his belief as *caused* by some factor which has unwittingly determined his reasoning processes, then I am treating him as less than rational. I may invoke his passions, his background, his obsessions, his race, his social traditions or many other such fancied causes, but in so doing, I always treat him as determined by a cause from which I implicitly exempt myself.[1] In other words, the idea of ideology reifies people. The philosophers of the ancient world believed the populace to be sunk in 'superstition': imperfect beliefs were inevitably generated by imperfect people.

The self-consciously critical tendencies of philosophy since the seventeenth century have been the soil in which the modern ideological project has grown. The idea is clearly animating Francis Bacon's project for an inductive method which could smash the four 'idols' whose worship has plunged men into error. Inherited doctrines, the distortions of language and limited individual points of view all dispose men to error, but perhaps the most portentous source of error was the idol of the tribe – human nature itself.[2] All men rely upon the senses, which may falsely mirror the world, and all are disposed to believe what they wish to believe. So comprehensive a range of causes means not merely that to err is human, but that to be human itself is to err. It is clear that one direction the project of ideology might have to take would be nothing less than an entire recasting of human nature.

Towards the turn of the nineteenth century, many *philsophe* projects culminated in Destutt de Tracy's famous coinage of the name, and elaboration of the project, of creating a perfectly formed system of knowledge.[3] Marx's scientific socialism was to reveal that the ideas of most people were inevitably defective because ideas reflect reality, and the social classes of the modern world impose limited points of view – that is, distorted perception – upon their members.[4] In perhaps the most famous twentieth-century version of the idea – that of Karl Mannheim – the rather simple elitism of the project becomes explicit.[5] Mannheim thought that ordinary people took on the cognitive colouration of their social position, but that intellectuals might to some extent tran-

scend it. One step beyond this, perhaps, is the view that a false body of thought actually *constitutes*, by 'interpellation', the individual subjects who have the capacity to make erroneous judgements.[6]

These examples make it clear that the project of ideology must always lead to a kind of *science* of belief. The opinions of others turn out to be causally determined rather than properly reasoned. The theory of determination invoked will point to some structure – psychological, sociological, possibly biological, and so on. But no such structure is self-explanatory. It can only be described from the outside. This explains one of the most significant features of the ideological project: it is invariably an explanation of the beliefs of others. The ideological projector on the trail of a universal theory must implicitly include himself within the total structure responsible for the error, while implicitly excluding himself by his critical posture. This fact leads to a set of familiar problems, at a variety of levels, and one general solution to them is to suggest that 'ideology' is actually the fluid medium which all thought necessarily assumes. What has happened when a thinker arises at this position is that the theory of ideology has been philosophically pushed far beyond its usual polemical employment and has arrived back at the arena from which it arose – namely, rhetoric.

The more normal use of the concept of ideology, however, is to establish a rhetorical advantage. Thus Marx, obliterating poor Proudhon to his own satisfaction, writes:

> He wants to soar as the man of science above the bourgeois and the proletarians; he is merely the petty bourgeois, continually tossed back and forth between capital and labour, political economy and communism.[7]

This is clearly not a view of himself that Proudhon could possibly take. The verb 'to be ideological' thus has no first-person application in this basic sense of 'ideological'. The whole ideological project is savaged by such problems as self-exemption, and they are central to the literature on the subject. At its least defensible, ideology merely collapses into dogmatism.[8] Whether or not we may judge Nietzsche an exponent of the ideological project, he certainly faces problems of this kind.

The ideological project is subject to a curious doom which has

led to immense confusion. It happened with immense speed to the inventor of the project himself. *Ideologie* was created by the liberal republicans who were early supporters of Napoleon Bonaparte. Power and knowledge, however, soon fell out, and it was Napoleon who then gave currency to the inverted use of the term 'ideology' to describe pretentious intellectuals whose unreal schemes caused most of the world's problems. The same oscillation is to be found in Marx's use of the idea. For Marx, ideology was already, *à la* Bonaparte, the name of the errors against which he juxtaposed his own scientific socialism. But he can also use 'ideology' to describe bodies of thought held, or ideally held, by the social classes he talked about. Bourgeois ideology, which is false, is contrasted with proletarian ideology, which is true. Marxism is thus both the ideology of the proletariat, and also the scientific analysis of bourgeois false consciousness.

Ideology thus begins as a cure for diseased thought, and its doom is to become the name for that very disease. It is a *pharmacon*, both poison and cure, and this terminology is appropriate because a medical metaphor underlies the whole project. But since we are concerned here with the special kind of medicine which emphasizes purification, we may suspect that a religious model is to be found at a level deeper than the medical. The roots of the ideological project are thus very deep indeed, and even its doom can be seen in the ancient world, when the superior wisdom claimed by philosophers who considered themselves above the superstitious herd, was inverted by the early Christians who affirmed the value of faith – indeed, of the folly of fools for Christ's sake. There is thus something inherently vulnerable about the whole project.

Such vulnerability is worth a moment's detour in the context of Nietzsche, a writer whose sense of tone makes him acutely aware of such matters. The vulnerability of the ideological project is not merely the absurdity to which all intellectual discourse is subject when punctured by juxtaposition with elementary human realities. It may be said of philosophers, as Montaigne said of kings, that no matter how high upon a throne they are, they still sit upon their own behinds. Everything, being human, is slightly absurd and no human performance is beyond the reach of parody. But the ideological project is essentially pretentious. It is peculiarly vulnerable to being exploded as a rhetorical device seeking an

argumentative advantage over those who do not hold the same opinion. Even in the midst of an enthusiasm, sometimes a virtual delirium, or relativism, the exponent of the project cannot succeed in concealing the fact that an Archimedean point is involved in his attempt to shift the terms of discourse. The critical posture must begin to dissolve as some founding belief-in-practice, or sensations, or some dogma about the constitution of minds and society, or even some simple abstraction such as 'domination' is to be discovered lurking in disguise behind – well, as Nietzsche might say, behind the mask.

NIETZSCHE ON TRUTH AND THOUGHT

The theory of ideology is evidently an unstable compound of scepticism and dogmatism. It belongs on the political periphery of philosophy but it lacks the rigour which would make it suitable for serious philosophical use. Virtually all its exponents have been writers for whom an external enthusiasm, usually for some kind of revolution, overshadowed the interest in exploring reality. Attempting to relate Nietzsche and the ideological project thus raises questions about Nietzsche no less than about ideology.

Nietzsche is dogmatic in manner but sceptical in content. He would clearly be dissatisfied with the kind of halfway house in which some true believer theorizes all competing doctrines as limited points of view, yet assumes a kind of simple universality about his own judgements. 'Truth', he wrote in one of the many versions of what he had to say on this subject, '*is that kind of error* without which a certain species of living being cannot exist.'[9] That truth is a kind of error is a view which evidently goes round in circles, since the term 'error' presupposes the idea of truth. It is necessary to press such logical squibs merely to follow the often confusing contours of Nietzsche's thought, for he would never be a thinker to fall at early hurdles such as these. Indeed, what is most characteristic of him is to contradict everything he says, in order to generate a kind of dialectical down-draught which will keep his enterprise going without having to rest upon any kind of vulnerable foundation. On the face of it, his aim is to avoid any kind of rationalist fundamental whose validity could become a battleground of philosophical criticism. Thus his constant criticism

of philosophy ('the brain sick fancies of morbid cobweb spin-
ners'[10]) does not prevent him identifying himself as a philosopher.
His hatred of priests and rejection of everything they stand for
does not prevent him from recognizing that man has become a
more 'interesting' animal in the course of the last two millenia.[11]
Although 'the will to power' is central to his understanding of the
human situation, the very idea of a will is subject to dissolution:

> At the beginning stands the great fateful error that the will is some-
> thing which *produces an effect*. . . . Today we know it is merely a
> word. . . .[12]

Every utterance helps to envisage the world as a swirl, as becoming. Every utterance will be denied elsewhere.

Nietzsche's remarks on truth cannot, therefore, be taken as
what we might call 'vulgar scepticism'. When Heidegger discusses
Nietzsche's opinion that truth is functional to some specific form
of life – a doctrine which might well be identified as an expression
of the ideological project – he makes rather heavy weather of it.[13]
We must not take Nietzsche, he remarks crushingly, to mean that
'everything that is an error [is] true'. Indeed not. But Heidegger
then rightly connects the remark with Nietzsche's 'fundamental
position in opposition to all Western philosophy since Plato'. The
idea of truth in both Nietzsche and in Heidegger's discussion
bifurcates. On the one hand, it refers to discrete propositions
believed to correspond to some condition in reality, the innumer-
able facts of utterance, the snow which is white if and only if snow
is white. On the other hand, it refers to some account of that
reality as given by the philosophers, without which such facts
would seem to be meaningless. The facts of the positivist without
a metaphysic are taken to be headless chickens hurtling pointlessly
around some nightmarish barnyard.

Nietzsche is interested both in the basis of this intellectual realm
of Being or Reality, and in the design of those who established
it. He is sceptical of the one and suspicious of the other. His main
suggestion is that it is the structure of language which generates
the illusory realm the philosophers call 'reality':

> The singular family resemblance between all Indian, Greek and
> German philosophising is easy enough to explain. Where there exists
> a language affinity it is quite impossible, thanks to the common philo-

sophy of grammar – I mean thanks to unconscious domination and directing by similar grammatical functions – to avoid everything being prepared in advance for a similar evolution and succession of philosophical systems . . . the spell of definite grammatical functions is in the last resort the spell of *physiological* value judgements and racial conditions. So much by way of retort to Locke's superficiality with regard to the origin of ideas.[14]

This is a version, or rather two possible versions, of the ideological project – one racial, one grammatical. And, like many other remarks made by Nietzsche, it encourages us to think of him as a philosopher pointing out that we are cognitively imprisoned, and thus suggesting to us a way of escape from the confines of our civilization. The reasons of the philosopher are swept away and replaced by the kind of causal determination typical of the ideological projector. The philosophers have been the unwitting victims of social composition and linguistic inheritance. Such a typical move promises us liberation, for the prison is in part constituted by our very ignorance that it *is* a prison, and this discovery itself – the grand cliché of contemporary intellectuality – constitutes the first step towards escape. But Nietzsche is, by contrast with the typical contemporary intellectual, a philosopher exploring a predicament rather than a rationalist propounding a liberation. The movement of his thought along these lines culminates in scepticism: there is no direct relationship between words and things, and the development of words into a language through whose mediation we understand the world result less from the impact of reality than the 'poeticizing' influences of the rules of language which we compose ourselves. In grasping what we take to be reality through the use of language and through reflection upon it, we succumb to 'the lie of language' which is the belief that the world of men is contained within some wider, benevolent cosmic scheme.[15] Such doctrines seem to spring out of language itself – as, for example, when a commonplace phenomenon like a flash of lightning is conceptually distinguished by the very structure of the language into a causal agent (the lightning) which produces an effect (flashes).[16] Language multiplies wills or agents and human passions work upon it, as in Nietzsche's suggestion that the doctrine of free will developed in order to make human doings more interesting objects for the gods.[17]

These gods, of course, are taken by Nietzsche to be nothing

more than phantoms of the human brain. They are a set of spectators whom this interesting animal man has imagined, and can be written off under the heading of a particularly comprehensive error: the belief that the universe needs man. In fact, it is utterly indifferent to him. This kind of error belongs to the specific kind called an 'illusion', and its natural corrective is some form of realism. 'Illusion' and 'reality' are the terms commonly used in the rhetorical version, in practical thought, of what, when it becomes somewhat systematized, we have called 'the ideological project'. Here again, then, Nietzsche appears to have taken that project one stage further in thinking that systematic forms of error are caused not by any special feature of human life, but by the human situation *tout court*. In this, of course, he resembles Marx and, in espousing a form of realism, he takes up a posture which he shares with most nineteenth-century *esprits forts*: a posture of boldly and courageously casting aside beliefs which are merely comforting:

> Under 'Spiritual freedom' I understand something very definite: it is a state in which one is a hundred times superior to philosophers and other disciples of 'truth' in one's severity towards one's self, in one's uprightness, in one's courage, and in one's absolute will to say nay even when it is dangerous to say nay. I regard the philosophers that have appeared heretofore as *contemptible libertines* hiding behind the petticoats of the female 'Truth'.[18]

One is tempted to dismiss such typical nineteenth-century German braggadocio as merely empty, but it is perhaps best seen as necessary to the elaboration of a conception of the human world which seeks to dispense with foundations. Truth is characterized as female because the philosophers, according it necessity, allow themselves to be dominated by it, whereas being essentially perspectival, truth comes from the 'male' knower rather than the 'female' known. Nietzsche is merely pushing a little further that technique of reversals which Feuerbach and others had applied to God: Man *makes* truth no less than he 'makes' God. The error (as it were) is the familiar one of man becoming victimized by his own creation. Behind the rhetoric of defiance is the deepest of all paradoxes: that reality depends upon us.

But what is 'us'? It is evident that Nietzsche is above all concerned with the character of modern life and thought. The cognitive ecology of his experience is not an economy or a state, hardly

even a society; it is principally a culture. It seems plausible to say
that he takes off from the familiar German preoccupation with
the relation between subject and object. In earlier times, mind
tended to 'reflect' the world in some relatively simple way, but
with the steady increase in the complexity and sophistication of
the inner life of modern peoples, it became possible to recognize
(in Nietzsche's view) that what was philosophically seen as 'the
external world' was no less complex and shifting than our own
inner fancies. The rhetoric of defiance is thus the nervous exul-
tation of a thinker kicking away not only religion but philosophy
– the entire realm of Being – as if they were crutches with which
we have hitherto learned to scamper round the domesticated
imaginings of our civilization, but which prevented us from strid-
ing boldly into new fields. To continue to rely upon such crutches
would be to put evolution into reverse, to abandon the adventure
of humanity.

In elaborating such a posture, Nietzsche eschews definition and
most of the techniques of philosophical precision. 'Truth' refers
indifferently to propositions and to metaphysics. But, when his
evolutionary way of conceiving all problems focuses on truth, we
discover that its origin is essentially moral. Truth emerged from
the self-characterization of the nobility as true and authentic crea-
tures by contrast with 'the lying plebeian'.[19] It is thus the self-
revelation of a type of man who has successfully imposed his
power on the world, and the truth of the philosophers is the
doomed attempt, which has been in progress since Plato, to detach
this authenticity from its source in the evaluations of a certain
species of man.

There is no mistaking the spirit which haunts Nietzsche in this
mood. He is a Vichian[20] storyteller uncovering layers of heroic
meaning beneath the prose of modern existence. The actual form
of the story is even older: it may be discerned, for example in Ibn
Khaldun's account of expansion and decadence in the world of
Islam. Since it is an evolutionary story, we may split it into the
traditional three stages. In the first, the conquerors impose their
vision of the world boldly and unashamedly on everybody. In the
second stage, this vision is detached from these moral and physical
foundations and set up by philosophers and priests as if it were a
self-sustaining canopy of understandings corresponding to reality
itself. But such rationalization, such a transposition of values out

of 'life' and into 'consciousness' erodes the source of this vision, which can only bubble up from an actual way of life. Consciousness consumes vitality. The nobility loses its character, and the intellectual emptiness of mere philosophy becomes evident. Thus, we find ourselves in the third stage, in which a virtually superstitious respect for mere facts and the abstract laws of science (mistakenly believed to be shored up by an external and impersonal reality) remain as the empty shells of a devastated life form. A sustainable philosophical vision depends upon heroic values and a class of nobles.

On the face of it, then, Nietzsche's argument, if taken to be of an ideological character, is the most radical version of that project imaginable. It is that *everything* we believe is ideological, in the sense of being an illusion sustained by some limited point of view. Some of his remarks read like direct echoes of the physiological reductionism of the original French *ideologues* themselves. That 'Consciousness is the last and latest development of the organic and consequently also the most unfinished and weakest part of it'[21] is a rather more sophisticated version of the idea that thought is a glandular secretion. But this latter idea, as affirmed by Cabanis, presents itself as a philosophical thesis about the nature of reality and Nietzsche wishes to sidestep any such doctrine by insisting on the personal character of all belief as an expression of the will to power. At every point where his opinions might seem to touch ground and rest upon foundations, Nietzsche is careful to remove the ground from under his feet. His intellectual motion results from never sitting on a branch without sawing it off. Yet there is one direction in which these equivocations are more difficult to sustain. We sense it wherever belief is connected to the moral qualities of superior people. Whenever we discern this pattern in his work, we are inevitably reminded of that special philosophical frenzy generated in German thinkers by the Hegelian heritage, which led them to look frantically for some external anchorage for the fantasms of the brain. They upstaged philosophy by the postulation (usually in a scientific idiom) of some external cause of thought: in Marx, the process of production in a class-divided society; in Gobineau, race; in Cabanis, glands. Nietzschean physiology appears to play the same role. In all cases, thought is being criticized in terms of its relation not to some foundational[22] metaphysic, but to some naturalistic touchstone of life. Nietzsche's

treatment of thought – his involvement in the ideological project – must thus be linked to another of the great intellectual enterprises of modern Europe: the project of human authenticity.

THE AUTHENTICITY PROJECT

The authenticity project resembles the ideological in being a modern preoccupation whose roots lie in Greek philosophy. It arises from the idea that in the modern world, man has lost touch with his own being. He is a divided creature whose technological prowess has been purchased at the cost of spiritual enfeeblement. Philosophers of many schools have diagnosed this complaint, suggested remedies and linked it to a variety of conceptions of the modern condition of humanity.

Machiavelli's account of Renaissance Italy is an early version of the genre. His conception of *virtu* might well be taken as a sketch for what Nietzsche was to call 'the will to power'. Remove the element of agency from it and *virtu* becomes activity expressing itself in a realistic response to its conditions of life. Machiavelli's version of inauthenticity takes the form of corruption, which happens when a *civitas* loses its patriotic cohesion and dissolves into a tangle of private preoccupations, such as ambition, revenge and greed.[23] In the modern world, argued Machiavelli, Christian moralism is a specific form of corruption because it inhibits healthy forms of self-assertion and makes men servile, caring more about some fancied individual salvation in the afterlife than about civic freedom and honour in this world.

There is much in this theme which has an aspect of the pagan's long-delayed revenge for defeat by Christianity a millennium earlier. Intellectually routed by St Augustine and the early Church, pagan themes lay germinating over the centuries before emerging at the Renaissance in a new form. Their natural milieu was a cyclic sense of contemporary corruption superimposed upon the continuing Christian idea of original sin. It is characteristic of the modern world that each new generation tends to strike out in directions which are commonly construed as decadent and corrupt according to the values cherished by their predecessors. Among the many versions of this conflict, the condemnation of monarchical and aristocratic usages in terms of classical republicanism may

be cited as especially persistent. It was, again, the classical idea
that luxury is the last stage in the collapse of power which led the
rising commercialism of modern Europe to be persistently seen
as a symptom of imminent collapse. More refined versions of such
theory detected in self-consciousness, or in individualism, a fatal
falling away from the vigour of a more communal past. The power
of Marxism lies in its promise to restore, at a higher level than
before, an authentic humanity which has been shattered by the
divisions of modern commerce. It is an idea which has all the
resonance of myth and, as myth, it has been entrenched in our
civilization by the early chapters of the Book of Genesis.

Vico was arguably the most talented modern exponent of this
theme, for he transposed it into a theory of cultural evolution.
The age of gods and heroes was past, and modern civilization, for
all its science, was an age of prose. In Rousseau we find this
theme stated in the familiar terms of mankind taking a wrong
road. His indictment of those responsible appears in many
versions.

> By nature (he explained to his followers) a man bears pain bravely
> and dies in peace. It is the doctors with their rules, the philosophers
> with their precepts, the priests with their exhortations, who debase
> the heart and make us afraid to die.[24]

Afraid, indeed, he would add, even to live properly. Modern man
is a divided creature in whom impulse diverges from precept and
rising technology is matched by declining spiritual vitality. Unable
to follow their instincts, moderns are swayed this way and that by
conventions and intellectual fashions. Rousseau, (whom Nietzsche
characterized as 'sensuality in spiritual things'[25]) framed his indictment in terms of the key ideas of nature and virtue, while Nietzsche attacked morality. This might suggest that they were affirming contradictory doctrines. In fact, they are precisely parallel.
'The terms *autonomous* and *moral* are mutually exclusive',[26] Nietzsche wrote crisply, in an extreme version of the diagnosis often
associated with the concept of alienation.

The authenticity project is a spiritual diagnostic, in which man's
conformity to the external forces of morality, custom, public
opinion and even the law of the land is taken to be a pathology
of the human condition. It is thus the source of all the vulgar

projects of liberation which have tormented the modern world during the last two centuries, for the simple-minded way of construing the problem – once modern life is actually seen as a problem – is that it consists in the frustration of whatever desires we happen to have. In this way, the authenticity project among philosophers has given rise to the most powerful demagogic techniques of our time. It is the stock-in-trade of all the more extreme versions of nationalist and socialist belief. Such uses of the idea are unmistakably vulgarizations because they take the discontents people suffer at their face value. Every frustration is evidence of the disease, liberation the universal cure. More subtle versions of the theme recognize that modern man is inauthentic even in his understanding of what he imagines to be his discontents. It is in this way that the authenticity project tends to slide into the ideological. How we live and what we believe are related in so complex a way as to be difficult to distinguish; on the other hand, they are not exactly two sides of the same coin. All manner of beliefs and convictions (often erroneous) are part and parcel of how we live, and often the very foundation of what we achieve. Many exponents of the project believe themselves to have the right beliefs. The problem then becomes one of making 'philosophy' rule the world, an idea to which many of the *philosophes* gave currency. The Marxist theory of ideology, which in its many versions straddles all possibilities, is often the argument that the way we live in late capitalism is not yet reflected in appropriate beliefs (that is, those of Marx himself) and that ideology is thus a set of inappropriate thoughts left over from earlier forms of life. Ideology may thus be construed as what stands between us and authenticity.

The distinction between life and thought accounts for the stream of paradoxes generated by the fusion – one might well call it a 'confusion' – of ideology and authenticity. A persisting strand of Nietzschean criticism of the modern Christian world concentrates upon its tendency to inhibit and frustrate natural reactions. As we shall consider, Nietzsche often writes as if authentic nobility lies in the natural expression of a certain type of will, and inauthenticity in all the apparatus of *ressentiment* which the Judao-Christian world has developed to repress it. Yet the new form of authenticity projected among the Supermen will involve new forms of sublimation and self-mastery.[27] It is an unavoidable result

of Nietzschean rhetoric that, in expounding this idea, he should sometimes sound like Nietzsche the Terrible, espousing the untrammelled rule of might over right, and sometimes Nietzsche the Mild, a prophet saving us from the involute frightfulness of revenge, resentment and envy – the prophet, even, of a reborn Christianity.[28]

More generally, it is characteristic of Nietzsche, no less than of Marx, Bakunin, Tolstoy and the whole line of nineteenth-century prophets that they should be explicable alternatively as critics of Western civilization, root and branch, and yet also as that civilization's most authentic voices, seeking merely to restore an original character from which we had strayed. And this particular ambivalence is matched by another no less striking. It is that they all affirmed the value of a world of simple authenticity which, as personalities, they themselves could not possibly share. The timid, neurotic Nietzsche whose life was one long succession of disasters mitigated by philosophical exaltation is hardly to be identified with the new men of Zarathustra, any more than the masterful and intolerant Marx could have found a place in the future communist society. The authentic nobility of which Nietzsche dreamed had a direct simplicity untouched by the inner conflicts and hesitations of the world to which Nietzsche himself belonged. He himself recognized that they made for a more interesting culture.

SCEPTICISM AND AUTHENTICITY

The ideological project, we have seen, depends upon a saving truth, and such dependence is the source of its intellectual vulnerability. Nietzsche is constantly hostile to the idea of truth, and it is thus plausible to seek his touchstone in some version of authenticity. He thus belongs, we may suggest, to the ancient tradition of scepticism. But in suggesting this, we run immediately into difficulties, and they do not merely result from Nietzsche's systematic ambivalence about asserting anything at all. That he is a sceptic has been plausibly denied by Mark Warren:

> . . . skepticism *follows* from holding the metaphysical presuppositions that underwrite the correspondence theory of truth. Nietzsche argues that when metaphysical foundationalists come to doubt their own

precepts, no other account of reality seems possible. This leads to skepticism and eventually nihilism. The mistake of skeptics, he argues time and again, is that they equate the reality of the world *as such* with the 'true world' as defined by an underlying metaphysical reality, while at the same time doubting its possibility. Skepticism can only emerge against the background of neo-Platonic and Christian metaphysics and for this reason is a mistaken position.[29]

Each step in this argument raises a host of questions, but the central point is that Warren has identified scepticism with the philosophical tradition which grew up in the wake of Plato. Such sceptics were a species of philosopher who rejected philosophy, and we may perhaps accept the suggested symbiosis with what Warren calls 'metaphysical foundationalism'. But scepticism is wider than this. It is a form of mistrust of intellectuality found in many situations, including notably that of the rhetoricians of ancient Greece, whose relativism actually preceded the grand universalism of Plato. A sceptic in this wider sense is one who prefers good practice to any thoughts about the world. The will to truth, Nietzsche remarks, is '*merely* the longing for a *stable world*.'[30] For Nietzsche, 'the reality of the world *as such*' is equated with 'existence'[31] but no formal theory of it is proposed. Nietzsche is certainly not a sceptic in the sense of believing that life is a dream, but the very perspectival insistence by which he criticized the static metaphysics of Platonic rationalism is an integral part of the sceptical tradition of thought in all its forms. And it is in his solution to the problems raised by truth that he is most firmly to be located there. The sceptical tradition affirmed that such basic forms of human vitality as instinct and custom constituted an anchorage for practical life which made unnecessary the grandiosities of truth itself; and so too does Nietzsche.

What marks him off from this tradition is not only his prophetic stance, but the fact that the idea of human nature which the sceptics used as a touchstone has turned into a solution to the problem of authenticity. The sceptics noted that however ill-founded our beliefs may be, we do manage to act successfully enough in the world. Instinct and nature sustain ordinary life, whereas thought commonly leads man to absurdities. As Nietzsche remarks: 'Consciousness is the last and latest development of the organic and consequently also the most unfinished and weakest part of it.'[32] Marx relies upon the same sceptical view of thought

in relation to practice in his eighth thesis on Feuerbach. But whereas in traditional scepticism, nature, instinct and custom had been an unpretentious recourse for which men who had abandoned the delusion of wild metaphysical flights were grateful, in Nietzsche and other prophets of his century, these humble capacities exploded into something much more ambitious. They constituted the solution to a problem of authenticity which had played no part in the thought of the early sceptics.[33] In Nietzsche, this authenticity comes in many forms. Perhaps the most concrete form is life itself realistically responding to its situation in the world. As against a sceptic like Hume, Nietzsche raises the tone of voice of the conversation of philosophy:

> . . . no act of violence, rape, exploitation, destruction is intrinsically 'unjust', since life itself is violent, rapacious, exploitative, and destructive and cannot be conceived otherwise.[34]

It is a theme which runs throughout his discussions of morality:

> . . . life itself is *essentially* appropriation, injury, overpowering of the strange and weaker, suppression, severity, imposition of one's own forms, incorporation and, at the least and mildest, exploitation – but why should one always have to employ precisely those words which have from of old been stamped with a slanderous intention?[35]

It is thus *natural* for life to be expansive and assertive, but life has been slandered by religion, and our thought is largely the expression of that slander. In order to understand the human condition, we must work our way back through the process which has brought us to our present enfeebled state. At the beginning of this process is to be found the Jews, a fateful people distinguished by the fact that, when their god could no longer deliver the goods, they failed to do what any vigorous and natural people would have done – that is, abandon that particular god and take up with another – and turned against the world itself. They created 'A God who *demands* – in place of a God who helps'. The result was the moralization under which we live:

> Chance robbed of its innocence; misfortune dirtied by the concept 'sin'; well-being as a danger, as 'temptation'; physiological indisposition poisoned by the worm of conscience.[36]

Christianity, far from being a revolt against this dispensation, was merely its logical continuation. Europe fell under the priestly power: "'God forgives him who repents" – in plain language: *who subjects himself to the priest.*'[37] Now there is, of course, a sense in which the development of this priestly power is as natural as the life which it subordinates, but in making this distinction, Nietzsche invokes another of his versions of the authenticity programme: the distinction between sickness and health. The priest is a *parasite* systematically concerned with destroying all natural values, everything, Nietzsche perilously adds, 'valuable *in itself*'. The triumph of life is steadily eroded by the onset of self-consciousness, whose content is the set of inhibitions Nietzsche identified with morality.

All of this has the familiar look of the ideology of unmasking, and its content is no less familiar: free-thought in the guise of cultural anti-clericalism. As he pushes back through this process – a fall of man into moralistic religion – he increasingly invokes the famously ambiguous term 'nature', and his account of the cycles of civilization takes on a familiar form. Asking how every higher culture on earth has actually begun, he tells us that:

> Men of a still natural nature, barbarians in every fearful sense of the word, men of prey still in possession of an unbroken strength of will and lust for power, threw themselves upon weaker, more civilized, more peaceful, perhaps trading or cattle-raising races, or upon old mellow cultures, the last vital forces in which were even then flickering out in a glittering firework display of spirit and corruption. The noble caste was in the beginning always the barbarian caste: their superiority lay, not in their physical strength, but primarily in the psychical – they were *more complete* human beings (which, on every level, also means as much as 'more complete beasts' . . .).[38]

The source of civilization, and its enduring claim on vitality, is thus not in ideals or higher principles, in divine influence from above or in platonic principles, but in animal vitality, and what is basic about animal vitality is its spontaneity, its lack of second order inhibitions, its almost fatalistic acceptance of the consequences of its vitality – pain, suffering and rank order. It is his constant theme that idealists have consistently seen the source of civilization in higher influences – religion, morality, or, in other (nineteenth-century) words, ideology – and have been almost

incapable of conceiving that the higher might emerge from the lower. And, like the ancient he really is (all of these romantic prophets have their roots in ancient Greece) he sees decline as the natural tendency of human affairs. Immediately on the heels of his account of the process of civilization comes exemplification, by a contemptuous invocation of the French aristocracy under the *ancien régime*, which 'throws away its privileges with a sublime disgust and sacrifices itself to an excess of moral feeling'.[39]

It is hard not to regard the argument as a little simpleminded. Life, nature, sickness and health – all of this is so much the stock-in-trade of the least interesting kind of nineteenth-century Darwinian that one would hardly be surprised to stumble across the idea of the survival of the fittest, which does indeed seem to be a possible summary of much of what Nietzsche has to say. At one level, there's not much to choose between Nietzsche on the one hand and Dale Carnegie and other upbeat American positive thinkers on the other: in both cases, there is the message 'stop worrying and start living, happiness is there to be seized'. But at this level, there is hardly much in the way of philosophical interest, and in order to revive that, we must look to the most abstract formulation Nietzsche gave to his theory of natural human energy: the will to power.

As with many other terms in this corpus of work, the expression 'will to power' tempts us to vulgar simplification. It tempts us to regard human life as a scramble for whatever benefit may be construed as 'power'. Just such a notion infests the vulgar ideas of liberation current in our time. However, there popular ideas take for granted that the active human agent is a fixed and stable entity seeking determinate benefits or advantages in the world. What Nietzsche affirms is a reversal of this relationship. The will to power is a reality principle in which organisms seek to grasp the world by exploring and exploiting such possibilities as the organism itself can recognize and construe. It is not so much that a determinate agent seeks to attain its purposes by subduing the world as that, in the process of exploring and exploiting the world, the organism is constantly discovering its own character, and in particular, reaffirming its character as a creator of meanings and values. The point of the process is not any determinate condition of the world, but rather the maintenance of a certain equilibrium between the world and the organism's active presence within it.

To talk in this way about an 'organism' follows directly from Nietzsche's propensity for abstract universals such as 'life', and further suggests he may be assimilated to the reductionist positivisms of his time. These implications are evidently misleading. Nietzsche's argument may best be taken as a case of *reculer pour mieux sauter*. Nietzsche seeks at the first stage of the argument to dissolve the apparatus of soul, self, subject and individual agent which had been inherited from the Western philosophical tradition. His objection to these entities is that they are metaphysical in the sense of being constructions above and beyond the evidence of man's organic nature. In this sense, Nietzsche is simply pushing much further Hegel's criticism of Kant, in whom the noumenon rose up like a Grail far beyond the here and now of human understanding – beyond what might appropriately be called the *lebenswelt*. The self or soul in this philosophical tradition might well be conceived by analogy with a radio receiver designed to cut out the static produced by the passions (that inference of nature with our precious human reason) in order to receive, loud and clear, the pronouncements of metaphysics and religion, each being conceived as the higher spheres which draw us upward away from our base animal inheritance. The *Genealogy of Morals* is a direct attack upon the notionally Platonic derivation of the specifically human from some higher sphere, and an affirmation of the notionally Darwinian derivation of human powers from what we must, in terms of these conventions, call 'below'.

Nietzsche steps back from the metaphysical, then, in order to dissolve it in the organic, and when he is performing this stage of the operation, he invokes life and physiology and sounds rather like a latter-day *ideologue*. But the point of stepping back is to jump better, and Nietzsche's leap is into treating the human world as a self-conscious empirical process. The self becomes a process of experience. 'I see a bird' becomes the less linguistically familiar 'There is a seeing of a bird conscious of itself as the seeing of a bird'. The self, as Mark Warren argues, is a self-reflective empirical process, a mode of self-reflective experience. He summarizes it as:

> . . . Nietzsche asserts that human beings (and perhaps all things) universally strive to constitute themselves through their experiental and interpretive worlds as causal agents, and that human beings will

power in this sense . . . (the will to power) . . . requires that self-reflective interpretations of agency be considered as realities insofar as they give rise to all possibilities of value. Accordingly Nietzsche arrives at a concept of value that is both an interpretation and objectively contingent upon practice.[40]

IDEOLOGY: CULTURE V. CIVILITY

We can only escape these oscillations of interpretation between the physiological and the philosophical by recognizing that there are two kinds of argument animating Nietzsche's writings. The first may be best signalled in his strident declamations against the classes of person he despises, as when he breaks into a dithyramb about freedom:

> The man *who has become free* – and how much more the *mind* that has become free – spurns the contemptible sort of well-being dreamed of by shopkeepers, Christians, cows, women, Englishmen and other democrats.[41]

This is the true ideologist's contempt for those who do not share his admirations, and it is essentially dogmatic. His view of Christianity is merely the simple and superior view that the objects of Christian belief are, in truth, fantasy, and the admirations of Christians contemptible. But Nietzsche, unlike Marxists, feminists, anarchists, nationalists and all the rest, is not recruiting for a movement and would have fled screaming had he ever come close to one. Hence it is best to assimilate this strand of thought to the status of a stimulating, but highly disputable, application of the deeper and more interesting thesis that authenticity entails realism. What is interesting about this thesis is its formal character. It need not become entangled in any of Nietzsche's highly contingent responses to his own time. This form of realism can be analysed in a variety of ways but, on any plausible account, the reality involved is entirely constituted by the responses of a properly functioning organism. It is 'perspectival', being oriented towards performances likely to yield strings of future satisfactions, but these satisfactions arise directly from within the endeavour of the originating agent itself. They are not to be identified with happiness, although to take pleasure in one's own happiness is

one sign of the authenticity Nietzsche is seeking to understand. One major strand of this realism is the capacity to liberate oneself from the dead hand of the past. Unrealism in this area is exemplified partly by the Christian tendency to dwell upon sin (which is likely to elicit an enfeebling remorse) and the Prussian tendency to turn history into a prop for the state. Nietzsche sees the past largely as the receptacle of brooding memories liable to induce one or other of the various forms of *ressentiment*. He speaks with admiration of Mirabeau, who never forgave a slight because it was not the kind of thing he could manage to remember in order to forgive it.

More generally, his view is that modern Europeans have fallen into self-contempt from having been indoctrinated in certain false ideas. These false ideas induce pangs of conscience and a general feeling of displeasure in the fact of the individual's being as he is. But even in someone largely subject to these feelings, there will be moments when he 'feels free and valiant' and begins to take pleasure in himself. Natural vitality thus breaks like a sun through this cloudy Christian consciousness, and the individual finds himself once more in a real relationship with himself and the world. Often the false theory is strong enough to induce him to think of such moments as if they were divine love, but what they are in fact is *self*-redemption, a breaking free from doctrinal constraints. And Nietzsche summarizes this argument:

> Thus: a definite false psychology, a certain kind of fantasy in the interpretation of motives and experiences is the necessary presupposition for becoming a Christian and for feeling the need of redemption. With the insight into this aberration of reason and imagination one ceases to be a Christian.[42]

The test by which this falsity may be exposed is life, or nature, or in its fullest formulation, the will to power. Natural propensities are weighed down by a heavy conscience[43] and the result is that mankind lives amidst phantoms. Philosophers have provided the intellectual support for this collapse of the heroic values into the inauthentic strivings of modern life:

> Wherever there have been philosophers, from India to England (to indicate the opposite extremes of speculative orientation) there has prevailed a special philosopher's resentment against sensuality . . .

every animal, including *la bête philosophe*, strives instinctively for the
optimum conditions under which it may release its powers. Every
animal, instinctively and with a subtle flair that leaves reason far
behind, abhors all interference that might conceivably block its path
to that optimum.[44]

The philosopher is a parasite on nature, drawing strength from
outside himself, but philosophy too is part of life, part of nature
no less than what it feeds on, and exhibits its own will to power.
Like the parasite pity,[45] the priests (who are the cleverest and
most conscious hypocrites[46]) have the simple confidence of every
sovereign instinct. Nature is thus the source both of truth, and of
falsity, and we are left with the view, however unsatisfactory it
may be, that everything is nature (that is, exhibits the will to
power) but that some things are more natural than others. The
first is Nietzsche the philosopher, the second is Nietzsche the
prophet.

But of what is he the prophet? To ask this question is to raise
a perennial difficulty in interpreting him. It is tempting to think
of him as a kind of political philosopher, in which case a view of
ideology might naturally fit into any exposition of his work. Those
attempting to discover Nietzsche's political doctrine in the past
usually came up with a set of proto-fascist exultations about the
noble and the base elements in politics, as if Nietzsche were simply
Callicles reborn at the height of the romantic nineteenth century.
But the Nietzsche who matches every doctrine with its opposite
is much too subtle to be captured in this way. We may perhaps
detect some idea of a good society in him: one where 'sovereign
individuals' are free to act as their natures dictate.[47] But as an
account of the modern world, his thought is marked by conspicuous gaps. He has no conception of an economy; we could still be
buckling on sword and shield for all the notice he takes of modern
industry. Nor is he, except fitfully, concerned with the state, or
any form of civil association. Everything dissolves into nature,
and the inhibitions upon it. For Nietzsche, every situation is best
understood as an unstable equilibrium of forces, and the ultimate
betrayal is the attempt to fix any particular constellation of such
forces as a timeless framework for living. Correspondingly, any
such timeless framework, any notion of 'the moral order of the
world' can at best be nothing else but some temporary moment

of ascendancy translated into an intellectual idiom in order to sustain the ascendancy. The attempt to create these timeless ascendancies is the pathology of consciousness. It is the sickness which has produced the metaphysician's yearning for a timeless world. Truth in one direction, history in another, are each forms of mediocrity seeking to avoid the constant alertness required by life, for 'the free man is a *warrior*'.[48]

No state, then, and no economy, but a culture construed as a ceaseless struggle against decadence, a culture largely aesthetic in form. When Nietzsche thinks of the state, he necessarily thinks of it as merely one more illicit attempt to 'fix' the unfixable, to impose an empty abstract form upon a substantial dynamism:

> To accept any legal system as sovereign and universal – to accept it, not merely as an instrument in the struggle of power complexes, but as a *weapon against struggle* (in the sense of Duhring's communist cliché that every will must regard every other will as its equal) – is an anti-vital principle which can only bring about man's utter demoralization and, indirectly, a reign of nothingness.[49]

At best, Nietzsche can manage ambivalence in his view of law and civil association. He denies that the idea of justice is merely a rationalization of the reactive emotion of vengeance, but he sees in it merely a form of domination: it is a code which the superior power imposes upon the forces of hostility and resentment. But the essence of a code of laws is its abstract character. Being abstract, it is subject to logic, and logic equalizes.[50] The very law which overcomes the reactive powers of hostility and resentment is simultaneously inimical to the rhythms of organismic vitality. What is it that might sustain those rhythms against the levelling power (as Nietzsche sees it) of law? Clearly his own thought, the inspiration of Zarathustra, setting itself up as a myth of oppositionality against the inevitable corruptions of modern civil association.

It is the contrast between *civitas* and *Kultur* which forces its attention upon the reader looking for that evidently whimsical object of attention – the politics of Nietzsche. Bewitched by the relation of master and slave (it has been observed) he did not understand

> . . . . that material as well as cultural practices are subject to reification

– in markets and bureaucracies, for example. This gap in Nietzsche's understanding of modern society caused him to explain the modern crisis of power solely as a cultural crisis.[51]

If there is such a thing as 'the modern crisis of power', then Nietzsche certainly saw it in cultural terms because, good German that he was, he saw everything that way. One clue to his interpretation of the world might be found in his highly ambivalent view of English thought and life, about which he most commonly made scathing comments. The English concern with happiness he takes to be a symptom of irredeemable mediocrity, and it would be above all the British bourgeois whom he might hope to shock with his wild declamations about the violence of life in the raw. Lacking a real grasp of civil life, he denies that there is any difference between abiding by a rule and submitting to domination. There is, indeed, little in his thought that might distance him from the supreme ideological vulgarity of the twentieth century: construing *all* human relationships in terms of domination. And starting from this point, he necessarily arrives at a concern with the question: what sort of person should actually dominate?

Ideology in Nietzsche's work is dead, life-denying thought whose time has passed. For all his recognition of sublimation and self-discipline as forms of gearing by which lower impulses are transformed into something noble, he remains forever hostile to any standing, external modifications of human striving. The only value of civility is as something to be transcended and transformed, and in this Nietzsche is entirely true to the whole project of ideology. It is consistently hostile to any civil apparatus which sustains a plurality of competing opinions within limited terms of competition, sustaining error no less than truth. The ideas of ideology and authenticity unite in seeking a culture superior to the inevitable makeshifts and compromises of an actual modern politics. In Nietzsche for whom only ideas were real, such a culture meant the constant ecstasy of an intellectual recreation of the world. His ideas begin the day as 'many coloured and malicious' but as the day wears on, they change, and Nietzsche apostrophizes them thus:

> You have already taken off your novelty and some of you, I fear, are on the point of becoming truths: they already look so immortal, so pathetically righteous, so boring . . . no one will divine . . . how you

looked in your morning, you sudden sparks and wonders of my solitude, you my old beloved – *wicked* thoughts![52]

There are ideas that are living, and ideas that are dead, and ideology is the graveyard of dead thoughts. A lively, laughing culture has its ears cocked for the new impulses bubbling up from the source of life. Yet, as the philosopher might also observe, such things only acquire their value by contrast with the old, the established, the conventions by which alone novelty may be detected; and of those things, Nietzsche had little conception, and certainly no affection.

NOTES

1. One must not be deceived by the false politeness of those who sweeten this pill by grandiosely universal utterances of the 'we are all the products of our background' or 'no theories are neutral' kind. These are never seriously operational when the argument gets down to specifics.
2. Francis Bacon, *The New Organon*, vol. I (New York: Bobs-Merrill, 1960), p. 41.
3. For an account of the content and background of the project, see Brian William Head, *Ideology and Social Science, Destutt de Tracy and French Liberalism* (Dordrecht: Martinas Nijhoff, 1985).
4. See particularly the early pages of *The German Ideology* (1846), as in *Marx and Engels Collected Works*, vol. 5 (London: Lawrence and Wishart, 1976).
5. Karl Mannheim, *Ideology and Utopia* (London: Routledge & Kegan Paul, 1936).
6. See Louis Althusser, *Lenin and Philosophy and Other Essays*, trans. Ben Brewster (London: New Left Books, 1971), p. 162.
7. 'The Poverty of Philosophy' in *Marx and Engels Collected Works*, vol. 6 (London: Lawrence & Wishart, 1976), p. 178.
8. Jorge Larrain in this volume, attempts to save Marx from the imputation of dogmatism: 'Is it not the case that all intellectual positions lay claim to validity? A theory . . . cannot be accused of dogmatism simply for claiming the truth of its arguments' (pp. 117–18). True enough. But the dogmatism in Marx, as in all theories of ideology, lies in the conjunction of (1) My judgement of the nature of reality is true; yours (2) is (a) false and (b) *caused* by determinants of which you are unconscious. The theory of ideology, in other words, is a standing muddle in which truth is confused with issues of either social determination or covert interest.
9. *The Will to Power*, p. 493, in Oscar Levy (ed.) *The Complete Works of Freidrich Nietzsche* (Edinburgh and London: T. N. Foulis, 1910), vol. 15, no. 493, p. 20. Cf. 'The criterion of Truth lies in the enhancement of the feeling of power', p. 534.
10. *Twilight of the Idols*, R. J. Hollingdale (ed.) (Harmondsworth: Penguin, 1969), p. 37. ('Reasoning Philosophy', p. 4.)
11. *The Genealogy of Morals*, trans. Francis Golfing (New York, 1956), vol. 1, p. 166.

12. *Twilight of the Idols*, op. cit., p. 38.
13. Martin Heidegger, *Nietzsche: Volume I: The Will To Power as Art*, trans. David Farrell (London: Krell, 1981), p. 29.
14. *Beyond Good and Evil*, R. J. Hollingdale (ed.) (Harmondsworth: Penguin, 1973), p. 20.
15. See Peter Stern's discussion of 'On Truth and Falsehood in an Extra-Moral Sense' in *Nietzsche* (Oxford, 1978), pp. 132 ff.
16. *The Genealogy of Morals*, op. cit., vol. I, p. 13.
17. *The Genealogy of Morals*, op. cit., vol. II, p. 7.
18. *The Will to Power*, op. cit., vol. 1, p. 465.
19. *The Genealogy of Morals*, op. cit., vol. I, 5, of I, p. 9.
20. See Thomas Goddard Bergin and Max Harold Frisch (eds, trans.), *The New Science of Giambattista Vico* (New York: Doubleday & Co. Inc., 1971) and especially the famous passage in paragraph 331 where Vico writes that 'the world of civil society has certainly been made by men, and . . . its principles are therefore to be found within the modification of our own human mind'.
21. *The Gay Science*; see R. J. Hollingdale (ed.) *A Nietzsche Reader* (Harmondsworth: Penguin, 1977), p. 158.
22. All metaphysics perhaps warrant the adjective 'foundational' but this redundancy, familiar in the literature, does emphasize the drift of Nietzsche's rejection of 'philosophy'.
23. Cf. Nietzsche on corruption as 'the indication that anarchy threatens within the instincts', *Beyond Good and Evil*, op. cit., p. 174.
24. J. J. Rousseau, *Emile* (London: Dent & Co., 1966), p. 22.
25. *The Will to Power*, op. cit., vol. I, 62, pp. 98–100.
26. *The Genealogy of Morals*, op. cit., vol. II, p. 20.
27. See for example, *Thus Spoke Zarathustra*, R. J. Hollingdale (ed.) (London: Penguin, 1969), p. 136 ff. and *passim*.
28. R. J. Hollingdale, in his introduction to *Thus Spoke Zarathustra* (London: Penguin, 1969), pp. 28–9.
29. 'Interpreting Nietzsche: A Reply to Alan Woolfolk', *Political Theory*, vol. 14, no. 4, November 1986, p. 663.
30. *The Will to Power*, op. cit., p. 585A.
31. Cf. ibid., 6.
32. *The Gay Science*, 11; Cf. R. J. Hollingdale, *A Nietzsche Reader*, op. cit., p. 158.
33. In one sense, of course, authenticity is an essentially classical idea, for the classical philosophers believed that only the rational element of man was authentically human. But nature, which posed this problem, also solved it by distinguishing the members of human societies into the rational and the superstitious. The modern problem, however, presupposes an idea of historical evolution different from anything entertained by the Greeks.
34. *The Genealogy of Morals*, op. cit., vol. II, p. 11.
35. *Beyond Good and Evil*, op. cit., p. 259.
36. *The Anti-Christ*, R. J. Hollingdale (ed.) (Harmondsworth: Penguin, 1968) 25, p. 136.
37. Ibid., 26, p. 139.
38. *Beyond Good and Evil*, op. cit., p. 257.
39. *Beyond Good and Evil*, op. cit., p. 258.
40. Mark Warren, 'Nietzsche's Concept of Ideology', *Theory and Society*, 13, (1984), p. 551.
41. *Twilight of the Idols*, op. cit., vol. I, 38 (p. 92).

42. *Human, All Too Human*, quoted in R. J. Hollingdale (ed.) *A Nietzsche Reader* (Harmondsworth: Penguin, 1977), pp. 171–2.
43. *The Will to Power*, op. cit., p. 295.
44. *The Genealogy of Morals*, op. cit., vol. III, p. 7.
45. *The Will to Power*, op. cit., p. 368.
46. Ibid., p. 377.
47. *The Genealogy of Morals*, op. cit., vol. II, esp. pp. i–3.
48. *Twilight of the Idols*, op. cit., vol. I, 38; p. 92.
49. *The Genealogy of Morals*, op. cit., vol. II, p. 11.
50. *The Will to Power*, op. cit., p. 501.
51. Mark Warren, op. cit., p. 561.
52. *Beyond Good and Evil*, op. cit., p. 296.

3.   Ideology and Political Reality

David Manning

The historian of ideas is confronted by a variety of considerations peculiar to the different intellectual ancestry of the disciplines to which his subject-matter belongs. To write a history of any one such form of understanding calls not only for a conception of historical investigation itself, but also for a clear conception of the place of the understanding under investigation on the map of knowledge. We expect the historian of philosophy or science to encompass within his study only what has been generally regarded by informed opinion to be germain to the subject chosen for investigation. It is therefore disturbing, if not altogether surprising, to discover the historian of ideas locating ideological thought in the domain of philosophical, scientific or some other territory of enquiry, and feeling obliged to penalize it for being unintelligible in the native language spoken there. It is obvious that, amongst students of ideological understanding, there is not the same consensus of opinion about its structural identity as there is about the structural identity of philosophy and science in the works of the students of these disciplines.[1]

Without this degree of certainty as to the parameters of the subject of investigation, the historian of ideological thought can be excused for being uncertain as to what does and does not belong to his narrative account. This toleration is all the more justified by the fact that ideological writing is crowded with arguments that appear, if not claimed, to be theological, philosophical, historical or scientific reasoning.[2] Nevertheless it can disturb the historian's conscience to witness what he instinctively recognizes as the degeneration of historical investigation into a polemic against ideology, if he seriously considers such work as Kedourie's *Nationalism*, Hayek's *The Road to Serfdom*, Popper's *The Open Society and its Enemies* or Talmon's *The Origins of Totalitarian*

Democracy as essays on the history of ideas.[3] Here the ideological understanding is denigrated as an enemy of truth, and the manner in which this is accomplished is puzzling, since Popper's, Hayek's, Kedourie's and Talmon's judgement on ideology evidenced in particular ideological writings – that it is a fraudulent representation of the right way for reasonable human beings to associate and live – has the characteristics of the ideological arguments in favour of the liberal/conservative convictions which Popper, Hayek, Kedourie and Talmon obviously consider to be justified.[4] The fact that these arguments appear to be respectable does not alter the implications of the fact that, from a philosophical point of view, they are as much arguments in favour of a way of life as those to which they are opposed, and ultimately rely upon the appeal of ethical evaluations rather than the compulsion of historical fact alone.[5] The problem is that the ideological understanding, as identified by Popper, Hayek, Kedourie and Talmon, has not been found a place on the map of knowledge that is, according to philosophical cartography, its legitimate home, and not an invasion of the territory of another form of understanding to be resisted by an appeal to the coherence peculiar to the conceptual framework of that indigenous comprehension. Ideology has been abandoned by philosophy to wander around as a potential vandal from the viewpoint of every established discipline. The damage it does is a matter of our own ideological judgement.

Popper, Hayek, Kedourie and Talmon clearly consider that properly understood politics is a form of practical understanding manifest in the legally regulated activity of governing a civil association. They conceive it to be a limited practice authorised to regulate the activity of associates exclusively intelligible in the liberal/conservative conceptions of politics. As such, the investigation of its intellectual ancestry by socialist historians of ideas such as Tawney, Carr, Thompson and Hill, whose conception of politics is one of the areas of class conflict where interested parties compete for power, must therefore be misconceived. It leads to a history of politics as the story of the conflict between government and the governed, both presumed to represent different social groups. We are familiar with the categorical exclusion of alternative ideological conceptions of this kind at more than this level of confrontation, but I shall not explore their many battlefields here.

In this essay I do not propose to travel very far in my investi-

gation of the ideological view of political reality. I have nothing ambitious in mind. I propose only to observe the play of political ideas in the political arena with a view to locating their ideological home. On the level of political debate there are, however, certain rules to be observed that govern the communication of political sense. These constitute the grammar of politics not in Laski's sense, as propositions about political reality,[6] but in Wittgenstein's sense as rules of a language game.[7] In so doing I hope to show precisely what is involved in the game of politics if any goals are to be scored. I have therefore taken a sample of ideological writing and given it the designation 'immigrant anglophilism'. What I want to do is locate chosen works of Popper, Hayek, Kedourie and Talmon in the English political scene of the mid-twentieth century; I will then spell out a more complete dictionary of political talk in that world of political discourse. This exercise is intended to help us locate certain grammatical features of the political utterance that are obscured by our incomplete command of its whole vocabulary, which tends to give us only a partial map of any political life. I offer this introduction to the cartography of ideology as a guide to revealing my chosen works of Popper, Hayek, Kedourie and Talmon which, by their critical omission of features of the geography of contemporary political debate, make excellent ideological persuasion. It is not so much what they do say (with which I take my reader to be familiar) as what they do not say that gives their works their individual identity. I hope that my map will assist the reader in locating their place in English politics at the time they made their distinguished and distinctive contribution to the formation of political opinion.

The ideologies of liberalism, socialism and conservatism took the field in the 1945 British election in the colours of individualism, collectivism and culturalism respectively. I shall see these doctrines as players in the game of politics, because all three will be seen to have the common concern with what men should try to be and do in a world of transient spatio-temporal experience to effect the creation and maintenance of permanent and universal human relationships of the kind that constitute a civil society and the state. I therefore propose to represent them as teams of ideas moving the goalposts in the arena of political life. Politics is a language game in Wittgenstein's sense and, in a very serious way,

individual ideological vocabularies are restricted languages which it is the business of philosophy to translate.

THE GAME

The game of ideological persuasion, I suggest, is one which identifies the individual with the cause of civilization in the service of which he can conceive of himself as a person worthy of respect (a player). This is the cause of a collectivity variously conceived to have the cultural identity of a society, a class, a nation, a race or community (a team). In each case a certain lifestyle is characterized as the criterion that determines whether a person belongs to, or can be judged to stand apart from, the social reality established by the collectivity (the supporters). To be at home in a social reality one has to be acknowledged to be a democrat, a proletarian, a patriot, an Aryan, a native inhabitant or to have some other consciousness peculiar to the approval of the arrangements that constitute its practices, particularly those which arrange its political life (the team spirit displayed on the home ground). Those who are entitled to participate in this life are primarily concerned with the preservation and future development of their economic, social and political conduct in a world in which there exist other political realities hostile to their survival (met at away games). Other political styles, classes, nationalities, races and communities are, ideologically, seen as threats to the temporal stability and territorial integrity of those who are associated and organized in a way peculiarly legitimized by their own beliefs (the visiting team and its supporters). Political survival calls for the cohesive autonomy and self-determination of a collectivity which in turn depends upon the persistence of its ideological identity, manifest in the continuity of its institutionalized and corporate life (the supporters' club).

Political stability within any one political reality calls for at least a degree of consensus of ideological conviction amongst its inhabitants, and its total absence makes legitimate government impossible and an identifiable way of life unattainable. However, this does not imply that, because the political realities of Nazi Germany and democratic Britain have had totally different institutional arrangements, the former must have enjoyed a political,

and the latter suffered an ideological, regime. The consensus or coincidence of liberal, socialist and conservative commitment represented by the British parliamentary government is not necessarily less ideologically inspired than was the monolithic commitment of the Nazi Party to Hitler's leadership. It is simply a liberal conviction that the politics of a liberal democratic society are naturally attractive to normal rational people who properly understand politics as the preserve of government, and that it is totalitarian leadership which is outside legal regulation and hence anti-political (anyone can play this game). The above-mentioned work of Popper, Hayek, Kedourie and Talmon is as capable of arousing political commitment with inhuman consequences as is the political thought of communists, nationalists and fascists – witness the plight of those in the Third World deprived of the necessary resources to pursue an effective policy to develop their economies by the capital control and technology of the industrial powers. The politics of poverty amount to very little (prevented rather than excluded from playing).

Ideological arguments of every variety are concerned to persuade the susceptible that the significant relationship between the past they have experienced and the future they believe to be within their grasp makes the present time the historic moment for shaping the course of desirable events (scoring opportunity). It is the moment in which the committed act will not only constitute a declaration of the authentic self in the political arena, but will also oblige others to make a similar stand for what they believe in, insofar as they too have a stake in the resulting world. The ideological communication is invariably a call for involvement. Unlike the universal processes of nature, and the particular circumstances of the past, the arrangements that constitute social reality can be changed by changed minds and redirected enthusiasm (goal).

It is the case that, like the supporters of a football team, the majority of adherents to every ideology do not play. They are extraordinarily intellectually lazy, leaving their political thinking to the professionals they admire, but who are names rather than texts. There is in fact a distinct anti-intellectualism amongst every ideology's adherents particularly when it comes to considering more than one point of view. The business of supporting ideological conclusions becomes an autonomous activity to the point that,

like football hooligans, supporters of a party attend to politics more for the confrontation than for the persuasion and spend little time considering the long-term implications of their received beliefs. Popular political activity is also a remarkably short-term engagement for most, being set aside between elections – as between Cup Final days – and the consequences of policies now pursued for generations to come are of little concern even then. Future generations do not vote.

Ideology is persuasive talk (tackling and scoring). It is about the business of changing minds, and, by changing minds, is not to be taken as implying a change of course in life of the kind made when one project is abandoned as impractical in favour of another that is not (tactics). This kind of decision is made in the light of new information as to the utility value of the alternatives before us that oblige us to admit that we have, in the past, made a mistake that could have been avoided.

A change of mind effected by ideological persuasion involves a change of life's significance, making what was the right choice at a time past no longer the right one in the time present (a new ball game). The change in question is a change in self-understanding, or the criterion of personal choice, and is not a change in what it is reasonable for any person to choose. To undergo this conversion is not an effort of the informed will to give up what should all along have been recognized as a bad habit, like giving up smoking and taking up chewing gum. It is more like the revelation that the way in which one has previously regarded others and the way in which one previously lived no longer appear as ethically justified as they did. It is to have a new regard for the value of life in the light of a new conviction, not to admit a final recognition of the established medical fact that smoking is harmful to one's health. Having a changed mind is not changing one's mind: it is not an admission that one has been acting irrationally and changed a habit. It is a realization that our values have changed, and that we no longer see ourselves and our relationships with others as we previously did. It is to have changed life's goals not to have changed course to make the journey longer. Of course, it is possible that a person decides to give up smoking at the same time that he finds that he is sympathetic to the environmentalist's cause, and this decision may occur at a point at which he has the opportunity to vote for a Green party which is committed to an

anti-smoking campaign on the grounds that it is selfish or bad habit (offside).

Voting for a party one has not previously voted for does not imply listening for the first time to what that party stands for; rather, it is realizing that what that party has to offer now makes sense of the growing dissatisfaction one has felt with oneself and one's social circumstances. It is as though changes in one's values have left one rightly feeling an outsider in company once enjoyed, frustrated in activities that previously gave satisfaction and disgusted with an environment that previously did not offend (the loss of the will to win). It is the focusing of one's attention on issues of common concern at an election (end of season) that provides the opportunity for reflection on persuasion and the occasion to declare oneself on another side (particularly if one has supported the losing team).

The recognition that the time has come to take stock of one's ideological commitment and, if necessary, openly come out as an advocate of a different lifestyle (changing teams) calls for a soul-search. It involves closing the gap between feeling and saying (scoring) rather than seeing the opportunity to put a theory into practice. Making a break with one's past of the kind that may be provoked by an event such as the Soviet Union's invasion of Hungary, or Britain's attack on Egypt in 1956, does not involve pulling up one's roots. It involves the realization that the ideological roots of the Communist or Conservative Party are no longer the roots of your political plant. No doubt some connections will then be broken and be a matter for regret, but the alternative is the meaningless self-deception and infertile imagination of the fellow-traveller (a leading player attracted to another team for financial gain). Being in politics calls for an ideological understanding of one's position, and one cannot make this stand with a foot in two different camps (scoring a home goal). Different ideological homes are not interchangeable at will.

Now, political persuasion concerns how to associate and live within legal regulation and organization that enables us as individuals, with different desires, understandings and feelings, to choose to transact, cooperate or coexist to acquire, produce or enjoy what is deemed valuable in life. In Western Europe these arrangements are the spatio-temporal coincident institutional realities of civil society and the state (the Football Association and the

national team). At this point it will be useful to outline these universal relationships between individuals, who are simultaneously both citizens and subjects, that are made intelligible in the vocabulary of democratic liberalism, socialism and conservatism (the principal teams). It is what is intelligible to the ideological mind that the historian of political ideas has to elucidate.

THE POLITICS OF CIVIL SOCIETY AND THE STATE

In a civil society, the function of government as a political activity is comparable with the limitation imposed upon the performance of an engine by its governor. The stability of the system sets a limit to, rather than directs, the performance of a range of acts by the governed and is itself governed by predetermined regulation (Football Association rules). Those who govern a civil society, whether they be elected, appointed or coopted, all work within defined terms of reference. For the most part their business is conducted in committees or assemblies, the chairman of which cannot overrule a majority of those having a right to vote on the issues considered. Responsibility for committee decisions is collective. Ideally, committee membership can be seen to be a microcosm of the society it represents, and although its debates and deliberations are not public discussions of the kind conducted through the media, they are held in public up to the point at which it is not the government of society so much as the direction and administration of the affairs of state that is under review (the National Selection Committee). The style of civil government is more convivial than confrontational, and the conclusions reached and resolutions adopted owe more to behind-the-scenes consultation and conventional procedures than to knock-down argument and public demonstrations.

Of course, insofar as what is at stake is the ideological acceptability of government policy, confrontation is inevitable. The politics of rank and file and of victory and defeat in parliamentary debate herald the declaration of an electoral contest. Failing institutionalized debate resolving the terms of our future coexistence in politics, politics can then be taken on to the streets with the prospect of victory moved to the battlefield of civil war.

What makes institutionalized political activity possible is the existence of a coincidence rather than a consensus of public opinion,
not on, but on what are the major political issues amongst those
holding, not a variety of compatible ideological beliefs, but a
variety of ideological beliefs that legitimize compatible activities.
The constitutional style of government we associate with a civil
society depends upon the shared spatio-temporal social reality of
civil society and the state rather than upon the existence of a
shared middle ground of political conviction. For example, it is
not the ideological consensus of British politics alone, to be found
in liberal, socialist and conservative thinking on the form of constitutional government, which is the precondition of the dual
relationship of civil society and the state. It is partly to be found
in the coincidence that the one form of government can serve the
political objectives of socialists and conservatives equally well, or
at least as well as indicated by the fact that constitutional reform
has not been their first priority, as electoral reform has not, for
both the Conservative and Labour Parties in Britain to date.

Comparable with this coincidence of interest, as distinct from
concensus of opinion, which forms the parameters of the centre
ground of civil politics is the tighter circle of the relatively uniform
conception of the national interest, variously ideologically conceived by different parties in power to be essential to the direction
of the state. This relative uniformity is to be found in the disci-
plined ranks of the party in power which is responsible for admin-
istering state affairs. Whether it be for the limited period in power
of an elected government in a multi-party state, calling for the
pretended political neutrality of its professional servants, or for
the indefinite period in power of a revolutionary government
leadership with a long political agenda calling for the declared
ideological commitment of its public servants, the style of politics
that characterizes the exercise of sovereign authority is that of
centralized decision-making – that is, decision-making within the
confines of authoritative circles of diminishing size the nearer they
approach the office of the effective head of state, the ideological
and administrative nerve centre. The executive mind of the high
command of state affairs does not so much represent a microcosm
of opinion held by the subjects of the state as the avant-garde
opinion of what it ought to be. As they reflect on the reports on
their desks, the minds of those in possession of a monopoly of

power tends to be pre-possessed and directed by the works of a school of ideological thought; these illuminate the steps they take when they tread the corridors of power in search of technical information and professional advice on how to achieve their objectives. This is as true of liberal, socialist and conservative governments in a pluralistic society with an elected government as it is of a totalitarian government in a one-party state. The extent of what is regarded as an affair of state may differ, but the model of rationality that is operative in decision-making is that of ideologically-determined objectives pursued by a professional organization with technical efficiency and the absence of political discord. The fact that there are potentially more fellow-travellers in the British civil service than in the Russian is about all that distinguishes one from the other. The history of the reform of both is the history of the organization of available human resources to get things done without members of the organization reflecting on the human consequences of carrying out those orders. In both cases the response to a queried order is that it has been decided elsewhere by those having the necessary authority. Should that answer not suffice, the civil servant is bypassed by alternative channels or go-betweens. In this connection, a comparison between the implementation of Chamberlain's policy of appeasement and Hitler's policy of the Final Solution is now instructive and a comparison between Mr Gorbachev's and Mrs Thatcher's administrative reforms will doubtless prove instructive in the future.

The paradigm of rationality that characterizes the agreement of two individuals to effect a transaction, (provided that this takes place in the department of human affairs: the marketplace) is not incompatible with the paradigm of rationality that characterizes the agreement of two ideologically committed persons to form a political party (provided that this takes place in the department of human affairs: the political arena). Equally, the paradigm of rationality that characterizes the acknowledgment of many that citizens have an obligation to comply with the law at all times when they are within the jurisdiction of a state is not incompatible with the paradigm of rationality that characterizes the acknowledgement that they, as subjects, have a duty to obey commands of servants of the state at particular times when they have violated the law. However, their being compatible when compartmental does not make them the same paradigm of ration-

ality. Exchange and voluntary organization, compliance and subjection involve different kinds of interpersonal relationship, implying that how we should associate and live is also a question of when and where, since the universality of any one such paradigm of rationality implies the unitarian or totalitarian conformity of one kind of relationship at all times and places.

Politics as the activity that determines how we should associate and live is therefore the business of persuading, in the political arena, who should be allowed or commanded to do what when and where within the association and organization of society and the state, or what degree of spatio-temporal compartmentalization of kinds of activities, if any, are compatible with the ideological convictions advanced by the politically conscious. Liberals, for example, have a compartment for religious observance – in church on Sunday. Communists do not. In their extreme forms liberal individualism, with its emphasis on the rationale of gainful transaction, socialist collectivism, with its emphasis on the rationale of corporate cooperation, and conservative culturalism, with its emphasis on the exclusivity of coexisting close-knit lifestyles, each reveal a tendency towards some sort of unitarian or totalitarian universalism of rigid singular compartmentalization. In their more restrained forms liberalism, socialism and conservatism do not represent unadulterated individualism, collectivism and culturalism respectively. There are elements of all three in each ideological tradition.

THE IDENTITY OF POLITICAL REALITY

Liberalism, as a doctrine, does not deny that the individual can only realize his full potential as a citizen in society; socialism does not deny that political achievement can only be assessed in terms of the quality of individual life; and conservatism does not deny that respect for law and order depends upon the individual's appreciation of an established way of life. Nevertheless the fact remains that what is generally seen to be genuine individualism, legitimate collectivism and authentic culturalism are associated with the ideologies of liberalism, socialism and conservatism in the minds of their adherents. All we have to bear in mind is that the exaggeration of the one-dimensional commercial, communal

or familial man is useful for advertising a match but is not an account of it.

Team One: Milltown Associated

For the liberal, civilization is the achievement of individual rational self-determination. His authentic being as a person requires freedom to act as he wills within the constraints of respect to which other persons are entitled under a rule of law that recognizes the sanctity of human rights. It can only be advanced by collective action where that action provides a good or service which the disadvantaged individual alone, or in restricted agreement with others cannot provide for himself. For the liberal there is, properly perceived, always a difference between the occasion for public assistance and the opportunity for private initiative. This distinction is to be borne in mind by those engaged in legislation that determines the relationship between civil association and the state. Their responsibility is to assemble to debate, deliberate and compromise in a parliament representative of the variety of interests and opinions in society which have, by regulation, to be conciliated and circumvented to prevent insult and injury to others. (On the face of it a nice team to play, but they are inclined to rig the rules and insist on the fairness of a preferred referee. They have difficulty keeping the team together, play in the fourth division, and talk about playing the game as it stands.)

Team Two: Marxville United

For the socialist, collective action in the form of the public administration of society and resources can alone effectively liberate the individual from otherwise inevitable forms of subjection and alienation that are the consequence of the condition of civility, particularly that aspect of the condition referred to as the free market economy. The distinction here between what is public and what is private is a matter of the difference between need and want. Establishing this difference in practice is something to be struggled for rather than bargained over with equanimity. It is a matter of principle. In its extreme form socialism supports popular demonstration, strike action and even revolutionary confrontation to effect a defence of the underprivileged. It calls for working-

class solidarity at all times to effect the recognition of the priority needs have over wants by making a stand against the vested interests of those possessing private capital in favour of the public ownership of productive resources and allocation of benefits. Where a universal franchise has been conceded by a show of force, a democratically elected socialist party can organize the state to appropriate and redistribute wealth in the name of social justice. (An exciting but potentially dirty team to play. Will break the rules when deemed necessary. Talks about revolution. Supporters to be avoided after the match.)

Team Three: Burke County

For the conservative, unless the individual is to be no more than a characterless drifting agent in a society of strangers, or an impersonal functionary in an administrative machine, he requires the cultural identity that alone can protect him from soul-destroying anonymity, insecurity and artificiality that together deprive him of any authentic feeling that he is leading a uniquely meaningful life. Here, the distinction between what is public and what is private is blurred by the idea that society is an organic whole of interrelated but different relationships between oneself and others. Preserving this inherent diversity is the responsibility of a national government of those experienced in ruling and hence having the intricacies of the inherited national character in view. Between the competitive relationships of the market economy and organizational relationships of the state there exist the familiar relationships of voluntary associations which preserve the diverse cultural identity of a chequered past. The continued coexistence of these strands of tradition holds together the fabric of society making attempts to change the human condition to achieve previously inexperienced human relationships as unnecessary as they are undesirable. (Positively charming to meet, but definitely out to deceive you on the pitch, particularly if you play for Marxville. Requires VIP changing rooms, and talk about horses.)

Team Four: Hitler National

(Not allowed to play again on account of supporter riot at last match and talk about war games.)

The minimal state is to the liberal what the welfare state is to the socialist and the nation state to the conservative. Each of these concepts is related to a concept of what constitutes a respectable person. For the liberal this is to have acquired by fair competition, superior property, position and reputation than competitors having the same legal opportunities as yourself. To be a respected person is to be honest, shrewd, hardworking, thrifty and trustworthy. To retain the right to acquire and be protected in possession a person must not deceive, steal, fail to pay debts, slander or otherwise intentionally harm others.

For a socialist, to be a respected person is to fabricate for use rather than profit. It is to have contributed to the community according to one's ability, and to have had to rely upon others only when unavoidably in need. It is to find dignity in work and pride in the quality of its product, rather than in possession and purchasing power. To which qualification is added that of having displayed determination for, and solidarity with, the cause of all those of one's kind who have sought to improve the condition of the working class.

The conservative definition of a respected person is to have professionally discharged one's duties to the community called for by one's station in life. Having compassionate feelings for others, who have to face the misfortunes of life, and benevolent intentions towards those less fortunate than oneself is to be dutiful. It is in public service that the loyalty and patriotism of the cultivated mind can best serve as an example of what it is to be an honourable person, and for the conservative it is to be honourable that calls for respect.

Each of the above ideals is related to a distinct concept of liberty, equality and justice. The liberal ideal of being free to compete in the marketplace without experiencing discrimination, and to consume in private without fear of interference, has its counterpoint in the socialist ideal of being free from exploitation in employment, and from market forces controlling one's leisure choices. In the case of conservatism the ideal of liberty is realized in being free for the purpose of the performance of one's duties as determined by one's social status, occupation or profession. Similarly, the ideals of equality before law, regardless of power, economic equality, regardless of status, and equal respect for equal rank, regardless of fortune, are related to the liberal, social-

ist and conservative ideals of justice as legal fairness, justice as
moral preferment and justice as due cultural respect respectively.

THE MATCH

Now it is clear that in the light of the brief foregoing synopsis that
the ideologies – liberalism, socialism and conservatism – present
different conceptions of human being and doing. The question is,
is there anything that we can say about political identity that
is not itself an ideological evaluation of human activities and
relationships? I have in mind something that will enable us to see
the sense in which ideological differences are not differences in
kind, making it unreasonable for the historian of ideas to declare
any one of them as a misrepresentation of reality and a restriction
on rationality, on account of its taking this form of understanding.
I propose to try and show that there exists such a common form,
and to locate it on the map of knowledge in a place where the
game of ideological persuasion can be played next-door to those
other forms of intellectual activity that are rarely abused by being
damned as the cause of some recent major human and man-made
misfortune, as Popper, Hayek, Kedourie and Talmon have done.

First, I wish to claim that it is not the existence of a consensus
of political commitment permitting parliamentary debate between
liberals, socialists and conservatives that makes it reasonable to
conclude that they all share a common ground on an existing map
of knowledge. The plurality of the convictions that legitimize the
governmental procedures and political activity of the dual legal
reality of civil society and the state does not make them any less
ideological than does the relative uniformity of the convictions
that legitimize the leadership of a totalitarian state. The constitution of the sense that legal relationships make, and the form
they take by virtue of the exercise of regulative or directive authority, power and force is everywhere the same kind of intelligibility that a political reality must have before it can be said to
exist. The doctrine of national socialism is not a threat to the
doctrine of liberalism in the history of ideas, and the practice of
national socialism could not be a threat to the practice of liberalism if it belonged to a different realm of understanding in the way
that scientific theory is distinct from historical narrative. To do

battle, armies have to meet on the same battlefield, and this implies that there must be something that can be disputed, as illustrated by the propaganda war of 1940–45 between Britain and Germany.

The objective of political persuasion is to gain the ascendency not by continuously arguing politics on the same centre ground, but on the ground between the goalposts of politics wherever they mark the changing parameters of political debate. This involves changing the vocabulary of politics so that the dominant medium of communication is that of an aspiring political organization (the winning team). The currency of talking politics in terms of social justice, the responsible society, the plight of those in need, common ownership, workers' participation and state benefit is the currency of talking politics of liberal-socialism within the political parameters of the democratic welfare state, just as the currency of talking politics in terms of private initiative, ownership, health, education and investment, and the nation's interest, defence, unity and pride is the currency of talking politics of liberal-conservatism within the political parameters of the minimum nation state. Political education is instruction in the meaning and use of such terms when discussing how we should associate, organize and conduct ourselves to lead a worthwhile life (training session). It is not learning how to put a knowledge of politics to good use. It is learning to articulate an existing attitude to human relationships with a view to conceptually recompartmentalizing human activities – in short, learning to persuade by gaining possession of the political ball in what is essentially a word game about the meaning of life.

In a general sense, ideological convictions may be described as a family of related ethical beliefs that enable us to locate our bearings in an existing world of conflicting regulations and directions that confuse all but the most determined minds. It is within their teamwork that we are able to discover our own consciousness of selfhood and communicate with, and relate to, other like consciousnesses in our own society and in other societies we wish to influence. It is this self-awareness in the ongoing present, with its retrospective past and projected future, that obliges us to act in the here and now to change or retain our political style and circumstances. The orientation inevitably leads to our seeing the relationships in which we feel at home differently to the way they

are seen by those who do not find them comfortable. It is not simply that our ideological understanding is arbitrary or subjective, because a variety of political beliefs qualify as commonly ideological as distinct from commonly logical or empirical. It is that the ideological understanding is, within the same logical and empirical framework, conceptually diverse rather than perceptually uniform.

All ideologies play the same language game of persuasion, but they each play it with a different vocabulary. It is not their geometry or their arithmetic that is at fault if they fail to score any goals, rather that their opponents have moved the goalposts by ideological persuasion. Politics creates its own time and space at will. That is its freedom and its historicity. The ideologically committed do not perceive political reality from different angles from outside its predetermined boundaries – there are no such parameters of political debate or boundaries to a state – but they see it differently from within the different conceptual limits they perceive it to have at any given time. They stand by different angles on political reality on account of their beliefs, and believing in a conviction is not the same thing as believing that something is the case. To claim that seeing is believing is not the same test as seeing as one believes. In the former case, reference can be made to observation of a preformed reality, in the latter to preferred conviction of the preformed mind. To claim to believe in the humanity of democracy, the destiny of the Aryan race or the victory of the proletariat, for example, is not to be able to show that democratic decisions are necessarily fair, that the Aryan race will justifiably dominate the rest of mankind or that a socialist revolution will lead to the creation of an egalitarian commonwealth.

Unlike the student of politics approaching the study of political activity from the point of view of a social scientist armed with a technical vocabulary, the politically engaged have a political experience conceived and expressed within the sense of terms which actually constitute the intelligibility of political reality at any given time from the participant's point of view. Being a believer or having beliefs is not the same as knowing what it is to hold a belief, not in the sense of having held one, but in the sense that one can specify what constitutes a kind of belief. Furthermore, knowledge of the internal sense of one's ideological beliefs

does not permit demonstration of the validity of claims about the nature of such beliefs in the way that a philosopher of social science can show what kind of sense sociological theories make of ideological change. The viewpoint of the philosopher of language about the reference of the concept of a person is not identical to the political utterances of the ideologically committed on the same subject. The philosopher on the field of politics plays the role of the referee; he may not kick the ball in play and can only blow his whistle if a player has been hoodwinked into believing that an opposing player is on his side.

The liberal, socialist and conservative perceive the authenticity of the individual differently even though in the context of civil society and the state there may exist a changing degree of overlap in their separate concepts. The political mind is not closed to the same degree as the scientist's is closed to history as an argument in science. It can be changed as a result of political persuasion. For example, in Britain classical liberals and the new conservatives currently have a consensus of opinion on the human value of the market economy.

At the beginning of the twentieth century, radical liberals and parliamentary socialists had a consensus of opinion on the human value of the provision of public welfare. And during the mid-nineteenth century both socialists and conservatives, albeit for different reasons, rejected the conclusion of social Darwinists that only the fittest had a right to survive. Not at every point in the history of England has there existed even a consensus or coincidence of opinion of a comparable kind on the quintessential issue of the constitutional right to rule, as the civil war and the Glorious Revolution in the seventeenth century indicate. On the other hand there have been periods, such as that of the years 1940–45, when a common hostility to national socialism, and fascism brought the Liberal, Labour and Conservative Parties together to form a national government.

On the occasion of a different crisis, the political and economic thought of one seminal mind proved influential in more than one circle of political consciousness. Keynes's remarkable influence on younger Liberal, Labour and Conservative Party members, interested in Britain's domestic policy before and after the Second World War, resulted in Grimond, Thorpe, Gaitskill, Wilson, Butler and Macmillan creating, although not occupying, the centre

of British politics. For a time, the goalposts of British politics had relatively settled positions either because of ideological consensus or ideological coincidence of opinion as to their right location.

Needless to say, prominent political leaders can also split a party over a crucial issue of party policy: Gladstone split the Liberal Party over home rule for Ireland; Macdonald split the Labour Party over the formation of a national government; and Peel split the Conservative Party over the repeal of the Corn Laws. And, because every party is a coalition of factions, any one of its fringe groups can either break away from, or be expelled from, it and form a new party on ideological grounds, as did the British Union of Fascists, the Social Democratic Party and the Workers' Revolutionary Party.

Now, changes of party political affiliation of this kind are a result of a change of political conviction either amongst the fringe group or in the mainstream of party opinion representing failure and success, respectively, in moving politic's goalposts. They are not like the changes that occur in a physical process that is both universal and atemporal – a process that cannot itself be changed wherever and whenever the physical conditions for its occurrence are present. Wars, revolutions and reforms are historical, not natural, events. They are brought about by motivation, intention and action, felt, formed and committed by persuaded agents, rather than by the existence of a set of contingent conditions causing their occurrence. It is not therefore possible to predict (as distinct from project) political change (the course of the game) in the same way as we can forecast a change in the weather. There are no empirically verified theories of politics, as there are meteorological theories based on observation of quantifiable condensation, that can serve as the basis of the kind of technological instruction in politics that enable us to take a rational course of action to avoid an otherwise inevitable consequence (like getting wet). For instance, corporal punishment may deter the liberal individualist from committing future crime, chastise the national socialist, humiliate the conservative and martyr the nationalist, but it is unlikely to reform an anarchist. The penalties inflicted may be the same, but the victim's reaction to the authority responsible for the infliction will be different. Whether or not it will be one of passive acceptance or violent defiance will depend upon ideological identity.

The liberal who believes intensely in the sanctity of human rights is unable to prefer a police state to a civil society because it supresses crime more effectively. The Marxist who believes intensely in the inevitability of social justice cannot rule revolution out on the grounds that it disrupts production, administration and trade, and the national socialist who believes intensely in the supremacy of the Aryan race cannot respect the policy of the 'Final Solution' on the grounds that it will hinder the war effort. The value the liberal finds in respect for human rights, the socialist in enthusiasm for collective action for the common good and the national socialist in the affirmation of the will to dominate, like the value the conservative finds in deference to tradition and the nationalist in the achievement of self-determination, are a matter of terminological location not of technical discovery in a location. In each case, their value is intrinsic and, in comparison, all extrinsic considerations are of secondary importance (the game comes first). The relevance of instrumental reasoning to political action cannot be compared with its relevance to technical innovation. Doing in practice is not like making in manufacturing. A political reality is not a contrivance able to be mass-produced because it cannot be engineered into existence to provide a convenience at any time or place. Our political activity is an integral part of a way of life, not a means to a particular end, and the meaning of this aspect of life is to be found in the province of ideology (location of play). It is those who feel wrongly alone and without comfort or cause, or wrongly threatened and without defence, who are susceptible to the persuasion that there is something that must rightly be done to change themselves or their condition – something worth making a stand for in terms of gaining self-respect and reaffirming one's selfhood – rather than merely existing in the world without historicity (staying at home on the day of the match). It is this determination of attitude that can be effected by ideological persuasion, a communication in the vocabulary of a particular ideology that makes sense of forming or joining a political party organized to act in the name of the persuasion to which its members have proved susceptible (the football club).

However, it must be stressed that joining a political party is an act and, as such, has historical consequences. If it is judged that the act will involve the acceptance of onerous obligations, even

distasteful and dangerous duties, then the timid adherent of an ideology may stop short of becoming a political activist (not go to the match on a rainy day). A wealthy socialist may be unable to bring himself to join a revolutionary party and abandon his previous lifestyle. In this case those who have made the decision to commit themselves to what may in its infancy appear to be a hopeless cause, or in its lifetime a lost one, can only conclude that, for those unprepared to make the sacrifices of total commitment, the affair is not one of the heart. The profession of a conviction is incompatible with inaction. Actions, and only actions, can demonstrate the sincerity and intensity of ideological conviction – protest may be, but dissent is never enough for those who would change the parameters of political debate (watch the match on television). If dissent is a right it is a perfectly useless one for the politically engaged who are obliged to reserve the right to action on account of the logic of ideological commitment that forms the essence of politics.

Joining a political party is like becoming engaged to be married (joining the supporters' club). The affirmation of political belief is comparable with the affirmation of love in that it involves a disclosure of feeling in a declaration of sincerity that calls for a commitment. Party political relationships, like marital relations, are exclusive of comparable relationships with others. They call for the surrendering of options previously open to us for the sake of an exclusive relationship, the value of which is regarded as intrinsic to the bond in question. Within this bond is tied the famous relationship between theory and practice in human life that has eluded all those political theorists who have vainly tried to treat it in the context of instrumental reasoning from explanatory hypothesis to practical plan of action (the utilitarian value of playing for reward). Human relationships can be exploited by those who see them as a means to an end. Those who are sincere are always vulnerable to those with ulterior motives, particularly those who have no respect for themselves let alone for others (supporters whose sole interest in the game is of the football pools). No doubt there will always be fellow-travellers and fifth columnists in political parties and fortune hunters and sadists in marriages, but the majority of party members and married partners are in a rewarding relationship and are not in such relationships in order to improve their career prospects or to hurt the

feelings of others. The toleration of, or assent to, both political parties and the institution of marriage is proof of this fact. It is not surprising, therefore, that a radical change of feeling in relationships of this kind can lead, if not to the separation of the parties involved, to a change in what is expected of those party to them. The traumatic experiences of civil war and divorce are the critical culmination of the frustration felt in the context of relationships which inevitably constrain the expression of the authentic feeling under the naked institutional restraints they then expose.

Ideologies form our conception of ourselves as persons and outline the sense of the appropriate way to associate and live. If we live in a multinational, racial, religious, cultural or class society, and this way of life makes no sense, then it is unlikely that the one that does make sense to us is compatible with a democratic society and a minimal state. We may well find it more congenial to live in a totalitarian state. To impose a uniform lifestyle on a subject population can be made attractive in any ideological vision of the true self, and a successful ideologically motivated movement can suppress opposition as an inappropriate political utterance by systematic genocide if necessary (taking over the pitch). Where we have more than one movement ideologically determined to change or retain an identity in incompatible ways we may expect violent confrontation. However, the fact that the conflict would be resolved by negotiation and compromise does not imply that the murderous feelings of Catholic and Protestant nationalists in Northern Ireland, for example, are futile emotions like the anger expressed when one kicks a car that will not start. Calming down and investigating mechanical or electrical faults is not like calming down and reaching agreements despite the fact that the British government would doubtless find it convenient if more of the Northern Irish believed that they have only the right to dissent and not the right to protest, leaving the business of government to Westminster. The violence involved in fighting for a cause is quite different to the violence of the frustration of the helpless. The ideological dispute as to the legitimacy of the Westminster government rule over Northern Ireland constitutes the problem of public order for the British government's security forces. As in the case of the Sino-Soviet ideological dispute over the right road to communism, it manifests itself in terms of the

question of sovereignty, the issue of self-determination and territorial jurisdiction (whose football ground). The Northern Ireland
problem is not the result of any psychological abnormality or lack
of rationality peculiar to its people. Amongst those who have
joined the Sinn Fein Party there is a shared feeling that their
aspiration to achieve a united Ireland is unjustly suppressed by
the 'foreign' government of the United Kingdom, and some of
those doubtless see themselves as 'freedom fighters' against the
forces of British occupation.

The Provisional Irish Republican Army member considers himself to be a patriotic Irishman, not a loyal British subject, in
the same way that some nineteenth-century radicals conceived
themselves to be parliamentary reformers and others proletarian
revolutionaries. Self-portrayal in this kind of imagery is picturing
a type of person not describing a man. Hitler's self-portrayal in
his autobiography *Mein Kampf*, for example, is one of an Aryan
ideal-type transcending the unjust and unnatural humiliation of
his race by struggle and self-sacrifice, emerging, like a phoenix,
as leader and liberator of his people from the desperate condition
to which they have been reduced by an evil Jewish conspiracy to
deprive them of their rightful superiority in the order of nature
(top of the first division). Stripped of this rhetoric, dramatically
symbolized in the rituals of the Nuremberg Nazi Party rallies,
Hitler's physical presence and psychological make-up does not fit
the tall blond-haired, blue-eyed calm ideal-type pictured in Nazi
ideology. There is, in fact, no class of persons who can be identified as Aryans as there are classes of persons who can be identified
as dentists, Etonians or criminals on account of their profession,
education or criminal record respectively. An ideological identity
can only be declared by one who lays claim to it. It is not one
that can be independently established by reference to credentials
(the colours worn). Not even party membership is proof of political conviction. It has to be admitted that manners, lifestyle and
dress give a clue to political inclination, but, like political utterance, they constitute a public declaration of the self and can be
easily imitated. Those who enthusiastically joined the Nazi Party
were not in any sense other than political on account of this. They
were simply persons who shared Hitler's ideological susceptibilities or political aspirations, and, persuaded to see themselves as

Aryans, acknowledged him to be their Führer. Those who did not share this bond could not perceive Hitler in the same way.

Similarly, the fact that persons of Jewish faith are portrayed as morally degenerate cannot be established by propaganda of the kind that suggests that they were responsible for Germany's misfortunes in both war and peace, and it is doubtful whether committed national socialists would have concluded that Germany's misfortunes had been brought on her own head by German ideological commitment and political mismanagement had it been shown that Jews took no part in it. The falsification of fact by totalitarian regimes, no more than the secreting of facts by enlightened absolutist regimes, may serve to locate a scapegoat, but they alone cannot justify his persecution as a socially undesirable or his starvation as a socially useless person. Final solutions to the German question, like final solutions to the Northern Ireland problem, call for ideological justification before persons can be put outside the protection of law without general protest.

The restriction of all kinds of free enquiry either by direct supervision or financial starvation is only a part of the policy of every autocratic regime. Ideological education like that offered by the BBC's 1988 New Enlightenment programme is as essential to the legitimacy of the present UK government as is the establishment of its surveillance by a government-appointed broadcasting authority. The extent to which liberals/conservatives do not see Minogue and Rees Mogg as comparable with Rosenberg and Goebbels matches the extent of their playing their private language game. Just as the shop steward's loving wife, who is not involved in union politics, will find it difficult to understand why her husband spends so much time at union meetings rather than relaxing with her at home, so the liberal will find it difficult to see what is so remarkable about the man Hitler (the admired centre forward). The fact is, of course, that seeing from the outside that which can only be appreciated from within an involved relationship, in terms of the ideological convictions that make the involvement meaningful, cannot reveal the relationship's rationale. Alternatively, just as friends may not understand why one of them forsakes their company in order to spend time with a lover whom they find unattractive, so those outside a political relationship cannot see its attraction for those who experience self-realization within it.

Ideological motivation is exclusive to the committed, and we cannot choose a commitment any more than we can decide with whom we will fall in love. For better or for worse it is something that happens to us that depends upon particular susceptibilities of which we may be largely unaware. The experience is more one of an awakening than the result of an effort on our part. It is not surprising, therefore, that when the committed come to give an account of how they came to have the beliefs they hold they do so in terms of the lines that the liberal Mill and the socialist Holyoake follow in their autobiographies. Here we have retrospective visions of past states of mind from the standpoint of present ones. What the liberal sees on his part to be a justifiable rational reaction to rigidity and intolerance, the socialist on his part sees as a justifiable gut reaction to unemployment and poverty, when, in fact, it is their own convictions which give their particular past circumstances their present emotive power (will to win). Others with different political beliefs may not see these same circumstances to be the formative experience that proved to be the decisive influence on their political consciousness. They are even able to draw different conclusions from any one historical event or any one political work. (Who has ever heard of two identical accounts of the same football match from opposing supporters?)

At the risk of stating the obvious, the relationship I hold to exist between the ideological writings of influential political thinkers and the formative political activities of their disciples is not the link between the vocabulary and the grammar of the political utterance – the evaluative word and the grammar of prescription on the one hand and the selection of political objectives and strategies on the other. It is not the link between political theories and political practice – the frequently assumed influence of the ideological mind on the plans and programmes of the politically engaged. Unlike party politics, where the latter are matters for decision by committee, the politics of the book are matters resolved in the study of its author and on the pages of his manuscript. And all that can be resolved there is the meaning and use of words. The power and currency of persuasive terms like constitutional government, natural rights, market economy, public interest, representative government, cooperative community, national unity, national self-determination, class-consciousness,

Aryan destiny and corporate state are, in a sense, given to them by the way in which they are used by writers like Locke, Paine, Smith, Bentham, Mill, Owen, Coleridge, Mazzini, Treitschke, Marx, Chamberlain and Gentile respectively. It is their direct contribution to the creation of political reality (the game). This direct contribution is historically, or contingently, related to the decision and careers of politicians like Pitt, Holyoake, Cobden, Chadwick, Gladstone, Disraeli, Garibaldi, Bismarck, Lenin, Hitler and Mussolini (star players) respectively which is itself an independent contribution to political reality in its own right.

The historical relationship between the political thinker and the political activist is not in any way a causal one that explains the event of political decisions and accounts for their consequences. Persuasion is not a physical change nor is it a logical link between ideas and actions of the kind that obliges us to hold the ideas responsible for any actions committed in their name. The rationale of persuasion does not have the grammar of command, but comprises the ideological sense the politically active make of the conduct to which they historically relate – when, what is for us the past, was the ongoing present of the political agent? This is the sense conveyed by their words to the minds of those who come to share the persuasion they communicate – the sense they have in the politics of the book (mental games and replays). Nevertheless, dominant persons in the political arena do not rise to the political platform hanging on the coat-tails or riding on the back of the ideological writer. The power of words is not the power of a conveyance; it is the power of an original mind. The writer is rarely to be found in the political arena, and when he is, his is likely to be too academic a performance to fire anyone's imagination. The political activist may drag the name of an ideologue from obscurity, but he does not owe his policies and programmes, as distinct from his inspiration, to the work of a 'theorist' whose inspiration may be something entirely different, and who may well find the historical association of his ideas with the political objectives of the activist alarming – as, indeed, Marx may have found the linkage of his name with that of Lenin and Stalin disturbing. Influence is not an impact. I suggest that attempts to prove that a political thinker would have approved of a political decision is as futile as attacking the politics of a book on account of the historical coincidence of its vocabulary with the intentional

standards set by the politics of a party: except for political reasons, that can only be articulated in the politics of another book (for example, Locke's *First Treatise* can be seen simply as an attack on Filmer's *Patriarcha* as the cause of the policy of James II).

Book wars constitute a large part of the history of political thought, but are something which the historian cannot sensibly engage in if he is trying to advance historical understanding. The exclusive relationship between the politics of the book and the politics of a party is that of two sides of the same coin that cannot be seen simultaneously except in the inclusive mirror of society without either of which it is a perfectly transparent glass, having either only the form or content of a way of life insufficient to give a picture of the historical reality in which men have experienced their being as politically conscious persons. It is to this transitory world of immediate experience that the political policy or programme has to relate, and in which political decisions continually to change them have to be taken (the course of the game). In this engagement, the politically active may read the political concepts of the political thinker into his practical actions in the process of evaluation that is the exercise of political judgement. At the same time it may equally be said that he may read his awareness of changing circumstances into his existing ideological conceptualization. It is an ongoing two-way influential process that independently constitutes the activity of politics seen in the mirror of society by the methodologically informed historian as a peculiarly historical phenomenon. In short, the ideologically informed political utterance is the act of speech that modifies the meaning of words like freedom, equality and justice which influence our understanding of legal regulation and political action, but do not alone change the legal framework of the way we associate and live. It is the historian's business to investigate the relationship between them in his biography of political life. The rationale of liberalism, socialism and conservatism is the reality of individualism, collectivism and culturalism to the extent that they are made manifest in the legal arrangements of civil association and state organization (the record of the game). Nothing can be done to change the rationality of transaction, cooperation and coexistence, but everything can be done to persuade us when and where the rationality of any one of them is appropriate. The persuasive power of ideological influence is the rationale of the ideological

utterance not the demonstrable facts of existing legal distinctions. Without the sword politics is but words, but it is equally the case that without the power of words the sword cuts no legal ties.

The art of persuasion displayed in ideological talk and political propaganda is essential to the vitality of political life. Exclusive persuasion and vetted information are readily combined in the presentation of a political programme. The emotive vocabulary, imagery and symbolism deployed calls for a soul-search on behalf of those who listen to political speeches, read political tracts and have their attention caught by political posters. If their response to the family resemblance of any one set of these is positive, they will learn from this how better to express their feelings in political argument and confrontation. The form of society is ultimately determined by the political consciousness of the ideologically articulate and literate, the informed political ability of leaders who bridge the gap between the politics of the book and the politics of the platform. It is their consensus or coincidence of opinion that promotes the acknowledgement of an authoritative and powerful relationship between government and ruled, party leader and member and sovereign and subject. No particular variety of these relationships can be shown to be supremely practical or universally desirable, but for those who believe in the capacity of this or that order of human interaction to realize what it is, in their view, to be an authentic person no such demonstration is required.

In pursuit of universal recognition the ideological imagination has attempted to fortify with proof what is claimed to be the right way to associate and live in order to be one's true self. Liberals have argued that they are armoured by the principle of civilization, socialists that they have harnessed the engine of class conflict and conservatives that they bear the shield of tradition. Yet, it is beside the point that they have claimed to have science, history or culture on their side, but still have not persuaded others, who hold different convictions, that their eventual victory is as inevitable as it is just. Just as a belief in the coming kingdom of God does not require proof of His existence, so the ideological belief in the coming best of all possible worlds does not require the demonstrable certainty of the arrival. The ideological conviction has human value. It is not an eternal truth. The influence of an ideological conviction lies in its ideological appeal – the generation of affection and the distillation of hate. It has the emotive

power of persuasion without which there is no influence on events. It determines motives rather than intentions. It gives us all the will to focus our attention on the immediate task in the pursuit of the immediate objective no matter what we hold to be man's ultimate destiny. Our ideological convictions establish the parameters of political, not religious, debate, and the priority of our political problems. It is within the area of both public and private decision-making that it focuses the attention of those it motivates on an immediate present that is transformed by their actions continually into a new relationship between the past and the future. This is the present in which we live – a world of transient experience that is always now, but never now for any length of time. In a world of conflicting and intermittent human interaction, only the projected ordering of human activity can provide the security of enduring and encompassing relationships we can claim to be our own. It is within relatively permanent institutions with which we can identify and for which we can feel affection that the significance of being and doing is to be found. This is particularly the case when in a political relationship, with utterance and action determining the form which that relationship takes.

The realm of ideological understanding on the map of knowledge is, then, the kingdom of our being in the world (the game itself – the enduring spatio-temporal reality that relates experienced past to the projected future. It is in strengthening the link with the past and forging the link with the future that the ideologically inspired action establishes the metaphysical boundaries of human relationships manifest in legal regulation and organization. The spatio-temporal limits of our private, social, economic and political life are all ideologically conceived in terms of our obligations and duties; at the same time, what they are is legally determined. To the extent that an ideological conviction is enduring and persuasive, it constitutes the rationale of the prevailing form and justification of the exercise of authority, power and force. Between the immediate past and future is the intermediate present of our own limited experience in which ideological conviction is the medium of communication of evaluated information about the ongoing present in which we all live. The political utterance is an invitation to others to see the world as we do, and a warning of the battle of words to come if they refuse to accept it. The ideological portrayal of circumstances and the

ideological dramatization of events points to a crisis in our affairs that calls for the decisive action that alone will save our skins, if not our souls, or make the great leap forward or next stumbling footstep into a new era of consciousness (the higher division).

Inevitably it seems that the work of the political enthusiast is a race against time. As his ordering of experience rolls out the carpet of the present he is obliged to walk upon it. His work will never be done. Every new critical situation calls for yet another crucial decision and even the ideological vision itself calls for constant revision and revitalization lest the link between the past the present and the future be broken, and the horizons of the ideological consciousness fade.

No doubt third parties who suffer the violent consequences of irreconcilable ideological conflict would welcome the prospect of pragmatic politics in the mistaken belief that it is possible to exchange for profit, produce for use and conform to coexist without ideological motivation, a view encouraged by Weldon in his book *The Vocabulary of Politics* (football without the ball).[8] But the rationality of transaction is not divorced from the rationale of possessive individualism, nor are the rationality of cooperation from the rationale of collectivism and the rationality of coexistence from the rationale of cultural autonomy – the sentiments of the self-made-man, workers' solidarity and patriotism respectively. The ideologies of liberalism, socialism and conservatism present us with different rationales of social, economic and legal rationality, not, as Oakeshott argues, rationalism versus reason in politics. Like all other ideological arguments they are forms of practical reasoning relating information, values and decisions in institutionalized associations and organizations within which we experience our spatio-temporal being. The fact is that all men are obliged to transact, cooperate and coexist. They may attempt to universalize, by ideological persuasion, the paradigm of value in life personified in a preferred activity at the expense of the value to be found in others. But any rigid adherence to such a rationale can prove destructive of the practicality of this totalitarian urge to the degree that any two of the concepts of voluntary transaction, cooperation or coexistence is eliminated from the social reality.

The technical recommendation of the philosophical investigation of political experience is that the concepts of freedom, equality and justice are interdependent when applied to human

relationships in space and time. This is not necessarily acknowledged to be the case by the distinctive ideological views that happen to constitute the centre ground of consensus politics at a particular time and place, but it would seem to be something like a necessary feature of political talk where we have the dual political reality of civil society and the state. Neither is it something that is altogether absent in political talk where one ideological paradigm or rationale is predominantly used to perceive one uniform social reality of personal, economic, political and cultural life. The rationality of individual transaction follows from the fact that persons have desires, the rationality of collective cooperation follows from the fact that persons have instrumental reason and the rationality of separate coexistence follows from the fact that persons have sentiments. Whatever is conceived to be a civilized life, it cannot be one in which everyone's desire, reason or sentiment are unnecessarily frustrated, as when the unfettered rationality of transaction produces an attempted total centralized control of wealth, the unfettered rationality of cooperation an attempted total centralized control of power and the unfettered rationality of coexistence an attempted total centralized control of culture by one over each and every other one of us in some practically inconceivable state of nature. The sovereignty of reason, as Aristotle perceived, precludes the possibility. A monopoly of capital, technology or communication implies totalitarianism – the frustration of the satiation of diverse wants, the disciplining of diverse aspiration and the denial of the diverse urge to be oneself (the attempt of any one team to play its own game). Any ideological inclination can run in the direction of imperialism of this kind: the liberal rationale can, to a degree, conceivably commercialize politics and culture; the socialist rationale can, to a degree, conceivably politicize industry and culture; and the conservative rationale can conceivably culturalize business and politics. But it is impossible to believe that possessive individualism, corporate collectivism or indigenous culturalism can and must take us all the way to imperialistic extremes. Liberalism, socialism and conservatism do not necessarily harbour any such wild dreams. These are only nightmares in the minds of socialist, liberal or conservative intellectuals who would persuade us that the alternative political convictions will lead us to a totalitarian destination in order to frighten us into retreating in their direction.

The conclusion I have reached is that, in relation to the political reality of civil association and the state, the consensus and coincidence of political opinion amongst British liberals socialists and conservatives for some time before, during, and far less time after the period considered is peculiarly apposite to the dual identity of 'citizen' and 'subject' possessed by the British national (making football as here understood the national game). He possesses civil rights the Soviet national does not, and state benefits the American national does not. The area of overlap between the concentric circles of liberal, socialist and conservative ideological consciousness provides the so-called centre ground of politics that a party must capture by forming, not conforming to, political opinion to form both a principled and a popular government. The acknowledgement of the legitimacy of the constitutional procedures it is obliged to follow and the support of the policies it pursues are neither to be found kicking about at the centre nor at the fringe of political opinion. They have to be kicked into the centre of political debate by the participants.

This, however, is not to suggest that there was not a comparable consensus or coincidence between nationalist and socialist opinion represented in the historical reality of Nazi Germany and between conservative and liberalizing socialists represented in the historical reality of the Soviet Union today. The distinctive feature of political consensus and coincidence in Britain is the extent of the nation's assimilation of the three principal ideological traditions that have dominated its political life for some considerable time. It is this extensive consensus and coincidence of opinion on the value of both the relationships of civil association and state organization of persons that underwrote the stability of the British system of government particularly after the Second World War (the way everyone would play). The extent of the respective sectors of regulation and direction may be disputed, but their interdependence is not. This fact, I claim, is the result of historical contingency and not the absence of ideological commitment. Certainly it is not the result of a native genius for political design. It cannot be successfully portrayed by anglophiles like Popper, Kedourie, Hayek and Talmon as the result of rational political conduct – the rational theory of democratic government put into practice. It was, and to some extent still is, the ideological conduct of British politics and, as such, it calls for no academic defence

as something superior to that – something Crick has described as
a defence of politics, Graham as politics in its place and Minogue
as politics defended against alien powers.[9]

Each of these conceive political activity as a governing activity,
in the same way that Greenleaf regards Oakeshott's view of politics as one of philosophical politics.[10] They confuse the government of the mind that investigates truth and value with the government of men who live in the real world. In the ideological
understanding, the mind gives meaning to, rather than finds it in
experience, and the place of ideology is in political life (there is
no game of games). The kind of understanding that can explain
any political tradition in particular, as distinct from political behaviour or political concepts in general, is the historical understanding, and the historical understanding has to take the world as it
finds it. In the case of the historian of political ideas he has not
only to locate the ideas, the character of which he would investigate, in their spatio-temporal location, he has also to locate their
conceptual place on the map of knowledge. I have tried to show
the sense in which the ideological understanding has such a place,
and the sense in which the British varieties inhabit at that level
the same territory as those of other times and places whether we
like it or not. Our politics are a matter of individual choice.

The philosophical explanation of the territory of politics as the
ground of ideologically oriented activity is not one from which we
are entitled to infer that philosophy can instruct the committed or
direct their political engagement. The philosopher is not obliged to
inform or reform the ideological utterance. His location of the
place of ideology on the map of knowledge as a form of imagery
peculiar to political consciousness may only serve technically to
warn those engaged in other intellectual activities of the consequences of an ideological invasion of their territory.

Ideological thought is thematic rather than systematic thinking
about the ethical significance of human life in which variations on
the main theme are orchestrated to give an ethically pleasing
portrait of experience. Without the meaning ideology can ascribe
to political conduct, its reason in politics is directionless, unless
ethical value can be successfully ascribed to rationality in itself as
attempted in ethical utilitarianism. To attempt to preclude one or
more ideological visions from the political arena by philosophical
censure is to risk admitting philosophy itself into political debate,

which inevitably, is to incite ideological evaluation into its own reasoning. Outside philosophy's own circle, it has yet to be demonstrated that philosophy can communicate the grounds of its preference for one alternative against any other project in life. In spite of Graham's sweet embrace it seems to me that philosophical reflection on politics is only just less partial than the non-political stance in politics. It is under no obligation to make a direct response to the ideological urge. No ideological persuasion is conducive to the pursuit of knowledge for its own sake. The enthusiasm it generates can all too easily interfere with the logical symmetry of the philosophical mind. I suggest that enthusiasm for philosophy generates empathy, but not sympathy, for the ideological understanding, and, even then, only when ideology remains on its home ground.

A belief in any ideological conviction obliges scepticism to be overruled by the acknowledgement of some seminal mind as having grounded a definitive statement of preferred conviction in a question of philosophy deemed to be determinate of that point of view, such as the metaphysics of market forces, the dialect of history and the wisdom of tradition. Notable ideological deliberations, such as Smith's *The Wealth of Nations*, Marx's *Capital* and Burke's *Reflections on the Revolution in France*, serve as authoritative reference books, rather than research works for those already persuaded of their conclusions. No veils of ignorance are available to those who find themselves politically motivated. Ideological masterpieces not only prescribe how human reality is to be perceived rather than describe its geography, they also presuppose that there is something on a grand scale that we want to know. The principles that are elaborated as authoritative guides to understanding politics and society are the confines of our political reasoning rather than the conclusions of its free play. They serve as the arbitrators of allegiance and alliance in politics and society rather than present allegiance and alliance as the subject of investigation.

NOTES

1. Cf., for example, the understanding of ideology presented in G. Graham, *Politics in its Place* (Oxford: University Press, 1985); K. Minogue, *Alien Powers: the pure theory of politics* (London: Weidenfeld & Nicolson, 1984).

2. See D. J. Manning (ed.), *The Form of Ideology* (London: George Allen & Unwin, 1978).
3. E. Kedourie, *Nationalism* (London: Hutchinson, 1960); F. A. Hayek, *The Road to Serfdom* (London: Routledge & Kegan Paul, 1944); K. Popper, *The Open Society and its Enemies* (London: Routledge & Kegan Paul, 1945); J. L. Talmon, *The Origins of Totalitarian Democracy* (London: Martin Secker & Warburg, 1961).
4. See D. J. Manning, *Liberalism* (London: D. J. Dent, 1976).
5. D. J. Manning and T. J. Robinson, *The Place of Ideology in Political Life* (London: Croom Helm, 1984).
6. H. J. Laski, *A Grammar of Politics* (London: George Allen & Unwin, 1929).
7. L. Wittgenstein, *Philosophical Investigations*, trans. C. E. M. Anscombe (Oxford: Basil Blackwell, 1972).
8. T. D. Weldon, *The Vocabulary of Politics* (Harmondsworth: Penguin Books, 1953).
9. B. Crick, *In Defence of Politics* (Harmondsworth: Penguin Books, 1964); Graham and Minogue op. cit.
10. W. H. Greenleaf, *Oakeshott's Philosophical Politics* (London: Longman, 1966).

PART II
Theories of Ideology

4. Ideology and its Revisions in Contemporary Marxism

Jorge Larrain

The fact that there is no such thing as a single conception of ideology within Marxism is hardly surprising to anyone acquainted with the complexity of this intellectual tradition and its vast, multiform influence upon other forms of thought. Yet this fact has never seemed evident to those who, from within or outside the Marxist tradition, tend to construe it as a monolithic orthodoxy which admits very little scope for variability and change. Hence, the idea of revisionism arises as a way of portraying and/or purging those who have ventured beyond the well-defined boundaries established by the founders. This is not, however, a satisfactory position to take if one does not accept Marxism as a revealed doctrine. It can be shown that the very Marxists, who by the turn of the century attacked the revisionism of Bernstein in the name of orthodoxy, did themselves revise Marx and Engels in other respects. The concept of ideology is a good case in point. Its evolution within Marxism shows that the epistemologically neutral conception of ideology initially sketched by Kautsky and Plekhanov and fully developed in Lenin's writings is fundamentally at variance with Marx and Engels's critical concept.

The differences in the conceptualization of ideology then did not start or end with the so-called 'revisionism' but affected the very core of Marxism from the beginning. Furthermore, it could be maintained that some of the reasons behind this change of perspective can be traced back to some ambiguities and tensions in Marx's and Engels's thought itself. It is therefore my contention that the existence of various concepts of ideology within Marxism cannot be reduced to the problematic of revisionism and that the seeds of many contemporary controversies on ideology were

91

already present in the thought of the founders. This is the reason why, in dealing with some contemporary theories of ideology which draw on Marx, to a greater or lesser extent I shall pay little attention to traditional distinctions between authors who should be considered proper Marxists and those who should not. The idea is rather to focus on some basic polarities, already present in Marx, which govern the main theoretical options about ideology and which at present continue to affect not only self-confessed Marxists but also authors in the periphery and critical of Marxism.

At the risk of oversimplifying the problem I shall argue that the discussion of ideology within the Marxist tradition and its periphery hinges on, and oscillates between, three partially over-lapping polarities. The first polarity is connected with the ontological status of the ideological phenomenon and generates an alternative between a subjective or ideal and an objective or material conceptualization of ideology. The second is related to the autonomy and effectivity of ideology and presents a choice between ideology as a determined superstructure or as autonomous discourse. The third polarity is related to the epistemological status of the concept and gives rise to two poles: the negative or critical and the neutral or positive understanding of ideology. Epistemologically negative conceptions are frequently associated with ontologically subjective and deterministic positions whereas neutral conceptions are often coupled with objective and non-reductionist positions. But there is no strict logic linking these alternatives and other combinations are possible.

The purpose of this chapter is to take these polarities as a basis to explore and critically assess the contributions to the conception of ideology of various contemporary authors and currents of thought which are directly or indirectly influenced by Marxism. The first polarity provides an opportunity to discuss Marxist structuralism, especially the contributions of Althusser and his followers, inasmuch as one of the main planks of their theoretical position is to substitute the primacy of the structures for the primacy of the subject. Within the second polarity the work of post-structuralists (Foucault, Hindess, Hirst, Laclau and Mouffe) can be examined as an attempt finally to liberate ideology from all economic determinations and to establish discourse as the constitutive principle of all social and political life. The last polarity allows us to explore Critical Theory, especially the work

of Habermas, insofar as they resurrect a negative notion of ideology, and also permits us to discuss Mannheim's critique of the Marxian concept of ideology.

THE SUBJECT–OBJECT POLARITY

The existence of this polarity within Marxism can be traced back to Marx himself. Under various forms, many authors have identified the existence of a tension in Marx's writings between the role assigned to the subject and the role attributed to objective circumstances in social change. Korsch described this tension in terms of two formulae. On the one hand, an 'objective formula' found in the 1859 Preface whereby history seems to be determined by the progress of productive forces which enter into contradiction with the relations of production. On the other, a 'subjective formula' supported by the *Communist Manifesto* whereby the historical process seems to depend upon class struggle (Korsch, 1938, p. 187). More recently, Anderson has characterized this disjuncture as the problem of the relationship between the structure and the subject in society (Anderson, 1983, p. 33). There can be very little doubt as to how the structuralist Marxism of Althusser proposes to resolve this tension. But what is really interesting and new is the fact that he transposes this tension from the plane of contradictions and change into the plane of ideology and reproduction. The question is no longer about the fundamental principle of social change but about the fundamental mechanism of social reproduction.

In effect, for Althusser the whole question of the base and the superstructure should be posed from the point of view of reproduction. He introduces his main discussion of ideology by raising the question about the reproduction of the relations of production and the reproduction of labour power both in its skills and its submission to the established rules. His conclusion is that, in addition to state power, they are mainly reproduced by ideology (Althusser, 1971, pp. 123–41). Ideology works by reproducing the conditions of production and it achieves this through interpellating individuals and constituting them as subjects obedient to the system. It is in the nature of the interpellation process that the newly constituted subjects will represent their conditions of exist-

ence in an imaginary form – that is, they will tend to see their
submission as freely chosen (p. 169). Ideology, therefore, cannot
produce true knowledge. Science, on the contrary, is 'always completely distinct from', and is able to 'criticise ideology in all its
guises' (Althusser, 1977, pp. 167 and 171). It is in this context that
Althusser proposes to resolve the problem about the subjective or
objective nature of ideology.

On the one hand it is possible to conceive of ideology as having
an eminently subjective character – that is, as a form of consciousness produced by a subject which could be either individual or
collective. Ideology would be made up of ideas (whether distorted
or not does not matter here) but, because it would consist of
ideas, ideology would have a spiritual form of existence only in
the minds of individuals. This conceptualization, according to
Althusser and his followers (Althusser, 1971, pp. 150–1;
Mepham, 1979, pp. 144–5 and Poulantzas, 1973, p. 20), can be
derived from some of Marx's formulae in *The German Ideology*
where Marx says that in ideology the world appears upside-down
'as in *camera obscura*', or 'as the inversion of objects on the
retina', as 'phantoms formed in the human brain'. Ideology would
originate in the thinkers of the ruling class, the conceptive ideologists, those 'who make the perfecting of the illusion of the class
about itself, their chief source of livelihood' (Marx and Engels,
1976, pp. 36 and 60). Ideology thus seems to be presented as an
illusion, as an inversion of reality, which is produced either by a
faulty cognitive process in the human mind or by self-deception
induced by class interests. Ideology would be a misperception, a
misrecognition of a reality which is otherwise perfectly intelligible,
standing the right way up. As Althusser puts it, Marx's formulae
in *The German Ideology* conceive of ideology 'as a pure illusion,
a pure dream, i.e. as nothingness. All its reality is external to it'
(Althusser, 1971, p. 150)

In contrast with the subjectivist position, which is assimilated
to historicist and humanist deviations, Althusser and his followers
propound a radically different conception which they find expressed in Marx's *Capital* and other writings of his maturity. This
conception amounts to a new scientific problematic which is
hidden, even from Marx himself, and which must be extracted by
means of a symptomatic reading. Whatever form the definition of
ideology may take among these authors, they all agree that ideol-

ogy has little to do with consciousness. For Althusser, ideology is a system of representations 'but in the majority of cases these representations have nothing to do with "consciousness" they are usually images and occasionally concepts, but it is above all as structures that they impose on the vast majority of men, not via their "consciousness" ' (Althusser, 1977, p. 233).

Althusser argues that ideology has a material existence; it exists in material apparatuses which he calls 'ideological state apparatuses', and in the practices and rituals with which they operate. According to this view, ideology is neither spiritual nor ideal, it is not subjective, but material and external; it is an objective level of society, an instance of the social totality, a structured discourse, which is not produced by any subject but which shapes and constitutes the subject. Althusser does not deny that ideology is a misrecognition of reality (or rather a representation of the imaginary relationship of individuals to their real conditions of existence), but he maintains that such misrecognition or representation of the imaginary is neither a product of the subject nor is it an illusion or false consciousness that inverts reality.

Althusser's theory of ideology can be criticized for its borrowing of functionalist premises and for two crucial antinomies. First, how is it possible to conceive of ideology as a comprehensive instance of society and at the same time as the opposite of science? Second, if ideology reproduces the conditions of production by constituting subjects who 'freely' submit to the established order, how can anybody become radically critical of that order? As a consequence of these criticisms Althusser eventually abandoned the opposition between science and ideology and accepted that ideology could also constitute individuals as 'militant subjects' against the system (Althusser, 1978, p. 99). However, I do not want to dwell on these problems for too long because they have been sufficiently analysed in the current literature. I rather want to concentrate my comments on Althusser's resolution of the subject–object polarity in comparison to Marx's.

Ideology conceived exclusively as either an objective instance separated from the subject, or as a subjective form of consciousness separated from objective reality, introduces a dualism between subject and object which Marx explicitly tried to overcome. Against an idealist kind of subjectivism Marx argues in these terms:

. . . man also possesses 'consciousness', but, even so, not inherent,
not 'pure' consciousness. From the start the 'spirit' is afflicted with
the curse of being 'burdened' with matter, which here makes its
appearance in the form of agitated layers of air, sounds, in short, of
language. Language is as old as consciousness, language *is* practical
consciousness that exists also for other men, and for that reason alone
it really exists for me personally as well; language, like consciousness,
only arises from the need, the necessity, of intercourse with other men.
Where there exists a relationship, it exists for me . . . consciousness is
therefore, from the very beginning a social product, and remains so
as long as men exist at all. (Marx and Engels, 1976, pp. 43–4)

But he also argues against the objectivism of vulgar materialism
by saying:

The chief defect of all hitherto existing materialism – that of Feuerbach
included – is that the things (*Gegenstand*), reality, sensuousness, are
conceived only in the form of the *object, or of contemplation*, but not
as *sensuous human activity, practice*, not subjectively. (Marx, 1976,
p. 3)

The reality of consciousness is, therefore, multidimensional. Its
existence is not merely physical as language and books, nor is it
purely social in the sense of an instance of society external to the
subject, but also, from the very beginning, it is internal to and
involves the subjects. It is not possible, and it does not make
sense, to oppose any of these three dimensions to the others.
Consciousness is simultaneously material, social, and internal to
the subjects. Consciousness is not imposed on subjects from without because it is social; rather, it is internal to the subjects because
it is social. The separation between subjectivity and objectivity
cannot apply to consciousness because consciousness is both at
the same time: it is internal only because it is social, and it is
social only insofar as it is internal.

The Althusserian interpretation conceives of ideology as an
object confronting subjects from without. In this perspective subjects are nothing but *supports*. They are the *bearers* of, and have
been constructed for, certain ideological meanings. Indeed, for
Althusser, social totality and history are conceived as processes
without a subject. In order to deny that subjects are the producers
of ideas and of the processes constituting the social totality,
Althusserians argue that subjects are rather produced and constituted for certain representations, they are conceived as the place

of crystallization of certain objective social practices. But it should be clear that these interpreters use a concept of practice which differs from that of Marx.

Whereas, for Marx, practice is a conscious human activity which realizes the unity of subject and object because through it human beings alter both material reality and their own nature, for Althusserianism practice becomes a hollow objective form rather like the concept of role in the structural–functionalist tradition, a given system of role expectations separated from, and shaping, the subject from without. Marx affirms in *Capital* that the human being 'by acting on the external world and changing it, he at the same time changes his own nature' (Marx, 1974, p. 173). This is very different from the Althusserian contention that the subject is produced for/in ideological representations. *The determination of consciousness by the subject's own material practice (which is Marx's proposition) has been transposed into the determination of the subject by ideological social practices conceived as external circumstances.* Marx explicitly rejects this conception: 'The materialist doctrine that men are products of circumstances and upbringing, and that, therefore, changed men are products of other circumstances and changed upbringing, forgets that it is men who change circumstances . . .'. (Marx, 1976, p. 7)

In attempting to give consciousness and ideology an unquestionable reality, Althusserian critics consider their reality only in the form of the object, as external materiality, not subjectively. Ideology becomes an object confronting subjects from without. It is as if the reality of ideology could be guaranteed only by its objectivation. Of course, I do not deny the objective dimension of social consciousness. Ideology, as a form of social consciousness, cannot be reduced to individual consciousness. The emphasis on this aspect and on the fact that consciousness exists in patterned material practices and rituals is an important contribution of Althusser which must be recognized. I only object to Althusser's one-dimensional approach. Consciousness cannot be reduced to an external form.

THE AUTONOMY–DETERMINATION POLARITY

This polarity presents an alternative between a conception of ideology as determined superstructure and a conception of ideology as autonomous discourse. The former may have a variety of connotations but it is frequently described as, and/or criticized for, conceiving of ideology as a simple manifestation or epiphenomenon of an essentially material and external reality, possessing little or no effectivity of its own. The latter, on the contrary, conceives of ideology as structured discourse whose reality is not external to it and possessing enough effectivity to be able to construct and constitute a variety of subjects and their relations for/by itself. The emphasis is not so much on ideology being determined by an external instance as on ideology itself being a determining instance.

The existence of this polarity can be related to a tension in Marx's and Engels's writings about consciousness which has to do with the degree of its relative autonomy. On the one hand many texts influenced by the principles of philosophical materialism describe consciousness as a reflection of material life: because the material world is prior to and exists independently of the human mind, consciousness can only represent and reflect that material world. As Marx put it, 'the ideal is nothing else than the material world reflected by the human mind, and translated into forms of thought' (Marx, 1974, p. 29), or in Engels's words 'we comprehend the concepts in our heads once more materialistically – as images [*Abbilder*] of real things' (Engels, 1970, p. 609). According to this view, consciousness is not autonomous but determined; it is the superstructure of a material base, for 'it is not consciousness that determines life, but life that determines consciousness' (Marx and Engels, 1976, p. 37). Inevitably, the base–superstructure metaphor and the theory of reflection tend to represent consciousness as a rather passive phenomenon which can only reproduce ideally external material processes which are constituted independently of consciousness.

On the other hand, many other texts seem to emphasize the active and anticipatory character of consciousness. The above-quoted first thesis on Feuerbach castigates philosophical materialism for not considering material reality subjectively as practice,

while it praises idealism for having set forth the active side of the subject. Insofar as the human practice which constructs material reality can only be conscious practice, consciousness is bound to be more than a simple passive expression of that reality; it must play an active role in the construction of that reality. This is recognized by Engels when he affirms that 'although the material mode of existence is the *primum agens* this does not prevent the ideological spheres from reacting upon it and influencing it in their turn' (Engels, 1975b, p. 393). But Marx is even clearer:

> . . . what distinguishes the worst architect from the best of bees is this, that the architect raises his structure in imagination before he erects it in reality. At the end of every labour-process, we get a result that already existed in the imagination of the labourer at its commencement. (Marx, 1974, p. 174)

It is interesting to note how in the context of the base–superstructure metaphor consciousness becomes more passive and determined whereas, in the context of the theory of practice, consciousness becomes more active and autonomous. It is therefore somehow paradoxical that the post-structuralist authors who assert the absolute autonomy of consciousness, should have started their intellectual careers very much in the structuralist mould and many should have been influenced by Althusser who from the start situated his struggle against economism and mechanism on the terrain of the base–superstructure metaphor.

In effect, Althusser's solution to the problem of reductionism was based upon a distinction between the dominant and the determining instances of society which allowed each instance or 'floor' of the superstructure a 'relative autonomy' and its own index of effectivity (Althusser, 1977, p. 213). This means that, for Althusser, the social totality was understood as a complex structure which was constructed through genuinely different and relatively autonomous instances and which was not reducible to the simplicity of one inner essence which either externally produces or manifests itself in all social phenomena. This is why Althusser rejected the notions of mechanical and expressive causality and proposed a new 'structural' or 'metonymic' form of causality in order to explain his conception of the social 'whole' (Althusser and Balibar, 1975, p. 97).

This understanding of the unity of social totality not on the

basis of a logic of identity but on the basis of a logic of difference
was pregnant with consequences for, although Althusser himself
kept the idea of totality and the ultimately determining role of
the economic structure, some of his followers took the logic of
difference to its extreme and ended up abandoning the very ideas
of structure and totality. What in Althusser was the articulation
of many relatively autonomous instances becomes in the post-
structuralists a necessary non-correspondence and heterogeneity
among absolutely autonomous spheres. The ideological instance
conceived as discourse is not only no longer ultimately determined
by the economy, but becomes itself constitutive of all aspects of
social life.

Hindess and Hirst start from a basic Althusserian distinction
between objects of knowledge and real objects. But they accuse
Althusser of neither applying it consistently nor drawing all its
consequences. According to Hindess and Hirst the distinction
means that:

> . . . the entities referred to in discourse are constituted solely in and
> through the forms of discourse in which they are specified. Objects of
> discourse cannot be specified extra-discursively. . . . There is no ques-
> tion here of whether *objects of discourse* exist independently of the
> discourses which specify them. Objects of discourse do not exist at all
> in that sense: they are constituted in and through the discourses which
> refer to them. (Cutler *et al.*, 1977, pp. 216–17)

Similarly, Laclau and Mouffe argue that because there is no possible distinction between discursive and non-discursive practices
everything in society is discursively constructed and every object
is constituted as an object of discourse (1985, p. 107). The unity
of discourse is purely relational and does not depend on a founding
subject, rather various subject positions could be constructed
within discourse, but these subject positions can neither be permanently fixed nor enter into permanently fixed relations. This is
why subjects cannot be the origin of social relations nor can their
discursive character specify the type of relations which could exist
among them. No identity or relation is necessary or ever fully
constituted in discourse; there can only be 'nodal points' which
are constructed as partial fixations of meaning by a practice of
articulation (Laclau and Mouffe, 1985, pp. 112–15).

The main conclusion Hindess and Hirst draw from their theory

of discourse is that all epistemologies are inevitably dogmatic insofar as, having posited a distinction between the realm of discourse and the realm of real objects, they go on to affirm a form of correspondence between them which is guaranteed by a certain privileged form of discourse that cannot be questioned or demonstrated and which entails that relations between concepts are transposed into relations between real objects. Because they are dogmatic, epistemologies must be rejected. As a consequence, all privileged forms of discourse and privileged basic concepts of a discourse must be rejected too. From here Hindess and Hirst derive their attack on the concept of determination: a relation between concepts, namely the concept of the economy and the concept of its conditions of existence, is proposed in such a way that the economy is supposed to be able to produce by means of its own effectivity the legal and cultural conditions of its existence, and this relation is transposed 'into a relation of determination between the objects specified in those concepts' (Cutler *et al.*, 1977, p. 210). For Hindess and Hirst this epistemological transposition is untenable.

The main conclusion of Laclau and Mouffe's theory of discourse is that the primacy of the working class and the centrality of class struggle within Marxism is untenable. As there can be no fixed relations or fixed subject positions in discourse all you can ever get is partially fixed and perpetually moving subjects and contradictions which are constructed by means of an articulatory hegemonic practice. Articulatory practices are essentially contingent and have no necessary 'articulating subject'. All that is required for a process of hegemonic articulation to take place is 'the presence of antagonistic forces and the instability of the frontiers which separate them' (Laclau and Mouffe, 1985, p. 136). Thus new subjects and struggles have recently appeared in Western Europe: feminism, anti-racism, ecologism, and so on. Marx would have made the mistake of reducing the presence of antagonistic forces to class struggles whereas 'class opposition is incapable of dividing the totality of the social body into two antagonistic camps, of reproducing itself *automatically* as a line of demarcation in the political sphere' (p. 151). For Laclau and Mouffe there are no privileged points of rupture, privileged subjects or privileged struggles. Plurality and indeterminacy are their banners.

Once the economic determination and the class origin of ideol-

ogy is denied the question arises as to what is then the role of
ideology within this perspective. For a start, ideologies lose their
unity of function and origin and their status will change according
to political circumstances. So their assessment is bound to be
provisional. According to Hirst ideological analysis entails political
calculation of the consequences of representations and social
relations, but this can be done from many political standpoints.
Class may come into it not as a reference to the origin but as a
consideration of effect. (Hirst, 1979, pp. 54–5) This means that
ideologies have become coextensive with discourse: the autonomous and free-floating space within which various political subjects and political alternatives are constructed, always in a provisional and non-necessary fashion.

The relativist perspective of Hindess, Hirst, Laclau and Mouffe
was initially inspired by Althusser's structuralism, especially his
theory of ideology, but as they progressively radicalized the logic
of its premises about discourse it became also indebted to, and
complemented by, the work of Foucault. This is not entirely
surprising, since he too was heavily influenced by structuralism in
the early 1960s and, as Poster has argued, his work could be
considered as a theoretical response to the difficulties of Western
Marxism (Poster, 1984, p. 1). A comparison of Foucault with
Althusser is instructive because it shows that they share certain
basic concerns: they both closely connect knowledge with institutional practices, they both tend to reject the centrality of the
subject and conceive of it as constituted by discourse and, what
is more important, they both want to expose various forms of
domination. But of course, the theoretical differences are very
substantial. Foucault rejects the categories of totality, base and
superstructure and has serious reservations about the very concept
of ideology. He refuses to accept the opposition between ideology
and science and between knowledge and power, and takes the
problematic of power beyond the sphere of class rule and state
domination.

Whereas Althusser analysed the mode of production as a totality made up of various social instances articulated according to
some specific determinations and ultimately determined by the
economic structure, Foucault emphasizes discontinuity, dispersion
and difference by affirming that the possibility of a total history
has begun to disappear as the possibility of a general history

emerges: 'a total description draws all phenomena around a single centre – a principle, a meaning, a spirit, a world-view, an overall shape; a general history, on the contrary, would deploy the space of a dispersion' (Foucault, 1977a, p. 10). While Althusser distinguished state power from state apparatuses and the repressive states apparatuses which function by violence from the ideological state apparatuses which function by ideology, Foucault affirms the omnipresence of power and the fact that power is not something that is acquired or seized or which is in a position of exteriority with respect to other types of relations. Power is something that circulates, that is never precisely localized or appropriated as a commodity (Foucault, 1980a, p. 98), 'power is everywhere; not because it embraces everything, but because it comes from everywhere' (Foucault, 1984, pp. 93, 92–4). Power cannot be conceived as separate from knowledge:

> No body of knowledge can be formed without a system of communications, records, accumulation and displacement which is in itself a form of power and which is linked, in its existence and functioning, to the other forms of power. Conversely, no power can be exercised without the extraction, appropriation, distribution or retention of knowledge. (Foucault, 1971, p. 131)

> . . . we should abandon a whole tradition that allows us to imagine that knowledge can exist only where the power relations are suspended and that knowledge can develop only outside its injunctions, its demands and its interests . . . we should abandon the belief that power makes mad and that, by the same token, the renunciation of power is one of the conditions of knowledge. We should admit rather that power produces knowledge . . . that power and knowledge directly imply one another; that there is no power relation without the correlative constitution of a field of knowledge. . . . (Foucault, 1977b, p. 27)

Insofar as the concept of ideology is concerned the comparison is not so easy. Although Foucault frequently uses the concept in a negative sense, which is not dissimilar to Althusser's usage, most references to ideology or ideological processes are in contexts where Foucault is arguing against reducing a particular phenomenon or process to ideology. For instance, Foucault points out that the formation of discourses need not be analysed in terms of ideology (1980c, p. 77), that the apparatuses of knowledge, the major mechanisms of power, are not ideological constructs

(1980b, p. 102), that the political question about intellectuals and truth is not alienated consciousness or ideology (1980d, p. 133), that power does not impose on knowledge ideological contents (1971, p. 131), and so on. Foucault's idea seems to be that the explanatory and heuristic capabilities of the concept of ideology have been greatly overrated. In fact he explicitly recognizes that, for him, it is difficult to make use of the notion of ideology, for three reasons:

> The first is that, like it or not, it always stands in virtual opposition to something else which is supposed to count as truth . . . The second drawback is that the concept of ideology refers, I think necessarily, to something of the order of a subject. Thirdly, ideology stands in a secondary position relative to something which functions as its infra-structure, as its material, economic determinant, etc. For these three reasons, I think that this is a notion that cannot be used without circumspection. (Foucault, 1980d, p. 118)

The scepticism about the concept of ideology is coupled with a strong rejection of the Althusserian opposition between science and ideology which is hinted at in his first reason. For Foucault discourses are not in themselves true or false, scientific or ideological. Each society has its own regime of truth, its own accepted discourses which function as true, and its own mechanisms and procedures for deciding what counts as true. Truth is not outside power (Foucault, 1980d, p. 131). Consequently

> Ideology is not exclusive of scientificity. Few discourses have given so much place to ideology as clinical discourse or that of political econ-omy: this is not a sufficiently good reason to treat the totality of their statements as being undermined by error . . . By correcting itself, by rectifying its errors . . . discourse does not necessarily undo its relations with ideology. The role of ideology does not diminish as rigour increases and error is dissipated (Foucault, 1977a, p. 186).

The rejection of the science–ideology opposition leads Foucault to underrate questions related to the epistemological validity of discourse and to replace them by questions related to the consti-tution of fields of knowledge which have their own 'truth' and which express a form of power. Thus psychiatry, criminology, clinical medicine, pedagogy and other human sciences arose in institutional settings such as asylums, prisons, hospitals, schools,

among others, which constituted their own power systems to control and discipline their inmates. But the institutional disciplines achieve subjection not necessarily by means of violence or by aiming at the minds of the inmates in order to deceive and conceal (ideology), it is the docility of the body that they aim at. They control by disciplining, extorting the forces and optimizing the capabilities of the body. This is what Foucault calls the political economy of the body (1977b, p. 25) or the anatomo-politics of the body (1984, p. 139).

A common feature of all the authors in this section is the fact that they not only concede to ideology and/or discourse an absolute autonomy but also, inevitably, the central role in social and political life. But as discourses – and the subjects and relations constructed therein – are eminently incommensurable, contingent and variable, a total relativism and indeterminacy seems to be the necessary outcome. The underrating of, and disregard for, epistemological questions may be a valid theoretical option but when Hindess and Hirst turn it into a radical attack on epistemology's supposedly inherent dogmatism, self-contradiction creeps in because their theoretical position presupposes its own validity and necessity. Hindess and Hirst are bound to fall into their own trap: in theoretically affirming the possibility of escaping epistemology they are reintroducing epistemological questions through the back door insofar as they are laying claims to know.

It is, of course, valuable to underline complexity and difference as against reductionism and essentialism, but these theories seem to find no alternative short of total contingency, indeterminacy and randomness. Post-structuralism transposes the structuralist attack on the subject into an onslaught on the structures themselves. The cost for social sciences is very high because it ultimately reduces society to a random arrangement of floating antagonisms between various forms of power and resistance to power. Such a position renounces all possibility rationally to explain these antagonisms by resorting to anything which is beyond their own closed discursive reality. The problem lies not so much in trying to investigate different institutional settings and their specific technologies of power, which is a valuable objective; but in trying to investigate them as totally and necessarily disconnected from the state and the class system. Yet, in this, not even Foucault can succeed: *Discipline and Punish* itself cannot but show the innumer-

able and important relationships between changing criminal and penal practices by the end of the seventeenth century and the emergence of the new capitalist mode of production.

THE NEGATIVE–NEUTRAL POLARITY

In general, negative or critical conceptions of ideology refer to a kind of distorted or false thought. Neutral or positive conceptions refer to either the totality of forms of social consciousness of a society or to the political ideas and the world-view of a class or party. A negative concept of ideology is inherently capable of discriminating between adequate and inadequate ideas, it passes epistemological judgement on thought, whatever its class origin or the expressed intention of its supporters. An ideological idea is a mistaken or distorted idea. The positive or neutral concept of ideology does not of itself discriminate between adequate and inadequate ideas, it does not pass epistemological judgement on them but links those ideas to some class interests. Thus one can speak of bourgeois ideology and proletarian ideology without necessarily wanting to establish or prejudge their adequacy or truth.

Within the neutral conception of ideology, critical judgement can be passed on ideologies but always from the perspective of a different ideology. Thus when Marxists criticize bourgeois ideology they do it from the point of view of proletarian ideology and what they criticize is its bourgeois character, not its ideological character which their own Marxist doctrine shares. In this conception, ideology of itself does not entail any necessary distortion. For the positive version the 'ideological' is the quality of any thought or idea that serves class interests, whatever they may be. For the negative version, on the contrary, the 'ideological' is the attribute of any thought or idea which distorts reality.

Although there can be little doubt that Marx and Engels's writings elaborated a negative concept of ideology, some ambiguities in their formulations and, especially, the fact that *The German Ideology* was not published until the 1920s, made it more difficult for the first generations of Marxists to apprehend the sense in which Marx and Engels had used the concept. In the absence of *The German Ideology* other more ambiguous texts

became central for the conceptualization of ideology such as Marx's 1859 Preface, Engels's *Anti-Dühring* (1975a) and various letters and prefaces. In the latter, a few references can be found to 'ideological spheres', 'ideological superstructure' or 'ideological domain', expressions which seem to cover the totality of ideas of a society. Equally, in the 1859 Preface, Marx speaks of the 'legal, political, religious, aesthetic or philosophic – in short, ideological forms in which men become conscious of this conflict and fight it out' (1970, p. 182), as if ideology encompassed most forms of social consciousness. By implicitly overlooking the context of these expressions,[1] Kautsky, Plekhanov and others began increasingly to use ideology in a neutral sense. Lenin, driven mainly by the urgent needs of the exploding class struggles in Russia, finally consolidated this usage when he wrote *What is to be Done?* (Larrain, 1983, ch. 2).

From then onwards and up to the 1940s, most Marxist authors, including Lukács and Gramsci, worked with and elaborated on neutral conceptions of ideology. Two contemporary currents of thought brought the negative concept of ideology back into the Marxist discussion, although from totally different theoretical perspectives. The most recent is the structuralist current inspired by Althusser who made the ideology–science opposition a central plank of his approach. The fact that Althusser himself abandoned this dichotomy after heavy criticism did not prevent many of his followers like Poulantzas (1973), Mepham (1979) and Pêcheux (1975) from continuing to uphold it. But paradoxically, it was Critical Theory which, while progressively moving away from the main tenets of Marxism, first resurrected and used a critical concept of ideology.

The Frankfurt School used the negative concept of ideology in order to analyse and criticize the emergence of an increasingly reified mass culture which controlled individual consciousness and promoted obedience and submission. According to Adorno and Horkheimer, Enlightenment and technology brought about a new form of subjection to reified relations. In the attempt to dominate nature reason became subjectivized, manipulative and purely instrumental. But this was paid for by the internalization of domination (Horkheimer, 1974, p. 93), 'by the obedient subjection of reason to what is directly given' (Adorno and Horkheimer, 1973, p. 26). However, this new form of ideology differs from the classi-

cal Marxist version of false consciousness. The critique of ideology could confront ideology with its own truth only insofar as ideology contained a rational element, as liberalism did (The Frankfurt Institute, 1973, p. 190). Contemporary forms of ideology lack that rational element and should be understood not so much as 'the autonomous spirit, blind to its own social implications, as to the totality of what is cooked up in order to ensnare the masses as consumers and, if possible, to mould and constrain their state of consciousness' (p. 199).

The new forms of ideology ever since Nazism have lost their theoretical status and have become a 'manipulative contrivance'. As Adorno put it, 'during the bourgeois era, the prevailing theory was the ideology and the opposing *praxis* was in direct contradiction. Today, theory hardly exists any longer and the ideology drones, as it were, from the gears of an irresistible *praxis*' (Adorno, 1967, p. 29). For Critical Theory, ideology has ceased to be a veil, it has become 'a face of the world', it converges with reality, or rather, reality has become its own ideology (The Frankfurt Institute, 1973, pp. 202–3). This is the idea which Marcuse will later expand and develop in his critique of the consumer society: ideology has become absorbed into reality, it has become an unassailable force which stems from the very process of production. Ideology may still be a form of false consciousness, but it has become immune against its falsehood (Marcuse, 1972a, p. 24). Reason and domination have ceased to be contradictory forces. By taking Adorno and Horkheimer's critique of instrumental rationality to its logical conclusion, Marcuse argues that:

> Today, domination perpetuates and extends itself not only through technology but *as* technology, and the latter provides the great legitimation of the expanding political power, which absorbs all spheres of culture. (Marcuse, 1972a, p. 130)

> . . . the very concept of technical reason is perhaps ideological. Not only the application of technology but technology itself is domination (of nature and men) – methodic, scientific, calculated, calculating control. (Marcuse, 1972b, pp. 223–4)

Habermas develops his approach to ideology within this theoretical tradition, but introduces new elements. He starts by accepting that in contemporary developed societies ideology is no longer

based upon the market economy and the principle of just exchange. That was the hallmark of liberalism in the nineteenth century. Today the legitimation of power is achieved by means of a new form of technocratic ideology (Habermas, 1971, pp. 99–101). However, Habermas argues that Marcuse went too far and could not properly reconcile the fact that technological rationality is the new ideology with the fact that it is also a progressive productive force. Habermas wants to affirm both that technological rationality is progressive, insofar as its continuous growth threatens the institutional framework, and ideological, insofar as it 'sets the standard of legitimation for the production relations that restrict this potential' (p. 89). Science functions as ideology inasmuch as it is connected with instrumental interests which in late capitalism have become predominant and have reduced the sphere of practical or communicative interests.

For Habermas, the problem of ideology arises in the context of the relationship between knowledge and human interests and is very similar to Freud's problematic of rationalization:

> From everyday experience we know that ideas serve often enough to furnish our actions with justifying motives in place of the real ones. What is called rationalization at this level is called ideology at the level of collective action. In both cases the manifest content of statements is falsified by consciousness' unreflected tie to interests, despite its illusion of autonomy (Habermas, 1972, p. 311).

This is why his model for a critique of ideology is psychoanalysis. Habermas distinguishes three types of interests: technical or instrumental, which corresponds with empirical sciences; practical or communicative, which governs historical sciences; and emancipatory, which is related to Critical Theory. He criticizes Marxism for having neglected the distinction between instrumental and communicative interests and having reduced the latter to the former. According to Habermas, the phenomena of domination and ideology just as much as the phenomena of liberation and critique of ideology take place in the sphere of communicative action. Ideology, in particular, makes reference to a situation where due to violence, censorship or repression no genuine consensus can emerge. Ideology is thus understood as 'systematically distorted communication' and arises out of a communicative framework which puts obstacles to discursively achieved and con-

straint-free consensus. The main feature of the ideological phenomenon is the fact that its operation cannot be easily recognized by the participants just as the neurotic patient cannot easily discover the real problem behind his/her disturbance. As Habermas puts it:

> The barriers to communication which make a fiction precisely of the reciprocal imputation of accountability, support at the same time the belief in legitimacy which sustains the fiction and prevents its being found out. That is the paradoxical achievement of ideologies, whose individual prototype is the neurotic disturbance. (Habermas, 1976, pp. 477–8)

Just as the psychoanalyst is required at the individual level in order to explain through language analysis the meaning of symptomatic manifestations (Habermas, 1970a, p. 207), the critical theorist is needed at the social level to help uncover through a process of self-reflection the real causes of pseudo-communication. In both cases, the psychoanalyst and the critical theorist have a preconception of non-distorted communication. In fact, in every communicative situation there is implicit the idea of a genuine consensus which makes reference not to actual reality where this rarely occurs, but to a counterfactual ideal situation, the 'ideal speech situation', the realm of pure intersubjectivity, where no barriers obstruct free communication, and hence rational constraint-free consensus is achieved (Habermas, 1970b, p. 372). Insofar as all discursive validity claims must be measured against this ideal norm, the critique of ideology can only find and pass judgement on situations of systematically distorted communication by comparing historical situations with the ideal speech situation.

In Habermas's most recent work the concept of ideology loses the centrality it had in his early writings. As we have seen, although Habermas detected an important change in the predominant form of legitimating ideology in advanced societies from liberalism to technological rationality, in either case he believed in the importance of a critique of ideology carried out by critical theory and governed by emancipatory interests. Conversely, in *The Theory of Communicative Action*, Habermas seems to maintain that the very notion of ideology should be restricted to the totalizing systems of the nineteenth century. This means that in contemporary advanced industrial societies ideology has finally

disappeared and has been replaced by a 'functional equivalent': 'in place of false consciousness steps *fragmented consciousness*, which precludes enlightenment about the mechanism of reification' (Habermas, 1981, p. 300).

On a superficial level this might be interpreted as a belated *rapprochement* between Habermas and the 'end of ideology' thesis.[2] This is unlikely insofar as fragmented consciousness seems to perform the same role as ideology, and Habermas is far from arguing that oppression and conflict no longer exist in contemporary society. One wonders then why Habermas does not see the connection between ideology and fragmented consciousness. No doubt he will eventually clarify his position. But in any case, as Thompson rightly argues, it is 'quite mistaken to maintain that fragmentation is an equivalent, "functional" or otherwise, for ideology and that these two equivalents operate *in exclusion* of one another' (Thompson, 1981, p. 301).

Although the analogy between the critique of ideology and psychoanalysis is suggestive, the difficulties of a transposition from the individual plane of neurosis to the social plane of class power and domination have been noted by many authors, especially in respect of the problem of positing individual psychoanalytic treatment as a model for political action (Gadamer, 1971, pp. 294–5; Giegel, 1971, pp. 278–9; Ricoeur, 1981, p. 85 and 1986, pp. 245–53; Held, 1980, p. 394; McCarthy, 1984, pp. 205–7). Habermas answers such objections by distinguishing the level of the processes of enlightenment, where the objective is the initiation of a process of group reflection and the model of action is the therapeutic discourse, from the political level, where the objective is the making of prudent decisions on the appropriate strategies and where there is no single model of action. Psychoanalysis is thus not intended as a model for political action (Habermas, 1974, pp. 32–3). However, Habermas's analogy does entail that the analyst–patient relationship is a model for the process of enlightenment which the critical theorist must initiate within the oppressed group. The difficulty with this comparison is that the neurotic patient is aware of his/her problem and is willing to submit to the therapeutic process, whereas the oppressed social group may not be aware of its problem and may not be prepared to listen to the self-appointed critical theorist. As Ricoeur puts it, 'in ideology-critique no one identifies himself or herself as the ill,

as the patient, and no one is entitled to be the physician' (1986, p. 248).

But, from a Marxist point of view, perhaps the most important problem of Habermas's conception is the fact that it does not make any explicit reference to the material interests and class antagonisms which are supposed to be at the basis of ideology. True, for Habermas the notion of systematically distorted communication entails the existence of discursive barriers to constraint-free consensus which in a vague and general manner refer to situations of repression, violence and censorship. But he hardly ever makes a specific reference to the material inequalities, power asymmetries and antagonisms of interests which divide contemporary society. Habermas tends to present systematically distorted communication itself as the problem of society. With a few textual substitutions, Marx could have applied to Habermas the same scathing comments he made on the German ideologists: '[Habermas] considers [systematically distorted communication and the barriers to genuine discursive consensus] as the real chains of men . . . he forgets that he is in no way combating the real existing world when he is combating solely the [systematically distorted communication] of this world' (Marx and Engels, 1976, p. 30).

If Critical Theory reasserted the crucial role of a negative concept of ideology within social sciences this move was strongly opposed and criticized in other quarters. I shall briefly focus on two relativist sources of opposition: one stemming from a branch of Althusserianism (Hirst), and the other coming from a branch of German historicism (Mannheim). As we have already seen, Althusser kept a negative concept of ideology but criticized the notion of false consciousness as a form of subjectivist idealism. Some of his disciples, though, extended his critique of false consciousness and began to attack the very notion of a negative concept of ideology. Hirst argues that ideology cannot be a distorted or false representation of reality, for 'how can something which has effects be false? It may derive from forms of the imaginary but it is not false. It would be like saying a black pudding is false, or a steam-roller is false' (Hirst, 1979, p. 38). This argument presupposes a peculiar concept of falsity; in fact it seems to equate falsity with non-existence or unreality. As Benton has cleverly pointed out, one might equally 'reflect that ideologies, though real and having effects, cannot be eaten nor driven' (Benton,

1984, p. 187). Hirst uses falsity as a synonym of 'illusion', thus transposing an epistemological reality into an ontological absence. There is no reason why one should oppose falsity to existence. A false statement is real; it exists and has effects.

At any rate, it is clear that the weakness of Habermas's concept of systematically distorted communication and the vagueness and imprecision of some notions of false consciousness, have served as the basis from which a more general attack has been launched against the very notion of a negative concept of ideology. This is why it is very important to emphasize that one cannot simply equate the negative concept of ideology with the notion of false consciousness and that Marx's conception of ideology, although negative, cannot be reduced to the idea of false consciousness. There are in my view three main problems with the notion of false consciousness. First, it is an equivocal expression for it can convey both the idea of a distortion and the idea that such distortion is an invention or a delusion of individual consciousness, a mirage without any base in reality. I contend that Marx's concept of ideology entails the former but not the latter idea. I underline the fact that the problem here is ambiguity and not that false consciousness, of itself and necessarily, entails the connotation of deception by individual subjects. Against the idea of an individual delusion Marx and Engels argue that:

. . . the phantoms formed in the brains of men are also, necessarily, sublimates of their material life-process . . . If the conscious expression of the real relations of these individuals is illusory, if in their imagination they turn reality upside-down, then this in its turn is the result of their limited material mode of activity and their limited social relations arising from it. (Marx and Engels, 1976, p. 36)

Second, if ideology is simply defined as false consciousness the impression is given that it is a mere cognitive or epistemological problem which can be put right by criticism or science. Just like the idea of systematically distorted communication, the notion of false consciousness does not make any explicit reference to the material practices and antagonisms in social reality which contribute to its emergence. Ideology appears disconnected from the real social contradictions which give rise to it and therefore it can supposedly be dealt with at a purely discursive level without

requiring any alteration of social reality. For Marx and Engels on the contrary, ideology

> . . . cannot be dissolved by mental criticism . . . but only by the practical overthrow of the actual social relations which gave rise to this idealistic humbug. (Marx and Engels, 1976, p. 54)

> The real, practical dissolution of these phrases, the removal of these notions from the consciousness of men, will . . . be effected by altered circumstances, not by theoretical deductions. (Marx and Engels, 1976, p. 56)

Third, and most important, the expression 'false consciousness' is vague because it does not determine the kind of falsity which ideology entails. Its apparently universal and general scope seems to encompass all sorts of distortions and falsities as if they were ideological. In fact, ideology is equated with error and loses its identity as a distinct concept. It must be accepted that many errors and mistakes could exist which should not be necessarily treated as ideological distortions. For instance, why should the clearly unsound rationalizations of a neurotic patient be considered ideological? For Marx, the ideological distortion is specific and makes a necessary reference to the concealment of social contradictions. This is the case, for example, of the attempt by the French newspaper *La Réforme* in 1848 to veil the contradictions between the bourgeoisie and the proletariat by invoking patriotic and national sentiments. Marx criticizes it thus:

> . . . the *Réforme* knows no better way of changing and abolishing these contradictions than to disregard their real basis, that is, these very material conditions, and to withdraw into the hazy blue heaven of republican ideology. (Marx, 1972, p. 142)

Marxism is therefore able to defend its critical notion of ideology against the attacks which confuse it with false consciousness. However, the main source of attack against the critical concept of ideology comes from a different tradition and has to do with the question of self-reflexivity. Some critics contend that Marx's negative concept is one-sided and dogmatic because it claims a vantage-point which is assumed to be beyond criticism. The classic formulation of this type of objection was elaborated by Mannheim, although his own relativist solution to the problem

was not entirely to abandon the negative connotation of ideology but to universalize its scope. According to Mannheim, Marxism completed a very important transition in the history of the concept of ideology from the particular to the total conception of ideology but was unable to achieve a general formulation of the total conception and remained a special formulation. The problem was that Marxism criticized all other points of view as ideological, but refused to subject itself to the same critique:

> As long as one does not call his own position into question but regards it as absolute, while interpreting his opponents' ideas as a mere function of the social positions they occupy, the decisive step forward has not yet been taken. (Mannheim, 1960, p. 68)

Two things are of interest here. On the one hand for Mannheim the critical character of the Marxist concept of ideology is given by the fact that it devalues the intellectual positions of its adversaries by showing them to be a function of their sectional interests. On the other, the decisive step forward Mannheim is talking about is the transition to the general formulation of the total conception of ideology which has been achieved by developing the simple theory of ideology into the sociology of knowledge. The change amounts to a movement from a partisan weapon to a general method of research.

The main operating principle of this new science is called 'relationism' because it seeks to relate thought to its social basis. Thought is taken as a function of existentially conditioned relationships (Mannheim, 1971, p. 121). According to such a method, the thought of all parties in all epochs is existentially determined. The question Mannheim faces though is how is this relationism, which bestows everywhere a functional meaning to thought, related to the truth of that thought. He is at pains to deny that relationism necessarily leads to relativism: 'one may well assert that thought is "relative to being", "dependent on being", "non-autonomous", "part of a whole reaching beyond it", without professing any "relativism" concerning the truth value of its findings' (Mannheim, 1968, p. 137). Mannheim points out that even the critical disintegration or unmasking of certain ideas does not necessarily entail the refutation of their truth. It is possible to 'achieve an "unmasking" which in fact represents no theor-

etical refutation but the destruction of the practical effectiveness of these ideas' (p. 140).

However, in *Ideology and Utopia* Mannheim seems reluctantly to come round to the idea that relationism does affect the epistemological status of thought and that consequently 'the analyses characteristic of the sociology of knowledge are, in this sense, by no means irrelevant for the determination of the truth of a statement' (Mannheim, 1960, p. 256). Mannheim still denies that this amounts to relativism. What he wants is to steer clear from two extremes: first that the social position of an author can say nothing about the truth-value of his statement; second, that the social position of an author can simply invalidate his statement. Mannheim propounds an intermediate path according to which the social position of an author 'particularizes' the validity of his statement and makes it inevitably partial (p. 257). Relationism thus leads not to a total rejection, but to a certain form of limitation of the epistemological claims to validity which each social stand-point can posit. This, he hopes, amounts not to a total relativization of the truth but to a necessary particularization or restriction of its scope.

The sociology of knowledge is not so much concerned with criticizing particular distortions as with tracing the limitations of all positions back to their social background. This is why, in the end, Mannheim proposes to avoid as much as possible the use of the term 'ideology' because of its moralistic and denunciatory overtones and suggests that it should be replaced by the more neutral notion of 'perspective' of a thinker (1960, p. 239). Paradoxically then, the transition to a general formulation of the total conception of ideology is simultaneously the end of ideology. In constructing and using a denunciatory theory of ideology Marx would have fallen in the same one-sidedness which he had criticized in bourgeois thought. He uncovered the relationships between bourgeois thought and its social basis but stopped short of applying the same method to his own thought.

Mannheim's objection to Marx's concept of ideology is based on a double misunderstanding about the fundament of the distorted character of ideology. On the one hand, as we have seen above, Marx identifies the nature of the ideological distortion with the masking of social contradictions. Mannheim, on the contrary, identifies ideological distortion with the social determination of

every standpoint. On the other hand, Marx clearly affirms the social determination of all ideas, including his own, whereas Mannheim seems to believe that Marx imputes that determination only in the case of his adversaries. That Mannheim is mistaken is clearly shown by Marx's description of the evolution of socialism as determined by the evolution of the working class and its struggles:

> Just as the *economists* are the scientific representatives of the bourgeois class, so the *socialists* and the *Communists* are the theoreticians of the proletarian class. So long as the proletariat is not yet sufficiently developed to constitute itself as a class, and . . . the struggle . . . has not yet assumed a political character, and the productive forces are not yet sufficiently developed . . . these theoreticians are merely utopians . . . But in the measure that . . . the struggle of the proletariat assumes clearer outlines . . . science has ceased to be doctrinaire and has become revolutionary (Marx, 1975, pp. 116–17).

For Mannheim, the epistemological partiality of each intellectual position is given by the necessarily limited social position of its author. This was never Marx's argument. For him, all forms of consciousness were socially determined, including his own theory, but this did not of itself entail an ideological distortion or any necessary 'particularization' of their claim to validity. Whether or not a thought was ideological did not have to do with the social position of its author but rather with the objective assessment about whether or not it correctly understood or explained away social contradictions, whatever its origins. This is why Marx could equally criticize bourgeois forms of ideology (liberalism) and proletarian forms of ideology (the Luddite movement). This is also why he could equally appreciate the scientific contributions of Ricardo or the literary contributions of Balzac and the political contributions of the Paris Commune.

So, the imputation of dogmatism, sustained on the notion that Marx excluded his own position from determination but attacked everybody else's, is untenable. Of course it is possible to pursue the objection from a more general relativist point of view and accuse Marxism of claiming absolute validity. This is, as all forms of relativism, a contradictory argument which presupposes its own absolute validity. Is it not the case that all intellectual positions lay claims to validity? A theory can be accused of dogmatism if

it makes arbitrary statements which it refuses to justify and give arguments for, but it cannot be accused of dogmatism simply for claiming the truth of its arguments. All theories, including Mannheim's, implicitly do that. Ultimately, Mannheim's struggle to distinguish relationism from relativism is not successful. This is the price he pays for replacing Marx's restricted critical concept of ideology by a new version which although keeping a negative connotation, universalizes its scope to cover the totality of socially determined thought. As Ricoeur rightly points out, Mannheim 'pushes the concept and the critique of ideology to the point where the concept becomes self-defeating' (Ricoeur, 1986, p. 159).

CONCLUSION

I have shown some important changes and controversies occurring within, and influenced by, the Marxist conception of ideology during the last five decades in Western Europe. My contention has been that these revisions and disputes are best understood when grouped around the three polarities which have guided my analysis. I have also shown that these polarities were already present in the thought of Marx and Engels as tensions which were not always satisfactorily resolved. It is hardly surprising, therefore, that followers and critics should have emphasized certain poles and underrated others to produce theoretical accounts which often seem to differ widely from one another and from Marx's original theory. These authors have sought, with varying degrees of success, to resolve the problems of Marx's concept of ideology by adapting it to the new historical circumstances, changing some of its emphases or, simply, by abandoning it altogether. Some of them, like Mannheim, Althusser, Foucault and Habermas, have made important contributions of their own. However, in the confrontation of these revisions and criticisms with the Marxian concept of ideology one can still admire the balance, complexity and inspirational power of Marx's theory.

NOTES

1. It can be easily forgotten that in the 1859 Preface Marx opposes those ideological forms of becoming conscious to his own scientific understanding of the conflicts, and that further down the text he argues that he and Engels 'resolved to work out in common the opposition of our view to the ideological view of German philosophy'.
2. In fact, E. Mandel has argued that Habermas's early work also reeks of the end-of-ideology thesis (Mandel, 1975, pp. 500–8).

REFERENCES

Adorno, T. (1967), *Prisms*, trans. S. Weber and S. Weber, London: Neville Spearman.

Adorno, T. and Horkheimer, M. (1973), *Dialectic of Enlightenment*, London: Allen Lane.

Althusser, L. (1971), *Lenin and Philosophy and other Essays*, trans. B. Brewster, London: New Left Books.

Althusser, L. (1977), *For Marx*, trans. B. Brewster, London: Verso.

Althusser, L. (1978), 'Nota sobre los Aparatos Ideológicos de Estado' in *Nuevos Escritos* (trans. A.R. Qui), Barcelona: Editorial Laia.

Althusser, L. and Balibar, E. (1975), *Reading Capital*, London: New Left Books.

Anderson, P. (1983), *In the Tracks of Historical Materialism*, London: Verso.

Benton, T. (1984), *The Rise and Fall of Structural Marxism: Althusser and his influence*, London: Macmillan.

Cutler, A. *et al.* (1977), *Marx's Capital and Capitalism Today*, vol. I, London: Routledge & Kegan Paul.

Engels, F. (1970), 'Ludwig Feuerbach and the End of Classical German Philosophy, in Marx and Engels, *Selected Works in One Volume*, London: Lawrence & Wishart.

Engels, F. (1975a), *Anti-Dühring*, London: Lawrence & Wishart.

Engels, F. (1975b), 'Engels to Conrad Schmidt in Berlin', (5 August 1890) in Marx and Engels, trans. I. Lasker, *Selected Correspondence*, Moscow: Progress.

Foucault, M. (1971), 'Théories et institutions pénales', *Annuaire du College de France, 1971–1972*, (Paris) quoted in A. Sheridan, *Michel Foucault, the Will to Truth*, London: Tavistock Publications, 1980.

Foucault, M. (1977a), *The Archeology of Knowledge*, (trans. A.M. Sheridan Smith), London: Tavistock.

Foucault, M. (1977b), *Discipline and Punish*, (trans. Alan Sheridan), Harmondsworth: Penguin.

Foucault, M. (1980a), 'Lecture 7 January 1976' in C. Gordon (ed.), *Michel Foucault, Power/Knowledge*, Brighton: Harvester Press.

Foucault, M. (1980b), 'Lecture 14 January 1976' in C. Gordon (ed.), *Michel Foucault, Power/Knowledge*, Brighton: Harvester Press.

Foucault, M. (1980c), 'Questions on Geography' in C. Cordon (ed.), *Michel Foucault, Power/Knowledge*, Brighton: Harvester Press.

Foucault, M. (1980d), 'Truth and Power' in C. Gordon (ed.) *Michel Foucault, Power/Knowledge*, Brighton: Harvester Press.

Foucault, M. (1984), *The History of Sexuality*, vol. I, (trans. R. Hurley), Harmondsworth: Penguin.

Frankfurt Institute for Social Research, The (1973), *Aspects of Sociology*, (trans. J. Viertel), London: Heinemann.

Gadamer, H.G. (1971), 'Replik' in J. Habermas *et al.* (eds), *Hermeneutik und Ideologiekritik*, Frankfurt: Suhrkamp.

Giegel, H.J. (1971), 'Reflexion und Emanzipation' in J. Habermas *et al.* (eds), *Hermeneutik und Ideologiekritik*, Frankfurt: Suhrkamp.

Habermas, J. (1970a), 'On Systematically Distorted Communication', *Inquiry*, vol. 13, no. 3.

Habermas, J. (1970b), 'Towards a Theory of Communicative Competence', *Inquiry*, vol. 13, no. 4.

Habermas, J. (1971), *Toward a Rational Society*, London: Heinemann.

Habermas, J. (1972), *Knowledge and Human Interests*, London: Heinemann.

Habermas, J. (1974), *Theory and Practice* (trans. J. Viertel), London: Heinemann.

Habermas, J. (1976), 'Vorbereitende Bemerkungen zu einer Theorie der kommunikativen Kompetenz' in J. Habermas and N. Luhmann, *Theorie der Gessellschaft oder Sozialtechnologie – Was leistet die Systemforschung?*, Frankfurt: Suhrkamp, 1971, quoted in T. McCarthy, 'A Theory of Communicative Competence' in P. Connerton (ed.), *Critical Sociology*, Harmondsworth: Penguin.

Habermas, J. (1981), *Theorie des kommunikativen Handelns*, Band II, Frankfurt: Suhrkamp, quoted in J.B. Thompson, *Studies in the Theory of Ideology*, Cambridge: Polity Press, 1981.

Held, D. (1980), *Introduction to Critical Theory*, London: Hutchinson.

Hirst, P. (1979), *On Law and Ideology*, London: Macmillan.

Horkheimer, M. (1974), *Eclipse of Reason*, New York: Seabury Press.

Korsch, K. (1938), *Karl Marx*, London: Chapman & Hall.

Laclau, E. and Mouffe, C. (1985), *Hegemony and Socialist Strategy*, London: Verso.

Larrian, J. (1983), *Marxism and Ideology*, London: Macmillan.

McCarthy, T. (1984), *The Critical Theory of Jürgen Habermas*, Cambridge: Polity Press.

Mandel, E. (1975), *Late Capitalism*, London: New Left Books.

Mannheim, K. (1960), *Ideology and Utopia* (trans. L. Wirth and E. Shils), London: Routledge & Kegan Paul.

Mannheim, K. (1968), 'The Problem of a Sociology of Knowledge' in P. Kecskemeti (ed.), *Essays on the Sociology of Knowledge*, London: Routledge & Kegan Paul.

Mannheim, K. (1971), 'The Ideological and the Sociological Interpretation of Intellectual Phenomena' in K. Wolff (ed.), *From Karl Mannheim*, New York: Oxford University Press.

Marcuse, H. (1972a), *One Dimensional Man*, London: Abacus.

Marcuse, H. (1972b), *Negations*, Harmondsworth: Penguin.

Marx, K. (1970), 'Preface' to *A Contribution to the Critique of Political Economy* in K. Marx and F. Engels, *Selected Works in One Volume*, London: Lawrence & Wishart.

Marx, K. (1972), 'The Paris *Réforme* on the Situation in France' in K. Marx and F. Engels, ed. B. Isaacs, *Articles from the Neue Rheinische Zeitung*, Moscow: Progress.

Marx, K. (1974), *Capital*, vol. I (trans. S. Moore and E. Aveling), London: Lawrence & Wishart.

Marx, K. (1975), *The Poverty of Philosophy*, Moscow: Progress.

Mark, K. (1976), 'Theses on Feuerbach' in *The German Ideology* in K. Marx and F. Engels, *Collected Works*, London: Lawrence & Wishart.

Marx, K. and Engels, F. (1976), *The German Ideology* in K. Marx and F. Engels, *Collected Works*, London: Lawrence & Wishart.

Mepham, J. (1979), 'The Theory of Ideology in *Capital*' in J. Mepham and D.H. Ruben (eds), *Issues in Marxist Philosophy*, vol. III, Brighton: Harvester Press.

Pêcheux, M. (1975), *Les vérités de la Palice*, Paris: Maspero. There is an English version entitled *Language, Semantics and Ideology: Stating the Obvious*, London: Macmillan, 1982.

Poster, M. (1984), *Foucault, Marxism and History*, Cambridge: Polity Press.

Poulantzas, N. (1973), *Political Power and Social Classes* (trans. T. O'Hagan), London: New Left Books.

Ricoeur, P. (1981), *Hermeneutics and the Human Sciences* (ed. & trans. J.B. Thompson), Cambridge: Cambridge University Press.

Ricoeur, P. (1986), *Lectures on Ideology and Utopia* (ed. G.H. Taylor), New York: Columbia University Press.

Thompson, J.B. (1981), *Studies in the Theory of Ideology*, Cambridge: Polity Press.

5. Phenomenology and Ideology in the Work of Merleau-Ponty

Diana Coole

In exploring the implications of a phenomenological approach for the question of ideology, I shall concentrate on the work of the French philosopher, Maurice Merleau-Ponty (1908–61). Merleau-Ponty is a useful vehicle in this capacity since he explicitly used phenomenology to address political questions. Here he was especially eager to confront Marxism and, in so doing, he was obliged to consider its understanding of ideology. A caveat is nevertheless in order. Merleau-Ponty does not employ the term 'ideology' with much consistency. It often appears as a mere shorthand referent to expressions of an ostensibly ideal kind, although it occasionally takes on additional pejorative connotations which associate it with a particularly moribund and obfuscating set of claims. Rather than developing a theory of ideology from Merleau-Ponty's specific references to the term, then, it is more helpful to see in them an illustration of the underlying phenomenological approach. It is this, I shall suggest, that offers criteria for discriminating between neutral and negative accounts of ideology, while simultaneously providing grounds for a critique of some traditional misconceptions of its nature.

I

In order to grasp Merleau-Ponty's phenomenological approach to ideology, it is necessary to situate it in relation to his criticisms of both Marxism and Cartesianism. In the case of his Marxism, the earlier and more explicitly phenomenological writings exhibit an attempt, shared by his friend Jean-Paul Sartre, to recast it as a

humanism. This meant rejecting the rigidities of the prevailing Stalinist orthodoxy, wherein Marxism was interpreted in a deterministic way as that science which had discovered history's laws and found their apogee in proletarian power. The central flaw here, as Merleau-Ponty saw it, was one of dualism. In expounding a crude materialism, it claimed that consciousness reflects economic arrangements which may then be treated as a merely technical problem. Since the Party understands and represents the truth of history, there is no need for the masses to appreciate or accord with the mission that is being undertaken in their name. The superstructure will catch up with the base when the latter has been reconstituted in the correct way. The state of mass consciousness is not therefore a problem unless it becomes subversive: if ideology is considered, it is as an instrument of propaganda, which might be self-consciously utilized to manipulate a recalcitrant population.

Merleau-Ponty identified such a Marxism as an example of rationalism whereby the subject (the Party) imposed a rational plan on the object (nature and society). It must spawn a politics of terror because, like the protagonists of the French Revolution, its executors found in history a medium to be reconstituted by an act of will. Of course, the latter would distinguish themselves from their Gallic predecessors by claiming that they were only implementing a predestined *telos*. But since they no longer engaged in those messy and difficult analyses of the present that might verify their interpretation, this ultimately amounted to no more than a piece of rationalistic *hubris*. They failed to recognize in history a milieu which is already structured, with a density and inertia that offer but limited opportunities for action. In order to take advantage of such possibilities, a careful reading of events as they unfolded would be required, along with an appreciation of their essential contingency.

It was with such a method of ongoing interpretation that Merleau-Ponty identified a humanist Marxism and, as I shall explain later, this meant presenting Marxism itself as a phenomenology. Its significance as far as ideology is concerned, is that it must eschew any break between consciousness and economy, since mass consciousness cannot be irrelevant to the outcome of a merely contingent history. If the future is shaped by the way in which millions of actors perceive their destiny and struggle to fulfil their desires, then a particular outcome can only be painfully forged by

tipping their weight in one direction rather than another. For the theorist, Marxism can at best mean a process of clarifying possibilities and suggesting fecund and progressive themes from within the ambiguities of experience. For the actor, it means engaging in audacious yet risky acts which succeed only to the extent that they open up a future and galvanize the masses into an action whose outcome remains unpredictable. The building of communism cannot then entail the imposition of a preconceived rational formula. Rather, it suggests bringing rationality into a world where it is not predestined, via a commitment to communication and to continued self-criticism. In other words, it means engendering reason from within existence and not imposing it from without. What Marxism required, according to this understanding, was a more adequate account of how consciousness arises, and is transmuted, within existence. The dualistic formulation of economy and ideology, base and superstructure, social being and consciousness, required a fundamental revision. It would be facilitated by Merleau-Ponty's phenomenological inquiries, whose primary target was Cartesian dualism.

As a preface to describing Merleau-Ponty's attack on Cartesianism, it will be useful to sketch how ideology itself has been conceived in a Cartesian manner, such that the critique of Cartesianism must also *ipso facto* imply a rejection of traditional conceptions of the ideological.

When the term 'ideology' is used, it is generally taken to refer (*pace* Althusser) to certain kinds of ideas, beliefs, ideal expressions, forms of consciousness: that is, to mental as opposed to material phenomena; to something subjective (or intersubjective). In this sense it must partake in broader epistemological questions regarding the relationship between ideas and the world (whether material or social) which they represent. Suggestions of some fundamental schizm or mismatch between the two invite scepticism and doubt, while the possibility of mere distortion opens the door to conceptions of ideology as a form of false consciousness. This latter case rests upon the belief that we can in principle attain true knowledge of the world but may fail to do so, due to reasons that are political as well as epistemological.

The prevalent condemnation of ideology as a form of illusion or deception makes sense only in the context of assumptions that some correct correspondence between ideas and reality can be

attained, although not guaranteed. If it could not be attained in principle, then there would be no grounds for distinguishing between knowledge and ideology; if correspondence were always guaranteed, there would be no room for ideological slippage. The aim of an objective knowledge or scientific Marxism is then to release this correspondence from the occlusions beneath which it lies buried. In the case of science it is to achieve a value-free account of reality founded on empirical observation; in the case of Marxism it is to articulate the dialectic which structures disparate appearances and weaves them into a rational totality. To speak of ideology in this way is therefore to subscribe to oppositions between truth and falsity or reality and appearance. Such contrasts are ultimately sustained by a Cartesian metaphysic in which ideas are of another order than the world they know. As long as this distinction survives, however, the problem of validating our knowledge remains highly problematic and the problem of ideology, which it adumbrates, endures.

Besides proposing a strict separation of subject and object, Cartesianism also contends that mind is superior to matter and dominates it by appropriating it conceptually. It is this belief – that reason can offer an exhaustive account of the objective realm by imposing rational concepts upon it – that translates into the sort of rationalism Merleau-Ponty had found so dangerous in Stalinism. But he rejects all theories of knowledge which suggest a correspondence theory of truth, whether truth is discerned as a creation of mind or a reflection of the real, since he perceives in both cases the arrogance and dislocations of rationalism:

> We do not have a consciousness constitutive of the things, as idealism believes, nor a preordination of the things to consciousness, as realism believes (they are indiscernible in what interests us here, because they both affirm the adequation of the thing and the mind).[1] (Merleau-Ponty, 1969b, p. 103)

Whether thought is believed to construct or to mirror the world, it is equally conceived as something alien to it, so it can never ultimately know where discoveries end and inventions begin. Both positions rely upon the chimera of an impartial subject who stands back from externality in order to gain an overview of it. Thinking is thus cut off from the living sources of meaning and enjoys none of that engagement in reality which would alone allow it to verify

or interrogate its ideas. Instead it can only assert them dogmatically or slide into an unassuageable scepticism. Metaphysical materialism and idealism are both implicated in this dilemma, since both posit a primary substance (matter or mind, respectively) whose antithesis is of a different, and heteronomous, order.

So far, then, I have suggested that vulgar Marxist and scientific denigrations of ideology are rooted in certain epistemological contentions regarding the possibility of true knowledge, although the dualism which underlies these claims makes highly problematic any verification of such putative truths because of the separation it sustains between the knowing subject and the objects of its knowledge. Merleau-Ponty's work is important to a reconceptualization of ideology precisely because it challenges the distinctions upon which it has come to rest, whether these be epistemological oppositions between truth and falsity or reality and appearance on the one hand, or ontological dualisms between consciousness and its objects on the other. Before proceeding to his alternative account, it is first necessary to outline the premises of the phenomenological approach he used.

To speak of phenomena is to refer to appearances. The term has been used frequently by philosophers, usually to suggest that beneath 'mere' appearances there lurks some more true or authentic reality. Kant spoke of the phenomenal realm as that which is constituted in consciousness, but contended that we can never know the noumenal in-itself which underlies it. Hegel had also spoken of phenomena, but had portrayed them as only superficial and contingent appearances of a reality we increasingly come to know through history. For him, phenomenology itself is that science which traces the journey of consciousness from its superficial understanding of seemingly alien phenomena, to its recognition that the world is created by mind and can therefore become transparent before it. Free self-consciousness is finally able to discard the phenomenal wrapping of the external world and to attain absolute knowledge of it, since it was all along only itself in self-estrangement.

It is this rationalistic distinction between appearances and reality that recurs in Marx. If he rejects Hegel's idealism and presents knowledge as a reflection of the material world, he also eschews empiricism by claiming, like Hegel, that we grasp reality only when we penetrate beneath the realm of appearances to the

logic which gives them meaning. To do this we need an adequate method and this is the dialectic, although the dialectic itself is ultimately only a mirror of reality since reality is claimed by Marx to have a dialectical structure. When he presents us with the laws and structures of history and with a single truth in genesis, he retains both the Cartesian belief that the omniscient subject can present a full account of the real, and the archaeological imagery of the rationalist, where the theorist penetrates beneath appearances to disclose the reality which lends them their true significance. In this form the distinction between appearance and reality may be equated with that between ideology (or false consciousness) and a scientific, if dialectical, knowledge.

Merleau-Ponty's phenomenology also offers a description of appearances, but he rejects any suggestion that they might be explained according to some other, more rational, level of meaning which underlies them. For him there are only phenomena, but these are not flat and one-sided data which require explaining; rather they embody rich but ambiguous meanings whose proliferation is inexhaustible. There is nothing else – no more true and certain reality that endures beneath. Phenomenology means exploring the levels of significance which radiate out from and enliven every phenomenon, rather than reducing each appearance to some rationalistic concept which is claimed to capture its truth. 'To return to the things themselves is to return to that world which precedes knowledge, of which knowledge always *speaks*, and in relation to which every scientific schematization is an abstract and derivative sign-language' (Merleau-Ponty, 1962, p. ix).

Phenomenology in its modern sense, and as originally conceived by Husserl, had been intended as a rigorous science which would overcome all doubts about the adequation of objects and their representation by returning to the things themselves as they appear in consciousness. By putting the world in brackets and carrying out a series of reductions, Husserl had hoped to disclose the invariable essences which appear to us. Despite the idealist foundations of this task, he was increasingly drawn to the conclusion that the realm to which his reductions led him was one of experience – what he called the lifeworld (*Lebenswelt*).[2] It was this notion which was taken up by Heidegger in *Being and Time*, when he described a primordial realm in which we are not first of all consciousnesses who constitute meaning by reflection, but

beings who are thrown into a world first grasped through practical activity. It was such claims regarding the primacy of existence over reflection, that opened the way for Merleau-Ponty's existential phenomenology.

What Merleau-Ponty added was the realization that it is our bodies which situate us in the world and that the most basic relationship here is one of perception. If phenomenology was to describe the appearing of meanings, it would therefore have to begin by looking at a *preconceptual* lifeworld where we are incarnate and engaged. Here, then, lay the challenge both to a Cartesian metaphysics that severed subjects and objects and minds and bodies, and to all those forms of rationalism which founded meaning in reflection. Here, too, lay the rejection of distinctions between appearances and reality. It is true that appearances are riven by shadows, hollows, lacunae and invisibility (by negativity), but these are integral to what it is to appear and cannot be dispelled. They are our access to truth although to no truths in particular. To articulate these radically incomplete meanings is, moreover, to generate new levels of significance and not to translate them into fixed essences. 'The phenomenological world is not the explicit expression of a pre-existing being, but the laying down of being. Philosophy is not the reflection of a pre-existing truth, but, like art, the act of bringing truth into being' (Merleau-Ponty, 1962, p. xx).

When Merleau-Ponty speaks of phenomenology in the Preface to his *Phenomenology of Perception* (1945), which is his clearest indication of this approach, it is as a *style* of thinking, which 'steps back to watch the forms of transcendence fly up like sparks from a fire; it slackens the intentional threads which attach us to the world and thus brings them to our notice; it . . . reveals that world as strange and paradoxical' (1962, p. xiii). It seeks no final conceptualization of the world, since it recognizes that 'our reflections are carried out in the temporal flux on to which we are trying to seize . . . there is no thought which embraces all our thought'. Instead, as Husserl had recognized, the philosopher is a perpetual beginner and philosophy a dialogue, or infinite meditation (Merleau-Ponty, 1962, pp. xiv, xxi). It recognizes its own reflections as incomplete and perspectival; as requiring unceasing development and criticism. Phenomenology therefore both reveals, and participates in, the irremediable contingency,

equivocacy and situatedness of all sense. From this perspective, it would clearly be impossible to sustain those distinctions – between mind and matter, subject and object, truth and falsity, conscious-ness and economy, superstructure and base, reality and appear-ance – on which conceptions of ideology have been found to rely. Let us next see, then, how Merleau-Ponty applied the phenom-enological method to ontological and epistemological questions and what status he was able to accord to the ideal as a result.

II

The purpose of Merleau-Ponty's ontological inquiry is to describe a non-Cartesian lifeworld, where meanings emerge prior to the appearance of a reflective consciousness. He begins with the body, which never inhabits an insignificant plane but at once finds itself situated in an environment which it perceives and structures in a selective manner. It is motivated by needs and tasks within the imperatives of adaptation and at once experiences its world as a milieu endowed with a practical significance that summons a response. 'Already the mere presence of a living being transforms the physical world, bringing to view here "food", there a "hiding place", and giving to "stimuli" a sense that they had not hitherto possessed' (1962, p. 189). Even at the most primitive levels of corporeal existence, then, the sensible is differentiated according to what might loosely be termed carnal interests. There is no sense of a more objective significance lying behind them, but nor are these pre-reflective meanings simply gratuitous impositions. At the biological level, the monotonous rhythms of need and instinct impose fairly strict limits on what the organism can experience as meaningful to it, and only those structurations which strike a resonance in the real will permit adaptation and further develop-ment. The world is experienced as 'an "open" situation, and "requires" the animal's movements, just as the first notes of a melody require a certain kind of resolution, without its being known to itself' (1962, p. 78). Each situation remains both con-strained and open to a variety of resolutions.

What facilitates this openness is the phenomenon of perception. Perception marks for Merleau-Ponty the most original relationship between body and world, arising from an intimate and irreducible

dialectic between the flesh of the body and the flesh of the world: 'the things attract my look, my gaze caresses the things . . . between it and them we catch sight of a complicity' (1969b, p. 76). There is no causal primacy in the visual field that emerges between seer and seen, but there is a dynamism and openness because the perceptual forms that emerge there remain provisional and incomplete. To see is to adopt an orientation that struggles to achieve both clarity and richness. Yet in permitting one form to emerge in equilibrium, perception must sacrifice others to the background. This ground is not however negated: it continues to affect the figure which has been raised. The red spot is experienced differently according to whether it is perceived against a green or a white ground. Perceptual syntheses are thus merely possible solutions to the visible: 'the perceived, by its nature, admits of the ambiguous, the shifting, and is shaped by its context' (1962, p. 11). Each figure drags in its wake a train of latent associations and differentiations which contribute to its sense.

The perceptual wholes which emerge from this process are described by Merleau-Ponty as forms, or *Gestalten*. These are wholes that are more than the sum of their parts and cohere according to an overall significance which is an existential one. That is, their principle of cohesion is a style, a way of existing, of being-in-the-world. It is this style of being that is meaningful to the body in perception. The body grasps the thing's physiognomy all at once, in an aesthetic rather than a logical way. This is why perception yields us whole objects, rather than collections of profiles or disparate corpuscles of data which must be constituted by consciousness: each quality is the symbolic equivalent of all the others. 'For example, the brittleness, hardness, transparency and crystal ring of a glass all translate a single manner of being. . . . There is a symbolism in the thing which links each sensible quality to the rest' (1962, p. 319).

Significance, then, inhabits appearances; it is not imposed upon them subsequently, nor is it something 'other' to them. It is here that we first discover a latent rationality: a patterning of the empirical which arises from within it. The affinity of parts is 'the central phenomenon of perceptual life, since it is the constitution, without any ideal model, of a significant grouping' (1962, p. 53). To perceive is already an expressive act since it differentiates the world according to style. Although the world always appears to

us via this accretion of forms, which must exhibit some internal law of organization, the nature of that law remains entirely contingent. As Merleau-Ponty warns, 'this law must not be considered as a model on which the phenomena of structure are built up. Their appearance is not the unfolding of a pre-existing reason' (1962, p. 60). When he claims that we are condemned to meaning, since no part appears outside of a configuration which evinces an inner logic, he is therefore claiming that we are also destined for reason. But it is a reason which remains open and menaced. There is no specific rational content that is ontologically sanctioned, only a hazardous process of rationalization – a way of relating parts according to a richer and more comprehensive significance. This is made possible because existence and essence, the sensible and sense, emerge as inextricably interwoven.

The meaning of each whole remains contingent because from a different perspective or interest, its significance and composition may differ. Parts can always be shifted or reconstituted to yield different wholes with a changed style. This openness arises from the ambiguous nature of every signification: no part has any positive significance on its own but relies upon its relationship with other parts and its differentiation from them. It is diacritical. Indeed, it is precisely this negativity, this *difference*, which sustains the radical incompleteness that allows meaning to evolve from within the labyrinths of the sensible. Perception is structured like a language. The ontology thus yields an epistemology: we begin with a being that is primordially differentiated, ever open to that synthesis, decay and reintegration of meaningful wholes which the body effects in its perceptual life. In his last writings, Merleau-Ponty attempted to move yet further from Cartesian formulations by speaking of one differentiated flesh rather than of body and world. For him, the latter is more than inert objectivity precisely because it is pregnant with possibilities, while the body is able to assimilate these because it shares the world's fleshy syntax. 'To experience a structure is not to receive it into oneself passively: it is to live it, to take it up, assume it and discover its immanent significance' (1962, p. 258). It is in this corporeal experience, and not in the abstractions of an autonomous rationality, that meaning is born. But Merleau-Ponty never goes as far as the structuralists or post-structuralists here: for him, meaning always arises for-us, in that interworld where the intentional, if incarnate, subject and

its environment meet. The subject is decentred rather than eliminated.[3]

At this point we might pause and ask what implications arise from the account of perception which might have relevance for ideology. In particular, it is useful to see what sort of qualities must cling to all forms of meaning if, as Merleau-Ponty contends, they continue to bear the characteristics of the perception in which they originated.

To begin with, it transpires that all meanings must be in principle provisional and ambiguous. For according to the perceptual model, any particular configuration is a response to certain questions that are posed by the body in its quest for adaptation. There is no flat panorama of which it might gain a bird's-eye view, but a visual field in which it is situated and within whose horizons it interrogates its environment from a practical perspective. Those horizons are in turn structured in terms of previous configurations and so there is a sedimentation of significance which always lends a context to the questions and answers that can be accepted as meaningful. Because each perceiver is situated, vision must remain partial and perspectival. While the world is always open to further investigations, it is not constructed like a puzzle which may one day be completed when all its parts have been discovered. Opening up new horizons and dimensions means occluding others. While richer syntheses may well emerge, these only raise new and previously inconceivable questions. All meaning is therefore contextual and open, never complete and exhaustive.

It further follows that if all meaning originates in perception, even the most abstract ideas must find their roots in experience, where they are clothed in facticity. The implication of *Gestalten* is precisely that while facts emerge steeped in generality, ideas only unfold according to the contingent configurations of the empirical. They can never be purged of the silence that lies at their heart, to be finally and exhaustively articulated. Part of their significance must always lie in a stylization of existence which they continue to convey. Once we interrogate our ideas in a phenomenological way, we will therefore discover that they can never be definitive or transparent. As in perception, they participate in larger structures where it is their relationship to, and

differentiation from, other ideas and facets of existence, that lends to them a particular sense.

Finally, while it is true that there are no pre-given absolutes because being is a vast latency, so that the body experiences freedom, it is equally true that it finds itself constrained. For habit and inertia are always at work and once an efficacious level of significance is attained, it is tempted to push no further in structuring its environment. Although the world is open, the structures which emerge there tend increasingly to crystallize and to harden into generality. In the generation of significance, there is therefore an interplay of freedom and constraint motivated by the opposing forces of adaptation and habit, development and inertia.

We can now see how these implications relate more explicitly to an understanding of ideology. If there are no absolutes, no final correspondences between meaning and world, neither is there any fatal disjunction between knowledge and its objects. Instead there is a process of fulminations within the flesh, in which significant forms flourish from within the interstices of the sensible. Rather than an objective distinction between true and false which might permit *validation* of meaning, there is a process of *verification*. That is, there is an opportunity for an ongoing questioning and exploration of the real from within it, where non-sequiturs are crossed out only in the name of more fecund but equally provisional developments, and where facts dismissed as irrational in one context might not be so in another. 'I call such and such a perception into question only in the name of a truer one capable of correcting it' (Merleau-Ponty, 1962, p. 360).

It is therefore nonsensical, from Merleau-Ponty's point of view, to seek a truth that lies buried beneath the partiality and perspectives which are often identified with a pejorative sense of ideology and seen as something to be dispelled. We can only interrogate and explore meanings according to their ability to open up and enrich our world. Those which fail are not false in relation to some objective truth, but irrational and impoverished in closing off our ability to develop and adapt. They do not open up a future, they cannot accommodate the new events and experiences that history throws up. If ideology means a set of particular and partial meanings, then there is no escape from ideology. But there are more and less fertile ideologies. To distinguish between them, however, we must first renounce the

rationalist illusion of a non-ideological reason and recognize that
it is possible to question meaning only from within an existence
that yields no final answers. Being is a meaning in genesis that
depends upon our creative expressions for its emergence; it is not
an already finished system of laws merely awaiting discovery.

So far, I have spoken of meanings as they appear at the level of
existence, but it is important to remember that when ideal reflections finally emerge, they are not of another type. Merleau-Ponty
is eager to show that those phenomena which we associate with
the ideal – such as reflection, mind, consciousness – are neither
autonomous nor ontologically novel, but emerge from within the
flesh. It is in the movement towards more integrated structures
that we find the genesis of mind. When a new level of significance
is extrapolated, then the world is suddenly perceived according to
a richer level of generality. 'The configurations of our world are
all altered because one of them has been torn from its simple
existence in order to represent all the others and to become the
key or style of this world, a general means of interpreting it'
(Merleau-Ponty, 1973c, p. 132). It is this restructuring on a higher
level that yields a more evolved level of what might be called
consciousness. Mind itself is 'not a new sort of being but a new
form of unity' (Merleau-Ponty, 1965, p. 181). Thinking finally
emerges when merely latent meanings are rendered explicit and
articulate by means of symbols.
    It is language which facilitates this development. Here, mean-
ings become apparently autonomous; far greater possibilities of
expression are unleashed. Yet language also tempts us into believing that stable essences can be fixed and experience translated
into clear and unequivocal signs. Merleau-Ponty warns: 'It is the
office of language to cause essences to exist in a state of separation
which is in fact merely apparent, since through language they still
rest upon the ante-predicative life of consciousness' (1962, p. xv).
Over time he came to recognize that the key to overcoming Cartesian dualism lay in the question of language itself, since the
danger of rationalism always arose at that moment when thought
turned back upon experience in order to articulate it. Here a fatal
rift between subject and object threatened to reappear; the task
was to see the articulated as continuous with the lived.
    This is achieved by denying that the language which speaks of

experience is itself wholly ideal or conscious. It is structured, like perception, as expressive of a style due to the arrangement of its parts.

> But what if language expresses as much by what is between words as by the words themselves? By what it does not 'say' as by what it 'says'? And what if, hidden in empirical language, there is a second-order language in which signs once again lead the value life of colours, and in which significations never free themselves completely from the intercourse of signs? (Merleau-Ponty, 1964b, p. 45)

Then, like the perceptual, it will communicate via a mute and existential symbolism as well as by what it explicitly says. It will retain a poetic sense: 'language as well as music can sustain a sense by virtue of its own arrangement, catch a meaning in its own mesh' (1969, p. 153). It is this that allows language always to communicate more than it says; to retain an ambiguity and openness which permit the endless proliferation of meaning. Language is not then a tool which would allow us to reduce the lived to clear and rational concepts; it is only a relatively more ideal way of laying down meaning and of engendering new levels of significance. It is in language that the split between existence and consciousness is healed because it is self-reflexive. It both evolves as existential meanings do, and is able to reflect upon those meanings while participating in their mode of appearing: 'language in forming itself expresses at least laterally, an ontogenesis of which it is a part' (1969b, p. 102).

Individuals born into a linguistic community are initiated into the style of a particular language. The relations, oppositions, crossings and counter-crossings of words build and affirm one another until a whole phonemic scale is suddenly grasped all at once: it snaps up the subject 'like a whirlwind', tempting him or her by its 'internal articulations' and the 'lateral liaison' of its signs (1964b, p. 40). To assimilate a language is therefore equivalent to our initiation into a perceptual field: it is not pieced together by consciousness or learnt as a grammatical structure to be applied, but catches us up in its expressive unity. For those who speak it, each language symbolizes a manner of being-in-the-world.

Each language has its own way of expressing different relationships,

like time and space. For example, the structure of Greek will indicate an 'architechtonic time' appropriate to the Greeks. Even the manner of distributing the accents, the flections, and even the use of the article are expressive of a world view (*une vue du monde*). (Merleau-Ponty, 1973b, p. 75f)

This account of language refines those points of relevance to ideology which a phenomenology of perception had offered. It suggests more compellingly how even apparently ideal and reflective meanings rely upon our commerce with an existence whose significance continues to breathe life into them. It is also important in showing that while language is no clear and objective medium in which the contingencies and ambiguities of the lived might be transcended, its perspectival and stylistic nature does not imprison us. It opens a world of significance and invites us to explore and express it more richly. Any rationalist aspiration to a completed and unequivocal system of signs would be both misconceived and impoverishing, just as the search for a non-ideological society, where relations were transparent and fully knowable, is chimerical and confused. Both would condemn us to endless repetition and therefore become false in the sense outlined above. The expressive systems which we inhabit, whether they be linguistic or ideological, are our point of contact with the world and not a veil which hides something else. This does not mean that all languages or ideologies offer equally rich opportunities for expression, but it does reject the illusion of somehow getting behind them.

III

In this section I will construct a phenomenological account of how ideologies emerge within social life, suggesting that we must understand the process as analogous to the appearing of perceptual or linguistic significance.

To claim that social meanings develop as perceptual ones do is to deny that we begin with individuals who live their lives in a certain way and at some point develop a reflective account of them which comes to be shared by all, or imposed by one group upon others. Rather, it is within the shared practices of everyday living that common meanings are engendered and these flourish long before they achieve any sort of articulation. Even when

articulation does occur, and as we would anticipate from the ontological studies, their existential richness rejects any simple translation into second-order theories and principles. To an important extent the latter will anyway participate in, rather than simply reflect upon, the particular way of existing that has emerged. Ideological formulae will mean more than they explicitly say and what they say will remain less than what is experienced. For the social meanings which emerge are existential ones and, like perceptual meanings, they signify a way of existing which is first assimilated pre-consciously. They represent a collective yet pre-reflexive choice about a way of being-in-the-world. This choice is distilled over time, again in much the same manner that perceptual wholes come into being. Contingent activities come to resonate with one another according to what Merleau-Ponty calls a 'historical imagination', reinforcing some aspects at the expense of others, until a recognizable style of living, an historical *Gestalt*, emerges. At some point it begins to crystallize and to dictate individual acts rather to evolve out of them.

At this stage we have what might be called an existential ideology, which lends to a particular society its rationality – its inner logic or 'spirit'. While it may seem odd to our dualist way of thinking to describe an ideology in existential rather than ideal terms, this is no problem for the phenomenologist who rejects any rigid distinction between thought and the lived. This living code expresses 'typical ways of treating natural being, of responding to others and to death' (Merleau-Ponty, 1973a, p. 16). It is 'a symbol system that the subject takes over and incorporates as a style of functioning, as a global configuration, without having any need to conceive it at all' (1963, p. 56). Again, however, these systems are not objective structures immune to intersubjective preference, even if those preferences are not conscious ones. The motivation which underlies each historical form is the problem of coexistence, which provokes each culture as the questions of adaptation had the body. While there are no correct solutions, there is some broad criterion of advance:

> The progress of socioeconomic history, including its revolutions, is not so much a movement toward an homogeneous or a classless society as the quest, through always atypical cultural devices, for a life which is not unliveable for the greatest number. (Merleau-Ponty, 1964b, p. 131)

If such choices constrain by limiting perspectives and horizons, they also open up a world, releasing structures of significance and opportunities for communication; they provide a contact with things which allows them to be explored and expressed more richly. The symbol systems which embody these existential choices are no distorting medium which intervenes between us and a perfectly rational social organization, then. They are what allows each culture its identity and its projects, a way of being, where there are no pre-given solutions as to how people might best exist and coexist but only a series of provisional configurations which emerge over time.

This phenomenological account of the emergence of existential significance at the social level allows the earlier conclusions which were drawn from the appearing of perceptual sense, to be refined. In particular it allows further criticism of dualist conceptions of ideology.

First, let us return to the Marxist presentation of ideology and in particular its relationship with the economy. To begin with, it is evident that on the basis of Merleau-Ponty's account, ideology can never be a purely ideal phenomenon to be distinguished from social being or economic practices. Its meanings first arise from within them. Nor can ideology be severed from those existential and practical activities as something that might become fundamentally disjoined from them. As meaning and matter are irreducibly intertwined at the ontological level, so ideological and economic aspects of existence are interwoven at their core. If they are taken apart and presented in Cartesian fashion, then their relationship becomes incomprehensible:

> . . . the frequently celebrated relationship between ideology and economy remains mystical, pre-logical, and unthinkable insofar as ideology remains 'subjective', economy is conceived as an objective process, and the two are not made to communicate in the total historical existence and in the human objects which express it. (Merleau-Ponty, 1964a, p. 131)

When Merleau-Ponty describes social formations, we have seen that he grants them an overall significance in terms of their way of existing. This existential style is, for him, something which suffuses all the various manifestations of existence. Ideology, even

where it is articulated in a series of abstractions, will therefore reveal the same perspective and immanent logic as other dimensions of a culture where the whole is more than the sum of its parts. It cannot then be a reflection of an economic infrastructure which determines it. There is instead a correspondence which is motivated – but not caused – by particular existential choices. Economic practices from this perspective are themselves ideological insofar as they embody certain solutions in the face of the world's adversity. The most that Merleau-Ponty will allow is that the economy may be privileged in shaping the overall *Gestalt*, because it is more inertial than ideas. That is, it bears symbols and habits more effectively since it is a depository for practical categories and in turn suggests to people certain ways of being and thinking. Indeed, when it avoids rationalism, Marxism is said to recognize this relationship:

> Economic life is not a separate order to which the other orders may be reduced: it is Marxism's way of representing the inertia of human life; it is here that conceptions are registered and achieve stability. More surely than books or teachings, modes of work hand the previous generations' ways of being on to the new generations. It is true that in a given society at a given moment, the way of working expresses the mental and moral structure just as a living body's slightest reflex expresses the total subject's fundamental way of being in the world. But economic life is at the same time the historical carrier of mental structures, just as our body maintains the basic features of our behaviour beneath our varying moods; and this is the reason one will more surely get to know the essence of a society by analyzing interpersonal relations as they have been fixed and generalized in economic life. . . . (1964a, p. 108)

Thus, economic practices are the bearers of ideological themes, while ideas express choices buried in economic behaviour. Their relationship, and what allows them both to be expressions of the same thing, is the fact that they are existential equivalents. They express the way in which interpersonal relations are organized in that culture. To describe ideology as purely ideal or superstructural is therefore to introduce a false and problematic dichotomy.

> Marx's materialism is the idea that all the ideological formations of a given society are synonymous with or complementary to a certain type of praxis, i.e., the way this society has set up its basic relationship

with nature. It is the idea that economy and ideology have interior ties with the totality of history, like matter and form in a work of art or a perceptual thing. (1964a, p. 130)

The implications of this relationship can be developed further by looking at Merleau-Ponty's evaluation of Marxism. In his earlier writings, he wanted to claim Marx as an adherent of the phenomenological approach. What it means to be a phenomenologist, in this context, is to interrogate ideological and economic phenomena in order to reveal their latent meaning: to understand and judge a society means 'to penetrate its basic structure to the human bond upon which it is built' (1969a, p. xxiv). Such a Marxism is an open and experimental approach which tries to make sense of history from within it. Recognizing that the theorist is situated and questions from a certain perspective, it is self-critical and always ready to question the meanings it articulates, since it eschews the possibility of a final formulation of historical truth. 'The dialectic is this continued intuition, a consistent reading of actual history, the re-establishment of the tormented relations, of the interminable exchanges, between subject and object' (1973a, p. 32). Such a Marxism claims to unearth no essence of history from beneath its appearances: 'It is not so much a certain truth hidden behind empirical history that it gives us; rather it represents empirical history as the genealogy of truth' (1973a, p. 57).

But as we have seen, there is also a vulgar, non-phenomenological strand to Marxism, when it is reductive and presents ideology as a mere mask for class interests and reflection of material being. This is the Marxism which associates ideology with false consciousness. Now, Merleau-Ponty is in full agreement with Marx's complaint in *The German Ideology* that ideology *qua* idealism distorts reality because it is cut off from it and misconstrues the relationship between ideas and practice. But he can subscribe to no materialist inversion of this position, where ideologies are reduced to pale reflections of economic life and explained by it. They must have their truth, even if it is a latent one, because they express something about a society. The phenomenologist cannot, then, afford to ignore them, nor can he or she dismiss them as merely epiphenomenal.

We see these two forms of Marxism at work in the example of religion.

One would say that Marxism refuses to 'understand' religion, to grant
it any significance, and consequently rejects the very principle of a
phenomenology of religion. Here we are on the brink of a 'fleshless
Marxism' which reduces history to its economic skeleton. (1964a,
p. 127)

The question that should be asked is what religious ideology tells
us about a certain way of being and what interpersonal relationships it reveals. By studying this, we come to understand something about feudal society which its economy alone cannot disclose. Religion is not a veil for some other, more true, meaning
which is hidden beneath it, even if it helps sustain a culture that
is closed and narrow compared with a possible socialist existence.
'Thus it is a question not of denying religion all human significance
but of treating it as the symbolic expression of the social and
human drama' (1964a, p. 128). Its truth is the concrete relations
it expresses. 'It is a matter of understanding religion as man's
chimerical effort to rejoin other men in another world and of
replacing this fantasy of communication with effective communication in this world' (ibid). Religion thus shows itself in a particular existential choice. But it is also a facet of that overall quest
for communication and coexistence to which every culture is a
provisional solution. It is in its efficacy here that it is vulnerable
to attack, since it offers a closed and 'irrational' set of meanings
that are powerless to yield a means of expression which might
advance its goals.

Bourgeois ideologies, to take another example, are not appearances which disguise the realities of a capitalist economy. They
may mystify bourgeois society by presenting their abstract ideas
as an account of unassailable historical absolutes, but that very
rationalism is an expression of the bourgeois choice of existence
and forms a single system with the economy. It is evident, then,
that ideology cannot be simply equated with false consciousness.
Participants in its bourgeois form have an immediate contact,
through the ideology itself, with the existential truth of their
culture.

Even illusions have some sort of sense and call for deciphering because
they always present themselves against the background of a lived
relationship with the social whole and because they are thus not like
something mental, opaque and isolated; instead, like the expressions

of faces or speeches, they bring with them an underlying meaning that
unmasks them, and they hide something only by exposing it. (1973a,
p. 42)

Thus, it is not by reducing ideology to some set of more true
meanings that false consciousness is assuaged, for in its rationalist
assumptions this aspiration is only a further example of the bourgeois project. The phenomenologist seeks the existential choices
which ideas express and then evaluates a culture on the basis of
them. In the case of bourgeois ideology, what is needed is not its
dismissal as a veil for the true economic meaning of capitalism,
but a critique of the rationalism which its ideology and economy
both express and which, like religion, offers a closed set of meanings and therefore limited opportunities for communication and
coexistence.

A further implication of the phenomenological account of how
ideologies emerge in existence, is of more relevance to end-of-
ideology and would-be scientific beliefs that ideology is a malign
and expendible phenomenon. For Merleau-Ponty, as we saw,
ideologies emerge out of the lifeworld and first exist more as a
common culture than as a set of ideas. They form a horizon for
our thinking, an unquestioned and therefore unexamined context
within which we perceive and interrogate the world. Paul Ricoeur,
also a French phenomenologist and Merleau-Ponty's younger contemporary, summarizes this view succinctly: ideology 'operates
behind our backs. We think from its point of view rather than
thinking about it' (Ricoeur, 1984, p. 137). It is the impossibility
of standing outside it or of bringing it entirely to our attention,
that guarantees that all awareness and thinking must occur within
an ideological context. This is not problematic for the phenomenologist, since the idea of a social grouping that would operate
according to some hygienic model of non-perspectival realism
is but another rationalistic fallacy (which itself reveals its own
ideological perspective). All societies are perceived by this approach as ideological, in so far as the shared symbols and ideas
that make social coexistence possible necessarily remain provisional, perspectival, equivocal and something less than a reflection
of some putative social reality. When critics of ideology attack it
for being a partial and perspectival distortion of objective life they
implicitly, and paradoxically, condemn in it something that is

intrinsic to all significance. Indeed, for Merleau-Ponty it is precisely the recognition that meanings are of this nature that is prerequisite to a political thinking and practice that would remain open and non-violent. In the concluding section of this essay, I therefore want to explore the sense in which Merleau-Ponty admits that some ideologies may be pernicious and to suggest that it is the very rationalism by which its critics would eliminate it, that is to blame.

IV

So far, I have developed a phenomenological account of ideology in order to attack some of the major positions of the term's critics. The main line of opposition which has emerged here is the following. For Merleau-Ponty, meanings first emerge on a preconceptual level, where they are available to us in a pre-reflective manner via perception and styles of living. Within this realm of experience, they always appear in a shifting, overdetermined and ambiguous manner. Ideologies are no exception: no level of significance escapes the contingency and partiality of its origins. It is therefore a fundamental misconception to believe that some objective level of social truth exists beneath ideology. Even if it did, our second-order theories could not give an exhaustive account of it. But in any case, the real is for Merleau-Ponty a multifaceted latency riven by incompleteness and possibility – there is no plentitude there awaiting reflective replication. All societies will exhibit an ideology insofar as they exhibit a particular choice regarding the way they live and perceive the world, encapsulated in a more or less explicit symbolism. This does not distort or occlude something more authentic which they might attain with clearer vision: it is their contact with the world, their means of bringing to expression something which did not previously exist.

What this suggests, however, is that ideology is an entirely neutral term, oscillating somewhere between existential and ideal articulations and opening up, as well as closing off, possible ways of creating meaning. And certainly Merleau-Ponty often intends it in this sense. Yet he does not believe that all cultures (or ideologies) are equally valuable in existentialist terms and sometimes refers to ideology in a pejorative way. We now need, then,

to see whether some phenomenological criterion is available for distinguishing malign ideologies from the general category of ideology.

When Merleau-Ponty writes about ideology, he remains faithful to his anti-Cartesianism. He must therefore resist any tendency to describe ideology as a purely ideal formulation whose relationship to the world it explains would thereby become problematic. We saw this in his rejection of a dualism between ideology and economy (superstructure and base). What we have, then, are more and less ideal ideologies, although none can become completely so. I think it may be helpful at this point to distinguish between three different levels on which sociopolitical meanings might appear.

The first level is one of experience. We saw how societies evolve into symbolic matrices where their particular ways of being become embodied in practices and culture. Here, I suggested, we have a mute and living type of ideology, which structures perceptions yet rarely reaches consciousness since it provides the horizon for all thinking and acting. It is this pervasive, experiential level of ideology that is irreducible and which manifests itself in all facets of a culture. Religious or bourgeois ideologies often operate in this way.

At the second level, ideology becomes more explicit in ideal terms: some disjunction between circumstances and the unquestioned practices of a culture may force a questioning that requires the articulation and interrogation of its basic orientation, in order that action may challenge moribund institutions. Now the previously silent and equivocal meanings of experience must be articulated and yet by their nature, they resist any simple translation into clear concepts. Marxism, for example, misconceives itself if it believes that it reveals the objective nature of capitalism and thereby dispels false consciousness by offering to the working class a truth to be realized. Among the masses, theory emerges from a praxis and catches on only if it manages to capture some meaning which was experienced before it was thought. But its birth is a creative as well as a reflective act. It formulates a sense from within the density and ambiguity of the lived and thereby restructures it, offering new possibilities for action towards the future. It succeeds insofar as it strikes a resonance within the real while casting it in a new light and inspiring those who live within

it, to action. In this capacity it is neither true in the sense of offering a science of the real, nor illusory in fabricating some fanciful interpretation of events. When it is articulated from within a praxis, it invites continual verification by those who would take it up.

Paradoxically, it is at the third level, where ideas attain their highest level of abstraction, or ideality, that we find the possibility of ideology in the bad sense of the word, and here the distinction that is to be drawn is between ideology and phenomenology itself. What I want to suggest here is that ideology in its negative sense is closely related to rationalism, and so it is useful to begin by looking more carefully at Merleau-Ponty's account of the latter.

Rationalism presents itself as a project of enlightenment, where-by obscurities and mysteries might be swept away by the bright light of reason. Its fascination with the phenomenon of ideology is an excellent illustration of this. Ideology first emerges as an Enlightenment concept, when Destutt de Tracy introduces it in 1796 to refer to a science of ideas that will permit the reconstruction of society on a rational basis. The fact that the term is subsequently reconceived as a form of distortion in no way detracts from the overall project, which is to uncover a value-free, objective body of knowledge. As rationalism presents itself here, its aim is to show how things really are, beneath the mystifications of sinister interests, superstitions and false consciousness. This is why it becomes seduced by the idea of a perfect language or an end of history, where meanings would be static, unequivocal and complete, perfectly translating the material world into ideal terms.

Now, it is evident that according to Merleau-Ponty's account of how meaning appears, this goal must be fundamentally misconceived, since it relies upon the very Cartesianism he has rejected. He also challenges rationalism's own perception of itself as an objective form of knowledge. It is in fact, he argues, the particular existential choice of the modern Western world. That is, it is the symbolic configuration which structures those cultures that organize their existence in a certain way – namely, by seeking in knowledge and action a means for dominating nature and eliminating adversity. The significance of rationalism is therefore as a provisional solution to the problems of coexistence and not as a definitive resolution to history. In other words, it represents one

possible way of living and of expressing ourselves and not a formula for disclosing the truth about the world.

When rationalism suggests that it can illuminate the external
world by conceptualizing it without remainder, its aim is to translate all levels of meaning into rational concepts. In this sense it
becomes ideological in a pejorative sense. The relevant criterion
in imposing this judgement is not truth versus falsity, but openness
versus closure. Rationalism is allied to closure because it claims
to offer a definitive set of meanings and thereby closes itself off
from the living, pre-rational sources of creative expression. It is
condemned to endlessly repeating itself. It discounts non-rational
and pre-rational forms as inferior and ultimately as nonsensical,
believing that all levels of significance, whether they lie in experience, or music, or aesthetics, or eroticism, can be translated into
ideal concepts without loss, and thereby rendered transparent. It
anticipates an unambiguous set of symbols, to be shared in perfect
communication. Its success would mean total sterility and its own
inability to appreciate anything outside of itself. It is in this sense
that it offers a closed set of meanings and functions as an ideology.

What Merleau-Ponty means by ideology in this context, then,
is a set of ideas which have been severed from their immersion
in experience and reified as abstractions. They lose their intimacy
with the lifeworld and are therefore no longer able to look there
for verification or novelty. In this sense, Merleau-Ponty's understanding of ideology is similar to that of Marx when he condemns
it for its idealism. Philosophy is always ideological, Merleau-Ponty
contends, when it is 'an abstract aspect of total historical life'
(1964a, p. 132). While it is imprisoned in concepts and rational
abstractions, it does mask concrete relationships, and this is why
idealism operates as a 'class ideology': it presents meanings as
closed and immune to the fermentations within socioeconomic life
that will transport them (1969a, p. 103). But this is equally true
of Marxism when it becomes a form of vulgar materialism: when
it presents meanings as mere reflections of the economic base, it,
too, rips itself out of history's contingencies to offer a set of closed
meanings which have lost touch with their origins.

Ideology thus gains its negative status precisely when it sustains
a Cartesian epistemology and separates subject from object. Then
we find presented a set of abstract ideas which have nothing to
do with experience. They can no longer advance as it does and

therefore increasingly freeze into moribund formulae. Either they harden into abstract principles and then try to crush historical contingencies into conformity with them, or they offer *ex post facto* justifications for events which no longer have the significance that is claimed for them. This, then, is where epistemological confusion translates into political violence, since events are now pushed into a form that is alien to them while institutions are devised that will suppress the emergence of alternative possibilities.

This is also where theoretical levels of meaning split between those which are ideological/rationalist/philosophical, and a phenomenology which is presented by Merleau-Ponty as the only authentic way of articulating significance since it remains inter-rogative and accepts its engagement in the unfolding of history, attempting to articulate meanings as they emerge there in all their ambiguity, rather than attempting to sum them up from an external vantage point. Thus in the distinction drawn above, between a phenomenological and a rationalistic Marxism, it is the latter which becomes ideological in a negative sense. In the former capacity, it is 'not primarily a system of ideas but a reading of ongoing history' (1969a, p. 52). Here, truth is 'conceived as a process of indefinite verification' (1973a, p. 53). Where it presents proletarian victory as the hidden truth of history and is used as a set of ideas to defend this meaning and the Party in power, however, it loses its open, interrogative stance and becomes ideo-logical, because it is reduced to a set of abstract formulae. Marx-ism is most ideological, then, precisely when it masquerades as truth. 'There was a vulgar Marxism which believed it could give a general genetic diagram and describe clearly distinct phases in an order of invariable succession' (1973a, p. 86).

We can now see the ways in which both communist and liberal ideologies can be called ideological in the pejorative sense of the word. In the former case, Merleau-Ponty begins with an authentic, phenomenological communism where there is a 'spontaneous con-vergence of proletarian movements and the truth of its own his-torical perspective' (1969a, p. xxi). As these begin to diverge, however, meanings are no longer extrapolated/engendered from within the real: the subjective and objective, ideological and econ-omic, move apart. The tension between intentions and acts, behaviour and the thought behind it, thus grows, until the doctrine

which was once a living and open one 'has ceased to be a confident interpretation of spontaneous history' and instead defends the Soviet Union (1969a, p. xxvii). The USSR 'no longer professes the ideology of its economy' and revolutionary themes 'become an ideology in the true sense of the word: a collection of *a posteriori* justifications' (1969a, p. 155f). The idea of the dialectic as a contingent unfolding of significance where subject and object meet is now lost as a critical instrument and itself becomes a 'point of honor, justification, and ideology' (1969a, p. 72). In fact it becomes a form of scientific rationalism. Of course, a living ideology in the first sense in which I described ideology above, continues to unfold: its meaning is one of bureaucratic socialism, and it is this that the phenomenologist can bring to light by looking to concrete relations rather than at the ideas espoused. The ideology which masks them is therefore of a rather different order from the bourgeois or religious ideologies which continued to express the incipient truths of their cultures.

The weakness of Merleau-Ponty's account here is that he gives us no sense of the role of power or group interests in this process, although this does at least allow him to avoid any sort of conspiracy theory. Instead there seems to be a sort of historical inertia and loss of will. He leaves open the question of how far Soviet ideology is consciously recognized as being at odds with reality and cynically propagated. Its fictions are more maintained, the more reality diverges from them

> . . . either because for some this fraud is consciously accepted as the heritage of a project which they do not want to betray or because, in the decadence of Marxist culture which results from it, the fraud ceases to be perceptible and is all the less conscious the more it is constantly lived. (1973a, pp. 222–3)

An equivalent process has occurred in the liberal democracies where once living and resonant liberal values have become abstractions that merely justify a reality which fails to embody them. In other words, liberty and its corollaries become ideological when they are no longer used to defend free persons and become but justifications for Western states. Here, too, we can compare ideas 'formed in contact with the present and in order to understand it' with the 'ideological tatters which we inherited from the nineteenth century and which poorly clothe the facts'

(1964a, p. 154). The ideas are not intrinsically ideological, but become so when they are taken out of history and detached from historical forces that might realize them. And this is precisely the problem of rationalism.

In conclusion, Merleau-Ponty's existential phenomenology has challenged the oppositions upon which the usual condemnations of ideology rest. His account of the body–subject who perceives and structures the world prior to reflection has rejected the primordial opposition between subject and object which rendered impossible any satisfactory appreciation of the relationship between ideas and the world. Instead of using true and false as criteria for distinguishing between ideology and science, his work suggests that all societies are ideological in terms of the provisional existential choices they make, but that it is possible to identify pernicious forms of ideological expression according to standards of openness and closure. When living ideologies, as they emerge from existence in an ambiguous and polyvalent form, are frozen into abstract formulae, they become increasingly moribund. They no longer strive to articulate meanings as they appear but instead attempt to shape the real according to their own images. The rationalism which believes it can eliminate ideology in favour of a rational and transparent culture is itself an example of such an ideology, since it is no longer open to a multivalent significance which is inexhaustible. It cannot invite that exploration, experimentation and expression that would broaden communication and accommodate a genuine engendering of reason in the world, because it misconceives its own relationship to experience.

NOTES

1. Husserl had made a similar point in his *Crisis* when he commented that 'we should not be mislead by the usual contrast between empiricism and rationalism': *The Crisis of European Sciences and Transcendental Phenomenology* trans. David Carr (Evanston: Northwestern University Press, 1970), p. 162.
2. This is especially evident in Husserl's *Crisis* (1970).
3. Peter Dews brings out a similar distinction well in relation to language when he writes that Merleau-Ponty 'clearly perceives that without some conception of a subject which expresses and comprehends meaning through language, and therefore provides a point of departure and return, we would become trapped in an infinite regress: "Signs do not simply evoke other signs for us

and so on endlessly" ': *Logics of Disintegration, Post-Structuralist Thought and the Claims of Critical Theory* (London: Verso, 1987) p. 32.

REFERENCES

Dews, Peter (1987), *Logics of Disintegration, Post-Structuralist Thought and the Claims of Critical Theory*, London: Verso.

Husserl, Edmund (1970), *The Crisis of the European Sciences and Transcendental Phenomenology* (trans. D. Carr), Evanston: Northwestern University Press.

Merleau-Ponty, Maurice (1962), *Phenomenology of Perception* (trans. C. Smith), London: Routledge and Kegan Paul.

Merleau-Ponty, Maurice (1963), *In Praise of Philosophy* (trans. J. Wild and J. Edie), Evanston: Northwestern University Press.

Merleau-Ponty, Maurice (1964a), *Sense and Non-Sense* (trans. H.L. Dreyfus and P.A. Dreyfus), Evanston: Northwestern University Press.

Merleau-Ponty, Maurice (1964b), *Signs* (trans. R. McCleary), Evanston: Northwestern University Press.

Merleau-Ponty, Maurice (1965), *The Structure of Behaviour* (trans. A. Fisher), London: Methuen.

Merleau-Ponty, Maurice (1969a), *Humanism and Terror* (trans. J. O'Neill), Boston: Beacon Press.

Merleau-Ponty, Maurice (1969b), *The Visible and the Invisible* (trans. A. Lingis), Evanston: Northwestern University Press.

Merleau-Ponty, Maurice (1973a), *Adventures of the Dialectic* (trans. J. Bien), London: Heinemann.

Merleau-Ponty, Maurice (1973b), *Consciousness and the Acquisition of Language* (trans. H.J. Silverman), Evanston: Northwestern University Press.

Merleau-Ponty, Maurice (1973c), *The Prose of the World* (trans. J. O'Neill), Evanston: Northwestern University Press.

Ricoeur, Paul (1984), 'Ideology and Ideology Critique' in B. Waldenfels, J.M. Broekman and A. Pazanin (eds), *Phenomenology and Marxism* (trans. J.C. Evans, Jr.), London: Routledge and Kegan Paul.

6.   Hannah Arendt on Ideology in Totalitarianism*

Margaret Canovan

According to Hannah Arendt, totalitarianism is characterized by ideology and terror. Terror is 'the essence of totalitarian domination'[1] and ideology is its guiding principle.[2] While the prominence given to 'terror' in an analysis of regimes such as those of Hitler and Stalin may seem relatively unproblematic, 'ideology' puzzles many of Arendt's readers, who find it hard to be sure just what role it plays in her account of totalitarianism. Does she or does she not believe that the leaders of totalitarian regimes took their ideologies seriously? Cases can apparently be made for both accounts. This essay is an attempt to spell out the problem of interpretation and to offer a solution which, it is hoped, may shed some light on the central themes of Arendt's account of totalitarianism. The question whether or not her account is historically accurate will not be addressed here: it is obvious, however, that any attempt to answer that question must presuppose an accurate understanding of what she meant to say.

TOTALITARIANS AS FANATICS

One way of reading Arendt's account is to see totalitarians as fanatics, men obsessed with what they believe to be the truth and dedicated to carrying it out regardless of constraints or consequences. Although, as Arendt points out, ideologies are scientistic and secular in form, the obvious analogy here is with religious fanatics and their heresy hunts and *autos-da-fe*. Some of Arendt's statements appear to support this interpretation. For example, in an essay on the concentration camps which appeared in 1950, a

151

year before the original publication of *The Origins of Totalitarianism*, she says of the unprecedented crimes committed in the camps that 'there is very little doubt that the perpetrators . . . committed them for the sake of their ideology which they believed to be proved by science, experience and the laws of life'.[3]

There are similar passages in *Totalitarianism* itself. In the first edition, Arendt suggested that it would have been easy for the Nazis to have secured hegemony over Europe, had that been their sole aim. It was their racism, forcing them into policies of extermination, that made their rule utterly unacceptable to the conquered peoples.[4] A little later she remarks that ideologies are harmless only as long as they are not seriously believed in,[5] implying that within totalitarian systems they were so believed. In the essay on 'Ideology and Terror' added to the second and third editions of the book she assures us that Hitler and Stalin did indeed take their ideologies 'dead seriously'[6] – although, as we shall see, this claim is not as unambiguous as it sounds.

So far, Arendt's position appears akin to familiar explanations of totalitarianism which attribute it to ideas and beliefs of a particularly fanatical type. There are two objections to this interpretation, however. For one thing, Arendt often criticized those who sought to find an intellectual ancestry for totalitarianism, insisting that ideas were not responsible for what happened in the concentration camps.[7] Another, and perhaps more fundamental, objection is that if totalitarian ideology were comparable to fanatical belief in a religion or an intellectual system, the concentration camps themselves could not hold the absolutely central place accorded to them by Arendt.[8] True fanaticism would make the camps a means, not an end. Thus a fanatically-held belief that Jews were bearers of corruption might lead its adherents to kill Jews as earlier religious fanatics had killed heretics, but the killing would be ancillary to the belief: having got rid of the Jews or heretics one would be able to call a halt to the killing. Arendt, by contrast, insists that terror is absolutely essential to the totalitarian system, which will find new categories of victims when it has exhausted the original supply.[9] This emphasis on the centrality of terror suggests rather that she thought of ideology as an *excuse* for the total domination practised in the camps, and in 'Ideology and Terror' she does indeed go so far as to suggest that in con-

ditions of fully realized totalitarianism and perfected terror, ideology would be redundant.[10]

Are we to suppose, then, that she regarded ideology merely as a tool used by totalitarian leaders to legitimize an essentially cynical drive for complete power? As we shall see, there are indeed passages in which Arendt apparently implies that the leaders did not believe their own ideology.

TOTALITARIANS AS CYNICS

One of Arendt's earliest published reflections on the concentration camps, a book review from 1946,[11] presents the ideological trappings of Nazism and Stalinism as mere 'clothes' in which power is 'dressed'. Although several years of intensive reflection lie between this and the completion of *Totalitarianism*, a similarly sceptical view of the role of ideology seems to underlie the chapter on 'The Totalitarian Movement', where she discusses the various layers within the onion-like structure of the party and the gradations of cynicism within it. One of the characteristics of totalitarian movements, says Arendt, is disregard for truth on the part of the leaders, who tell monstrous, uninhibited lies for public consumption. While ordinary party members are not taken in by this propaganda, they do believe 'the standard cliches of ideological explanation'.[12] Further in, towards the heart of the movement, however, are élite formations who know better than to take these seriously, or even to be interested in whether or not they correspond to reality. Instead of believing, for instance, that Jews actually are inferior, they see such a claim as a programme, meaning that Jews are to be killed. As for the higher ranks of the hierarchy, those close to the Leader enjoy 'freedom from the content of their own ideologies'[13] and believe only in human omnipotence, that 'everything is possible'. Although Arendt does not at this point comment upon the beliefs of Hitler and Stalin themselves, her model appears to imply that in their cases cynicism must have been complete. This chapter therefore leads one to attribute to her the view that Machiavellian leaders use ideologies merely as tools with which to manipulate the masses for their own ends. Clearly, this directly contradicts the evidence already cited in support of an Arendtian picture of totalitarians as fanatics. Like

other people, Arendt is not invariably consistent. Nevertheless, her thought is a great deal more consistent than the casual reader is tempted to suppose, and what may seem at first sight to be contradictions often turn out, on careful reading, to be aspects of a consistent view which has escaped notice because of its originality and complexity. Let us see, therefore, whether that applies to her understanding of ideology.

TOTALITARIANS AS ARTISTS

In discussing whether or not, in Arendt's account, the totalitarian leaders took their ideology seriously, we have so far asked only whether or not they believed it to be true in the sense of corresponding to reality. But that is only one way of taking ideas seriously. There is another way that would fit much better with Arendt's remarks about cynicism within the totalitarian movement, and would provide us with an interpretation for which there is a good deal of support in *Totalitarianism*. For one may take an ideology seriously not as something that is already true but as something to be *made* true in place of what actually exists. In other words, one may reject reality in favour of an alternative structure – a fiction to be realized. This is certainly in line with the emphasis Arendt lays on the totalitarian belief that everything is possible, and with her continual references to the 'fictitious world' of totalitarianism. In her account of the totalitarian movement, she describes how it attracts the disoriented masses by offering them a new world by means of its propaganda and organization: a fictitious world, much more consistent than the real one, in which 'uprooted masses can feel at home and are spared the never-ending shocks which real life and real experiences deal to human beings and their expectations'.[14] Once in power, the totalitarian leaders alter the real world to suit their fiction, for example by reducing Jews to manifest inferiority and making racial descent all-important in social life.[15]

Within this interpretation, therefore, the seriousness with which the leaders take their ideology is a seriousness of purpose rather than a belief in truth: their 'unwavering faith in an ideological fictitious world'[16] is in fact a commitment to it, the determination, backed by their sincere belief in unlimited possibilities, to make

their dreams come true and to work out consistently the fiction presented during their struggle for power.[17] This suggests a picture of totalitarianism as a kind of hubristic Prometheanism, a gigantic and utterly unrestrained assertion of human power. George Kateb, who interprets Arendt's account along these lines, says that she sees totalitarianism as 'the disposition to live a fiction . . . or make the world over into a fiction', and he links this to the artistic impulse to remake reality and to 'the latent murderousness inherent in aestheticism'.[18]

Although there is considerable support for this reading of Arendt, I shall argue that it still misses the point of her account of totalitarianism. Even if we discount its inconsistency with the passage quoted earlier from the essay on 'Social Science Techniques and the Study of Concentration Camps' about how totalitarians believed their ideology to be proved by science and experience, there are other and stronger objections. For while no-one was more alive than Arendt to the dangers of an artistic approach to political action, and of the tyrannical potentialities implicit in a view of the world and other people as clay to be moulded,[19] totalitarianism as she conceived it was something else again. The artistic impulse to change the world implies a sense of freedom and a confidence in human mastery that may be hubristic but is certainly humanistic – which totalitarianism most certainly is not. Towards the end of *Totalitarianism* Arendt makes this contrast, briefly but quite clearly. As she points out, both revolutionary political action and civilization itself, 'the erection of the human artifice'[20] rest upon a 'contempt for reality', a 'proud assumption of human mastery over the world' – an assertion, in fact, of human creativity.[21] But what is distinctive in totalitarianism's transformation of the world is a contempt for reality devoid of this human pride, and linked instead to an attempt to destroy all human dignity and creativity. Totalitarianism contrives to act on the belief that everything is possible *without* asserting humanism, creativity and freedom; and the difference, it seems, lies in the role of ideology. 'What destroys the element of pride in the totalitarian contempt for reality (and thereby distinguishes it radically from revolutionary theories and attitudes) is the supersense which gives the contempt for reality its cogency, logicality and consistency.'[22] What we find at the heart of Arendt's conception of totalitarianism, therefore, is a conception of ideology as something that is

taken seriously, but taken seriously in a very special way, neither as something true in the ordinary sense (that is, as a statement about how things are) nor as a fiction in the ordinary sense (that is, as a free creation to be enacted) but as something different again. Let us now try to clarify what this is.

TOTALITARIANS AS ROBOTS

Reflecting at the end of the first edition of *Totalitarianism* upon the insanity of totalitarian ideology and how it differs from humanistic efforts to change the world, Arendt claimed that it was the distinctive *logicality* of such ideologies that excluded respect for human dignity and the creativity of men,[23] but in that passage the precise significance of logicality remained unclear. Arendt clarified it to some extent in the essay on 'Ideology and Terror' which she added to later editions, and which contained 'certain insights of a strictly theoretical nature' which, she said, she had not possessed when she finished *Totalitarianism*.[24] This essay is too compressed, however, to be easily comprehensible. Fortunately there are, among her surviving manuscripts, drafts which help to explicate her meaning.

The first point to note is that when Arendt talks of 'ideology' she uses the term in a particular and restricted sense. An ideology is not just any set of political ideas and beliefs, but one which purports to supply the key to the past and the future. Thus, as Arendt explains in an unpublished paper, racist anti-semitism is not yet an ideology while it is simply a matter of praising Aryans and hating Jews, but becomes one only when it purports to be able to explain the course of history in terms of racial struggles and Jewish manoeuvres. Similarly, socialism in the sense of struggling for justice for the working class is not an ideology: it becomes one only when it presents claims about the inevitable struggle between classes, leading to the classless society of the future.[25] Arendt claims that, once a set of political ideas is accepted as an ideology, the specific ideas involved fade into insignificance compared with the underlying belief in inevitable laws of historical development – which is why some of those who had accepted one ideology for a time found it easy enough to switch to another that was supposed to be the opposite of the first.[26]

Created in the nineteenth century, ideologies were harmless enough, according to Arendt, until their totalitarian potential was discovered by Hitler and Stalin. Of what, then, did this consist? Arendt points to three aspects.[27] In the first place, it is in the nature of ideologies, concerned as they are with the whole historical process, to be exclusively interested in change and motion, not with what actually is in existence but with what is coming to be. Claiming to know the future, they regard all existing reality as merely temporary. This is linked not only to the dynamism of totalitarianism but also to its contempt for factuality, for the way things actually are. Second and consequently, ideological thinking becomes uncoupled from reality, disinclined to accept our experience of the way things are,[28] for behind what we perceive, according to the ideology, lies the real secret meaning of the process. Third, this uncoupling from reality culminates in the way ideologists *think*. Instead of reflecting upon experience, ideologists take their axiomatic premises (such as the claim that race or class struggle is the order of nature) and proceed to deduce implications without referring back to experienced reality. This generates an automatic process of deductive consistency that is quite impervious to genuine thought or experience, and which is supposed to correspond to those fundamental natural or historical processes that doom to death 'dying classes' or 'lower races'.

The simple operation by which Hitler and Stalin transformed these ideologies into principles of totalitarianism was, according to Arendt, by taking them 'dead seriously'.[29] What they took seriously, however, was not the original political content of the ideology, but the inexorable laws of nature or history that gave it its ideological form. In their hands the original messages of the ideologies disappeared. Stalin was not guided by fanatical concern for the proletariat, nor Hitler for the German people, while neither of them was interested in ideas as such. Instead, what fascinated them was the remorseless process of logic whereby, simply following 'ice-cold reasoning' or the 'irresistible force of logic' one could conclude that groups were condemned to death by nature or history. In other words, the important point about totalitarian ideologies is not their specific intellectual content[30] (which is why Arendt could equate Hitler and Stalin, for all their supposed ideological differences) but their automatic, *inhuman* character, which excludes thought and experience, judgement and

responsibility, and sanctions terror that seems to grind on remorselessly like a natural process, without the need for human decision or action. Their ideologies 'transformed Nature or History from the firm soil upon which human life and action moved into . . . forces whose movements race through humanity and drag every individual willy-nilly . . .'.[31]

The central feature of the insane logicality with which totalitarians spell out their deductions from the laws of history is that it is not at all like genuine human thought, which reflects freely upon experience. Instead it is an automatic, unfree process. 'You can't say A without saying B and C and so on, down to the end of the murderous alphabet.'[32] As such, it is a compulsive way of thinking, unchecked by judgement or common sense, forcing the mind on to ever more preposterous conclusions for fear of contradicting itself. One example Arendt gives is that of the Bolsheviks purged by Stalin who, rather than abandon their belief that the Party delivered the verdicts of history, denied their own experience to the extent of confessing to crimes they had not committed.[33] Similarly, the Nazis who organized the Final Solution of the Jewish Question were following the logical implications of premises that had (in a less consistent way) been accepted by many highly respectable Europeans who had not been tempted to mass murder. The point here, of course, is that whatever the ideas they may occasionally profess, properly functioning human beings are restrained from following them to their remote and insane implications by a multitude of other considerations, among them the abilities to see other points of view and to reconsider ideas in the light of their practical consequences. It is just such capacities that ideological thinking destroys. 'Inner compulsion' by the 'tyranny of logicality' removes the capacities to think again and to react to experience[34] and turns men into robots, perfectly fitted for the role of executioner or of victim as required by the all-devouring process of totalitarian terror.

At this point in 'Ideology and Terror' Arendt is principally concerned with ideological logicality as a device for mobilizing the subjects of a totalitarian regime and inducing them to fall into line of their own accord. 'Totalitarian government can be safe only to the extent that it can mobilize man's own will power in order to force him into that gigantic movement of History or Nature which supposedly uses mankind as its material.'[35] She

stresses that compulsive thinking of this kind, which she attributes particularly to lonely mass-men who have, in their isolation, lost their hold upon reality and common sense, is not the same thing as genuine conviction. Totalitarian rulers do not want convinced Nazis or Communists, that is to say people who have reflected freely upon their own experience and come into agreement with these doctrines. What they want is people who are no longer capable of either experience or thought but only of computer-like deductions. This stress upon the role of ideology among the subjects of totalitarianism is therefore not inconsistent with the statements quoted earlier about the cynicism of the élite formations within the movement. That cynicism consists above all in an indifference and imperviousness to truth, facts, reality; 'the outstanding negative quality of the totalitarian élite is that it never stops to think about the world as it really is and never compares the lies with reality.'[36]

So much for ideological conviction among the supporters of totalitarianism, but what of the leaders? When Arendt says that Hitler and Stalin took their ideological logic 'dead seriously', does she nevertheless mean only that they took it seriously as a political device to mobilize masses while allowing themselves to exercise arbitrary rule? Arendt's discussion of terror in the earlier part of 'Ideology and Terror' strongly suggests an answer which is confirmed by her unpublished papers. Her first point, upon which she lays great stress, is that it is a mistake to regard totalitarianism as a form of tyranny, that is, as lawless rule in the interests of the ruler. Totalitarianism is different because it claims to execute the law of history or nature regardless of *any* human interests at all. The terror which is the heart of the regime is at the service of these 'laws', forever eliminating 'the unfit' or the 'dying classes'.[37] Within this section of her discussion, which is particularly abstract and general, Arendt does not refer to Hitler and Stalin themselves as the perpetrators of terror, but rather speaks of 'terror' itself as the ruler, blindly executing the laws of nature or history. The implication is that for all their arbitrariness in building a fictitious world and in selecting the next category of victims for the terror to swallow up,[38] the rulers do not believe themselves to be acting freely. Unlike despotism, in which (according to Hegel) *one* is free,[39] in totalitarian regimes none is free, for even the leaders are merely the servants of suprahuman processes.

The totalitarian dictator, in sharp distinction from the old-time tyrant and dictator, does not believe himself to be a free agent who has the power to execute his arbitrary will and whims, but to be the executor of certain laws which are higher than . . . himself.[40]

It seems that totalitarianism not only rules over robots, reduced to something less than human either by the internal compulsion of ideology, or by the terror which produces 'ghastly marionettes with human faces':[41] according to Arendt's account, totalitarianism is actually directed by robots as well. The leaders are not mighty tyrants revelling in their freedom to create and destroy as they please, but nonentities[42] allowing 'the force of nature or of history to race freely through mankind'.[43]

What makes Arendt's position so paradoxical and hard to grasp is that totalitarianism, as she describes it, seems to have two contradictory characteristics, namely an aspiration to omnipotence on the one hand and a sense of powerlessness on the other. On the one hand totalitarian leaders such as Stalin believe that 'everything is possible' to the point of despising reality as something that can always be changed, and are prepared to deploy the resources of total domination to fabricate a new society that will exemplify the principles of their ideology. Nevertheless, the sense of human mastery over the world that this demonstrates is deeply ambiguous. Not only is total domination primarily employed, in those camps that are the 'laboratories' of the regime,[44] to manufacture a new species of man too predictable and lacking in spontaneity to challenge the new order: more than that, even those who wield this unprecedented power do not believe in their own freedom, but see themselves as merely speeding up developments that are actually inevitable. At the bottom of their actions lies a 'belief in the omnipotence of *man* and at the same time of the superfluity of men'[45] – their superfluity, that is, as beings who are capable of originating action and making free choices. In the manuscript just quoted Arendt goes on to speculate that, while Hitler and Stalin did have genuine commitment to their respective ideologies, totalitarianism might ultimately function without even this vestige of human thought, directed by leaders who would not even know the difference between believing and not believing.

In Arendt's eyes, therefore, the totalitarian belief that 'everything is possible' is an attitude of a paradoxically anti-humanist

kind. Instead of stemming from a pride in human creativity, the totalitarian contempt for experience and disregard of facts rest upon 'the assumption that everything that *is*, is in constant movement and that dialectical materialism has discovered the law of this movement . . . totalitarianism assumes only the validity of the law of a moving History or Nature' and acts accordingly. This last quotation comes from a symposium first published in 1954[46] in which Arendt concisely restated her view of totalitarianism as a compound of omnipotence and subservience to suprahuman forces. When she says, therefore, that 'human nature as such is at stake'[47] she means that in totalitarian regimes human freedom and spontaneity are destroyed and all human purposes disregarded, not only at the level of the dehumanized victims in the camps but at the level of the rulers as well. 'Totalitarianism strives not toward despotic rule over men, but toward a system in which men are superfluous.'[48]

How, then, should we answer our original question, whether Arendt believed that the totalitarian leaders took their ideologies seriously? The answer is that Arendt's account is complex and easily misunderstood. Hitler and Stalin were cynics to the extent of disregarding most of what ordinary Nazis or Communists would regard as articles of faith (a freedom from dogmatism symbolized by their alliance at the beginning of the Second World War), but each was also a fanatic in that he genuinely believed he had found the key to history in the endless struggle and destruction of races or classes.[49] As Arendt put it in *Totalitarianism*,

> it cannot be doubted . . . that the Nazi leadership actually believed in, and did not merely use as propaganda, such doctrines as the following: 'The more accurately we recognise and observe the laws of nature and life . . . so much the more do we conform to the will of the Almighty. The more insight we have into the will of the Almighty, the greater will be our successes.'

Sustained by a conviction of omnipotence, each was prepared to destroy existing reality and to remake the world according to his vision: but far from displaying the hubris of the artist, this merely revealed their shared belief that, for those who knew the suprahuman laws of destruction and drew their logical implications, everything was possible – for the force was with them.

ROBOTS, NOT RATIONALISTS

In scholarly discussions of 'ideology' Arendt is often lumped
together with other political thinkers who distinguish in one way
or another between a deplorably 'ideological' approach to politics
on the one hand and a practical, open-minded, common sense
one on the other.[50] Ideology in this usage is closely associated
with rationalism and revolution,[51] and the whole line of thought
has its roots in Burke's critique of the 'abstract' thinking and
'armed doctrine' of the French Revolutionaries.[52] In view of
Arendt's stress on the 'logicality' of totalitarian ideology, it is not
surprising that her views should have been assimilated to those
of the modern Burkeans, but this classification is nevertheless
misleading. Arendt's 'logicality' is a much more narrowly defined
category than Oakeshott's 'rationalism', her 'ideology' is much
more of a special case than Burke's 'abstract thinking', while
above all 'totalitarianism' in her sense is not in the least equivalent
to revolution. Indeed, one of the signals that should make us wary
of assimilating Arendt's theory of ideology to the conservative
critique of rationalism is her attitude to revolution, and particularly to the French Revolution. At the time when she was writing
Totalitarianism, what she called 'the stern Jacobin concept of the
nation based upon human rights'[53] represented for her a pinnacle
of political civilization from which Europe had slipped under the
impact of bourgeois society and imperial expansion. Clemençeau,
the hero of her account of the Dreyfus Affair, is praised for his
'old-time Jacobin patriotism', his loyalty to 'such "abstract" ideas
as justice, liberty, and civic virtue'.[54] Arendt was certainly not
prepared to go along with the Romantic conservative critique of
such abstract ideas, and her political thought as a whole can be
seen rather as a return to the ideals of the Enlightenment than as
an endorsement of the conservative position.

We can clarify this contrast between revolution and totalitarianism by looking more closely at her 'formula' for totalitarianism,
'ideology and terror'. In the essay of that title which she added
to the second edition of *Totalitarianism* she asserted in the clearest
terms that totalitarianism was a new and unprecedented form of
government with its own specific essence and principle of action.
In so doing, she was consciously amending the theory of Montesquieu, who had distinguished in *l'Esprit des Lois* between three

basic forms of government, monarchies, republics and despotisms, and ascribed to them their characteristic principles, honour, virtue and fear.[55] It is highly likely, however, that she was following not only Montesquieu but Robespierre, whose speeches she read while writing *Totalitarianism*.[56] For Robespierre had himself meditated upon Montesquieu's categories in a momentous attempt to articulate the principles of the revolutionary government at the head of which he found himself. Remarking that 'the theory of the revolutionary government is as new as the Revolution itself',[57] he hit upon a variation on Montesquieu that catered for the difference between an established republic and one in the process of revolutionary formation. Montesquieu had said that virtue was the hallmark of republics and terror of despotism, and Robespierre agreed that:

> . . . in times of peace, virtue is the course from which the government of the people takes its power. During the Revolution [however] the sources of this power are virtue and terror: virtue, without which terror will be a disaster; and terror, without which virtue is powerless.[58]

It is in implicit contrast to Robespierre's claim, with its awe-inspiring hubris, that we should read Arendt's formula for totalitarianism: terror, indeed, but no longer linked with the misguided but still humanist aspiration to establish the reign of virtue; instead, terror hand-in-hand with an inhuman submission to inexorable laws of nature or history.[59]

It is true that by the time she wrote *On Revolution*, Arendt had come to see Robespierre rather differently, and even to view him as a remote forerunner of totalitarianism, but that was for reasons diametrically opposed to those of the modern Burkeans. Contrasting the French Revolution unfavourably with the American, she attributed the French slide into terror and disaster not to abstract thinking or rationalistic hubris but to something much more akin to the totalitarian worship of the laws of nature or history – namely to the forces of natural necessity let loose when the poor emerged on to the public stage, welcomed by revolutionaries blinded by compassion. Such leaders 'surrendered the "artificial", man-made laws of a not yet constituted body politic to the "natural" laws which the masses obeyed, to the forces by which they were driven, and which indeed were the forces of nature herself'.[60] Unlike

totalitarians, the Jacobins did not believe in historical necessity. Nevertheless, in abandoning the foundation of a free constitution in favour of the Social Question, Robespierre 'substituted an irresistible and anonymous stream of violence for the free and deliberate actions of men'.[61]

The point of *On Revolution*, however, is that this descent into inexorable force is a perversion of revolution, not its essence, which is 'the foundation of freedom',[62] as seen, however imperfectly, in America. In *On Revolution* as in *Totalitarianism*, revolutionary action seems to Arendt to manifest a human creativity that has nothing in common with the robot-like behaviour of totalitarians.[63] Conversely, totalitarianism, in Arendt's understanding of it, is not an extreme version of revolutionary rationalism to be avoided by eschewing abstract principles and radical action. Instead, it has much more in common with Romantic notions of immersing oneself in the soul of one's people and drifting with the stream of history, and only an assumption of political responsibility for man's future can combat it.[64] In this respect Arendt's stance could be labelled, awkwardly but appositely, 'Neo-enlightenment': a reassertion of the principles of the Enlightenment, but without the carefree optimism of the eighteenth century, and overshadowed instead by Nietzschean philosophy and twentieth-century history.

TOTALITARIANISM AS AN ESCAPE FROM RESPONSIBILITY

Although Arendt kept her distance from existentialist philosophies[65] and did not use their characteristic terminology, her books are haunted by a thoroughly existentialist view of the human predicament. Her assumption is that we find ourselves in the present age flung into a situation in which inherited structures have broken down. Traditional beliefs no longer make sense, no authorities are left to guide us, and we must act into an open future as best we can. One of her clearest statements of this predicament comes in the 'Concluding Remarks' to the first edition of *Totalitarianism*, where she says that 'totalitarianism became this century's curse only because it so terrifyingly took care of its problems'.[66] While one of the problems she referred to was

'superfluousness', the mass experience of having no place in the world as a result of overpopulation, political upheaval, and social dislocation, she went on to talk about another problem with which 'superfluous' masses are singularly ill-equipped to deal. This is the challenge posed by modern man's loss of tradition and authority as foundations for political life. Neither the old religious myths nor the eighteenth century's faith in nature now have authority over us, for modern man, as Arendt often remarked, is blessed or cursed with a 'deep-rooted suspicion of everything he did not make himself'.[67] We therefore find ourselves having to take responsibility for our future in a world where, for the first time, 'mankind' as a whole is an inescapable reality, and in which, like it or not, we cannot fall back upon divine commands or natural laws to relieve us of responsibility for whatever rules and systems we decide to adopt. Arendt's statement of this position is characteristic of the bleak, disabused style of her humanism: 'From now on man is the only possible creator of his own laws and the only possible maker of his own history', and Arendt comments, 'the greatness of this task is crushing and without precedent'.[68]

The idea that man can, and must, make his own history of course recalls Marx's much less apprehensive view of the same prospect. The point of Arendt's remark is the profoundly ironical way in which it differs from Marxism, even from what she herself in another place calls the 'humanist side of Marx's teachings',[69] let alone from the totalitarian version developed by his followers. According to Arendt, Marxism could be developed into a totalitarian ideology 'because of its perversion, or misunderstanding of political action as the making of history'.[70] Marx himself, who was not totalitarian, misunderstood political action as a form of fabrication in which, while doing violence to one's material, one controls the result of one's work and 'makes history'. This approach to politics is already fraught with danger because political action, involving as it does the interactions of plural men, is intrinsically unpredictable and uncontrollable. In the hands of Marx's totalitarian followers, however, this overconfident humanism becomes an equally confident but robot-like evasion of responsibility, the idea that the violent 'making of history' can be done according to a preordained script in which men act out what history prescribes. As Arendt expressed it in an article published in 1953, 'Communism in its politically effective totalitarian form

. . . treats man as though he were a falling stone, endowed with the gift of consciousness and therefore capable of observing, while he is falling, Newton's laws of gravitation'.[71]

Arendt's own view of the human condition shared neither this assurance of predestination nor the exhilarating confidence in man as the maker of history. While she believed that the future is open and that we are responsible for our own destiny, she stressed that we have no guarantee that this will turn out to be a blessing. History does not have a plot: 'nothing has been promised us, no Messianic Age, no classless society, no paradise after death'.[72] The plurality of human beings guarantees the permanent possibility of new beginnings, but also makes the outcome of all action unpredictable. No basis for political authority or human rights is provided by nature or tradition: they will not exist unless we succeed in establishing them.[73] Her bleak reflections recall Sartre's dictum that we are 'condemned to be free'.[74]

It is to this predicament that totalitarianism is a 'solution' precisely because it combines a sense of infinite possibility with a total lack of human freedom and responsibility. Seen in this perspective it looks like a gigantic piece of Heideggerian inauthenticity or Sartrean *mauvaise foi*, a disastrous refusal of human responsibility for one's actions and for the world. Arendt does not press the point, and the existentialist-sounding 'Concluding Remarks' are omitted from later editions of *Totalitarianism*. Nevertheless the book as a whole is haunted by her fear that, since men are not given a home on earth but have to build one in a hostile wilderness, they may be strongly tempted to refuse the responsibility. Her picture of the totalitarians echoes on the one hand her account of primitive savages who avoid human responsibility by living as part of nature,[75] and on the other those pre-totalitarians, whether adventurers like Lawrence of Arabia or bureaucrats like Lord Cromer, who surrendered themselves to the stream of history and let themselves be carried along by it.[76]

VARIETIES OF INAUTHENTICITY

We have seen Arendt arguing in 'Ideology and Terror' that total domination requires ideological logicality in its subjects because this deprives a man of his inner freedom, rendering him incapable

of thinking about his experience and making him function auto-matically. Later, observing the trial of Adolf Eichmann, she came round to the view that many of those who supported Nazism needed no such compulsion. The case showed her, as she wrote to Mary McCarthy, that she had overrated 'the impact of ideology on the individual'.[77] Eichmann, she found, had not been an ideo-logue, nor had he needed logicality to stop him thinking and responding to reality. On the contrary, he seemed to be consti-tutionally incapable of thinking at all, or even of avoiding straight self-contradiction,[78] while his mind was stocked with clichés that protected him against the impact of reality. Generalizing from his case, instead of a mass society of lonely individuals bound together by terror and ideology, Arendt now portrayed a society of phili-stines, protected by self-deception and sheer stupidity from any clear realization of what they were doing.[79] Far from needing ideological self-compulsion to stop them thinking, it seemed that many people were immune from the temptation ever to start thinking in the first place – a revelation that set Arendt off on another train of thought about the relation between thinking and morality[80] which eventually led her to *The Life of the Mind*.[81]

As George Kateb has pointed out, if sheer inability to think can account for some, at any rate, of the acquiescence in the Final Solution by so many respectable people, then ideology becomes less important in explaining totalitarianism, and so does the mass-man for whose loneliness ideology provides its spurious comfort.[82] And in fact Arendt's original account of German support for Hitler, published in January 1945 in an article on 'Organised Guilt and Universal Responsibility', did not rely on notions of mass loneliness and ideology but pointed instead to the civic irresponsi-bility of the bourgeois (especially the German bourgeois): the 'job holder' and 'good familyman' who is not interested in politics but will do literally anything to safeguard his private life. 'For the sake of his pension, his life insurance, the security of his wife and children, such a man was ready to sacrifice his beliefs, his honor, and his human dignity'.[83] Such an account of the behaviour of many inhabitants of Nazi Germany or Stalin's Russia is not actu-ally incompatible with the 'mass and ideology' account advanced in *Totalitarianism*, for it could be that the two are complementary in that mass-men might be found among the more enthusiastic Nazis and philistines in the ranks of the fellow-travellers. Eich-

mann's mindless preoccupation with his career seems to imply, however, that philistinism might be more important and ideological logicality less so than *Totalitarianism* suggested. *Pace* Elizabeth Young-Bruehl,[84] however, such a revision of Arendt's standpoint would not necessarily be a comforting one, for in terms of inauthenticity and refusal of responsibility for the common world there is not much to choose between ideological consistency on the one hand and cliché-ridden stupidity on the other. Either will serve equally well to prevent us actually seeing what is under our noses, judging and acting upon it. In the end, the only comfort Arendt found is that men are not robots in spite of all the efforts of totalitarians to make them so. Instead, every person who is born represents the capacity to think new thoughts and to interrupt the automatic processes of nature by starting something new. In the plural, human beings can act together, and sometimes (despite all the complexities and frustrations of action) manage to agree among themselves to establish a new political structure. At the heart of Arendt's later political thought lies the problem of how plural human beings can take responsibility for an open future and can establish a political order: how, in other words, they can face the challenge that totalitarianism so nightmarishly evaded.

NOTES

* I am indebted to the British Academy for a research award which enabled me to consult the Hannah Arendt manuscripts in the Library of Congress, Washington.

1. H. Arendt, *The Origins of Totalitarianism*, (3rd edn.) (London: George Allen and Unwin, 1967), p. 464.
2. Ibid., p. 468.
3. H. Arendt, 'Social Science Techniques and the Study of Concentration Camps', *Jewish Social Studies*, vol. 12, no. 1 (1950) p. 62.
4. H. Arendt, *The Burden of Our Time* (London: Secker and Warburg, 1951) p. 430. This first edition of *The Origins of Totalitarianism* (published under different titles in London and New York) is referred to hereafter.
5. Ibid., p. 431.
6. *The Origins of Totalitarianism*, op. cit., p. 471.
7. See, for example, 'A Reply' by Arendt to Eric Voegelin's criticisms of *The Burden of Our Time*, *Review of Politics*, vol. 15, (January 1953) pp. 80–1; 'Approaches to the "German Problem"', *Partisan Review*, vol. 12, no. 1 (Winter 1945) p. 95; 'Martin Heidegger at Eighty' in M. Murray (ed.), *Heidegger and Modern Philosophy* (New Haven and London: Yale University Press, 1978) pp. 302–3.
8. *The Origins of Totalitarianism*, op. cit., pp. 438, 456, 464.

9. Arendt, 'Social Science Techniques', op. cit., p. 53; *The Origins of Totalitarianism*, op. cit., pp. 391, 424, 443, 451.
10. *The Origins of Totalitarianism*, op. cit., p. 467.
11. H. Arendt, 'The Image of Hell', *Commentary*, vol. 2, no. 3 (September 1946) p. 294.
12. *The Origins of Totalitarianism*, op. cit., p. 384.
13. Ibid., p. 387.
14. Ibid., p. 353; see also pp. 362, 381, 382.
15. Ibid., pp. 363, 391–2, 413, 415.
16. Ibid., p. 417.
17. Ibid., p. 436.
18. G. Kateb, *Hannah Arendt: Politics, Conscience, Evil* (Oxford: Martin Robertson, 1983) p. 79.
19. H. Arendt, *The Human Condition* (Chicago and London: University of Chicago Press, 1958) pp. 139, 228–9.
20. *The Origins of Totalitarianism*, op. cit., p. 458.
21. Ibid., p. 192.
22. Ibid., p. 458.
23. *The Burden of Our Time*, op. cit., p. 432; *The Origins of Totalitarianism*, op. cit., p. 458.
24. *The Origins of Totalitarianism*, op. cit., 'Introduction' p. viii.
25. H. Arendt MSS, Library of Congress, Box 69: 'On the Nature of Totalitarianism' (second version) pp. 10–11. This paper is referred to henceforth as 'Totalitarianism', MS 2.
26. Ibid., p. 14.
27. *The Origins of Totalitarianism*, op. cit., p. 470.
28. Cf. Arendt's remarks in C.J. Friedrich (ed.), *Totalitarianism* (New York: Grosset and Dunlap, 1964) p. 228.
29. *The Origins of Totalitarianism*, op. cit., p. 471.
30. Cf. Arendt in Friedrich, *Totalitarianism*, op. cit., p. 134.
31. Hannah Arendt MSS, Library of Congress, Box 69: 'On the Nature of Totalitarianism' (first version) p. 32. This paper is referred to henceforth as 'Totalitarianism', MS 1.
32. *The Origins of Totalitarianism*, op. cit., p. 472.
33. Ibid., p. 473.
34. Ibid., p. 473.
35. Ibid., p. 473.
36. Ibid., p. 385.
37. Ibid., pp. 460–8.
38. Ibid., p. 378.
39. G.W.F. Hegel, *Lectures on the Philosophy of History*, trans. by J. Sibree (London: G. Bell and Sons, 1910) p. 19.
40. 'Totalitarianism' MS 2, op. cit., p. 9.
41. *The Origins of Totalitarianism*, op. cit., p. 455.
42. H. Arendt, *Men in Dark Times* (London: Jonathan Cape, 1970), p. 34.
43. *The Origins of Totalitarianism*, op. cit., p. 465; cf. p. 436.
44. Ibid., p. 437.
45. Hannah Arendt MSS, Library of Congress, Box 64. 'Ideology and Propaganda', p. 24.
46. Friedrich, *Totalitarianism*, op. cit., p. 228.
47. *The Origins of Totalitarianism*, op. cit., p. 457; cf. Arendt, 'Understanding and Politics', op. cit., p. 386.
48. *The Origins of Totalitarianism*, op. cit., p. 457.

49. Ibid., p. 346. In a note on the same page, Arendt gives other examples of the Nazi adherence to supposed laws of nature, and claims that Stalin was similarly deferential to the laws of history and class struggle. (p. 346) See also H. Arendt MSS, Library of Congress, Box 60, 'Einleitung: Der Sinn von Politik', pp. 3–4.

50. For example, M. Seliger, *Ideology and Politics* (London: Allen and Unwin, 1976) pp. 31–2; G. Sartori, 'Politics, Ideology, and Belief Systems', *American Political Science Review*, vol. 63, no. 2 (1969) pp. 399, 403.

51. M. Oakeshott, *Rationalism in Politics* (London: Methuen, 1962) pp. 1–36; K. Minogue, *Alien Powers: The Pure Theory of Ideology* (New York: St Martin's Press, 1985) *passim*.

52. *Works of the Rt. Hon. Edmund Burke* (London: Holdsworth and Ball, 1834) vol. I, pp. 384, 404; vol. II, p. 280.

53. *The Origins of Totalitarianism*, op. cit., p. 106.

54. Ibid., p. 110. See also H. Arendt, 'The Ex-Communists', *Commonwealth*, vol. 57, no. 24 (20 March 1953) p. 598.

55. Baron de Montesquieu, *The Spirit of the Laws*, trans. T. Nugent (New York: Hafner, 1949) pp. 19–28.

56. *The Burden of Our Time*, op. cit., p. 295.

57. *Speeches of Maximilien Robespierre* (New York: International Publishers, 1927) p. 62.

58. Ibid., p. 74.

59. Reading the formula as an ironic reference to Robespierre also enables us to understand why, although her account makes ideology secondary to terror, Arendt puts it first, thereby inadvertently encouraging interpretations that assimilate her account to those that blame totalitarianism on rationalism.

60. H. Arendt, *On Revolution* (London: Faber and Faber, 1963) p. 106. In *The Origins of Totalitarianism* she blames the bourgeoisie for developing the notion that history is a necessary process, and credits 'the French Revolution, with its conception of man as lawmaker and *citoyen* with having blocked this development for a time' (p. 144).

61. Arendt, *On Revolution*, op. cit., p. 109.

62. Ibid., p. 121.

63. *The Origins of Totalitarianism*, op. cit., p. 458.

64. Fear that men are abandoning their freedom to act and surrendering themselves to automatic processes of one kind or another is one of the most persistent themes of Arendt's work, and appears in many contexts other than in *The Origins of Totalitarianism*. See, for example, her remarks on the rise of 'society' in *The Human Condition*, op. cit., pp. 45–7, 255–6, 321–3; on the force of material necessity, represented by the needs of the poor during the French Revolution in *On Revolution*, op. cit., pp. 40–3, 53–5, 105–10; her interpretation of Kafka's work as a humanistic protest against inhuman forces (H. Arendt, 'Franz Kafka: A Revaluation', *Partisan Review*, vol. 11, no. 4 (1944), pp. 412–22); and, in the context of her persistent calls to her fellow Jews to act and take political responsibility for their future, her understanding of the Jewish settlements in Palestine as a great human achievement precisely in being 'artificial', and not dictated by 'necessity' (H. Arendt, 'Peace or Armistice in the Near East', *Review of Politics*, vol. 12, no. 1 (1950) p. 68).

65. Cf. H. Arendt, 'What is Existenz Philosophy?', *Partisan Review*, vol. 8, no. 1 (Winter 1946) pp. 34–56, and 'French Existentialism', *Nation* (22 February 1946) pp. 226–8. When young, Arendt was a pupil both of Karl Jaspers and of Martin Heidegger, and her debt to the latter was particularly great,

though complicated by Heidegger's support for Nazism. See Arendt, 'Martin Heidegger at Eighty', op. cit., and L.P. and S.K. Hinchman, 'In Heidegger's Shadow: Hannah Arendt's Phenomenological Humanism', *Review of Politics*, no. 46 (April 1984) pp. 183–211.

66. *The Burden of Our Times*, op. cit., p. 430.
67. Ibid., p. 434; see also *The Origins of Totalitarianism*, op. cit., p. 301, and *Human Condition*, op. cit., ch. VI.
68. *The Burden of Our Time*, op. cit., p. 437.
69. H. Arendt, 'Religion and Politics', *Confluence* vol. 2, no. 3 (September 1953) p. 115.
70. Arendt, 'The Ex-Communists', op. cit., p. 597.
71. Arendt, 'Religion and Politics', op. cit., p. 109.
72. *The Burden of Our Time*, op. cit., p. 436.
73. Ibid., p. 437.
74. J.-P. Sartre, *Being and Nothingness* (New York, Philosophical Library, 1956) p. 439. On Arendt's combination of humanism with an acute sense of its pitfalls, see M. Canovan, 'Hubris and Nemesis: Arendt's Story of Modernity', Keele Research Papers in Politics, no. 25 (1987).
75. *The Origins of Totalitarianism*, op. cit., pp. 190–4.
76. Ibid., p. 216; *The Burden of Our Time*, op. cit., p. 431.
77. E. Young-Bruehl, *Hannah Arendt: For the Love of the World* (New Haven and London: Yale University Press, 1982) p. 367.
78. H. Arendt, *Eichmann in Jerusalem: A Report on the Banality of Evil* (London: Faber and Faber, 1963) pp. 23, 29, 49.
79. Arendt, *Eichmann*, op. cit., p. 47.
80. H. Arendt, 'Thinking and Moral Considerations', *Social Research*, vol. 38, no. 3 (Autumn 1971) p. 417.
81. H. Arendt, *The Life of the Mind*, vol. I: *Thinking* (New York: Harcourt Brace Jovanovich, 1978) pp. 3–4.
82. Kateb, *Hannah Arendt*, op. cit., p. 73.
83. H. Arendt, 'Organized Guilt and Universal Responsibility', *Jewish Frontier* (January 1945) p. 22.
84. Young-Bruehl, *Hannah Arendt*, op. cit., p. 367.

PART III
Beyond Ideology?

7. Beyond Ideology: Politics and Pragmatism

Gordon Graham

The view that in the conduct of political affairs, especially perhaps on an international level, ideological commitments are inescapable, is one that is widely held. Indeed, so widely held is it, that it is rarely argued for explicitly, but taken to be obvious. Yet it is a belief that needs defence more than most, since it is this which very often constrains and inhibits the free exchange of ideas between politicians and individuals from widely different political systems.

One powerful line of thought which is sometimes employed in defence of this claim about the inescapability (and hence the practical relevance) of political ideologies turns upon the suggestion that, in some sense or other political action is impossible if we dispense with them, that without some overall ideological conception we cannot *do* anything. If this is true, any attempt to engage in 'non-ideological' or, as I shall call it, purely pragmatic politics is always fraudulent and consequently the only important question to ask is whether pragmatism's misleadingly non-ideological appearance is given and maintained deliberately or in ignorance. But I shall argue that this line of thought does not bear out the contention it is intended to support, and that purely pragmatic politics *is* possible. First, however, there are initial problems to be dealt with.

I

One difficulty in the way of assessing the truth of the suggestion that ideological conceptions are indispensible in political life, and

political pragmatism accordingly impossible, arises from uncertainty about where the burden of proof lies. Some theorists have written in a way which plainly assumes that the ideological character of opposing beliefs will inevitably emerge under scrutiny and as a consequence the resulting discussions tend to put the so-called pragmatist under constant pressure to demonstrate the non-ideological nature of his commitments. Other theorists have written as though it is the ideologist, with his strange pseudo-theoretical constructions, who is naturally out of place in the deliberations of politics, and who must demonstrate that his message is relevant, still more essential, to normal political debate. Given these different assumptions, it is obviously important to know who is required to prove what, especially since in this, as in most disputes of the sort, the best conclusion we are likely to reach is that one side or other has not established its case. And it is only if we know, as we do in a court of law, who should be proving what, that this sort of conslusion will be any use to us.

A second difficulty arises from uncertainties about the word 'ideological', which can mean different things to different writers. Indeed the flexibility of the term makes it easy for the dispute between pragmatists and their critics to be settled by stipulation in favour of *either* side – 'ideological' is used in such a way as to make ideology indispensable, or dispensable – and this is something which in its turn suggests that there is between them no real dispute.

The third obstacle resides in the fact that the view I have called pragmatism has itself become associated with a recognizable ideology – conservatism (of a certain sort) – so that any defence of, or attack on, pragmatism very quickly takes on the character of a dispute between conservatism and its critics, and hence the character of an ideological dispute. To address the question of this paper properly, therefore, we must begin by resolving these three difficulties.

The first is the hardest. There may have been a time when talk of ideology was so new that anyone wanting to insist that all political argument is ideological would generally be expected to make good his claims. But both politicians and political theorists have told each other of the ineliminability of ideological 'commitments' and 'perspectives' for so long that it has come to seem self-evident, and now the suggestion that we can conduct political

argument simply on the grounds of what will and will not be wise or successful, is likely to be greeted as highly implausible and plainly in need of argument. And yet, there is good reason to think that the current view about who needs to do the arguing is wrong, just because while there can be, and is, contention about the role of ideological thinking in political deliberation, *there is and can be no argument about the necessity for deliberative reason over means to ends*. Even the most ardent ideologues must admit that they have to reason carefully about the most efficient means to the practical realization of their political schemes. But given the incontestable necessity of *deliberative* reason, it seems plainly possible to ask whether anything more is needed. And this way of raising the issue puts the burden of proof on those who want to say that there is. Of course it must be admitted at the outset that this conclusion constitutes a very small victory, since the place of the burden of proof says nothing about the ease or difficulty of proving, any more than the presumption of innocence makes it hard to prove that anyone is guilty.

The second difficulty can only be dealt with, it seems to me, by making plain what for the purposes of this discussion 'ideology' is going to be taken to mean. Any other strategy – arguments in favour of preferred use for instance – must rest upon the somewhat absurd idea that other people's use of a term can be fixed by the recommendation or insistence of a single writer. Of course there is always reason (outside of poetry and the like) to avoid highly fanciful or unusual uses of familiar words, but in the long run, the only thing that can commend particular uses of words is the fruitfulness of the arguments that result from their being used in that way.

By 'ideological' I shall mean any argument, doctrine, theory, principle or conception which is concerned with more than facts about particular circumstances and which can be plausibly associated with the doctrines, principles, arguments or theories of any recognizable ideological tradition. These will generally be found to consist in evaluative conceptions of history and society, but we need not insist that anything called an 'ideology' must take this form. Such a generous use will, I hope, dispel any suspicion that I too am settling disputes in my own favour by stipulative definition, but any such suspicion will only be laid to rest finally, I think, by the cogency of the arguments that use 'ideological' in

this way. However, the suggestion that my arguments amount to little more than the manipulation of words is one to which I shall return more directly at a later stage.

In the meantime, something needs to be said about the third obstacle to discussing the topic of this chapter, namely the association of political pragmatism with conservatism,[1] an association on occasions so close that conservatism has come to be thought of as the anti-ideology ideology. But however close it may generally be thought to be, we can nevertheless distinguish between those who hold that political conduct need imply no commitments to fundamental theories or doctrines of an abstract and general kind, and those whose fundamental commitment is merely to the irrelevance of such general theories to the efficient conduct of political affairs. The difference between the two positions lies in their implications. The first holds that what I am calling pragmatism is a possible basis for political action, while the second holds that this sort of pragmatism is the *only* possible basis. The first is compatible with a belief that social science, for instance, may produce politically valuable theories, while the second is not: this means that to have established the possibility of purely pragmatic reasoning in politics, is not to have established the truth of conservative ideology.

It is only the first of these – the possibility of pragmatism – in which I am interested and which, as I suggested in considering the first of the three difficulties, I have identified, since I consider the burden of proof to lie with those who wish to deny it. It is to this largely negative task of refuting the best arguments against it that I now turn.

II

The most obvious general argument against pragmatism is that, since deliberative reasoning is reasoning about means to ends, without some assumption of ends to be pursued it is therefore powerless. In politics, thought and argument about ends to be pursued just *is* ideological. *Ergo*, non-ideological deliberation in politics is impossible.

The trouble with this argument is that, even if the claims it makes are true, it lacks a vital premise. Suppose we agree that

some assumption of ends is essential for significant deliberative reasoning and that arguments about ends in politics must indeed be ideological, the conclusion that political deliberation is necessarily ideological does not follow without the added premise that political ends can only be supplied by argumentation, and this may plausibly be denied. To put the matter most plainly, by this argument the pragmatist is merely required to *have* ends, not to acquire them. They may in fact simply be *given*.

But what it will be asked, could they be given by? The answer is – contingent circumstances. Indeed, it is plausible to think not only that political ends *can* be given in this way, but that some of our ends always *will* be. This is because political agents must function in a world in which political demands and objectives are not theirs alone to determine. Riots, wars, floods, famines, epidemics, civil strife, economic stagnation and so on, are all problems with which those in charge of the state must deal, regardless of their ideological views, and consequently to the question 'What shall we do?' political agents always have available the answer 'Do something about these problems'. In this way, there *are* what we might call 'ideology-transcendent' ends. But if there are these ideology-transcendent ends, there seems no logical reason why there should not be *only* these ends, from which it follows immediately that the first argument we have been considering does indeed employ a false premise. Ideology is inessential to the formation of political ends.

In response to this, someone is certain to argue that these problems are only problematic in the light of some ideological conception. Is famine a problem, for instance? Does not our answer depend upon whether the political ideology to which we subscribe gives the state a place in the alleviation of suffering for its own sake? Famine is a political problem for the socialist, no doubt, but not for the libertarian who thinks that each individual must take care of himself and may only call upon the state to defend his rights.

But such a reply attributes to ideological beliefs and conceptions far more power and influence than is realistic. Famines, wars and so on, are made politically problematic not by the opinions and belief of those in power, but by their effect upon the state's ability to control affairs. Political rivals can take advantage of such emergencies and crises quite irrespective of the beliefs of the

ruling class, provided that they are the sorts of things which create social and political uncertainty – which they are.

Critics of political pragmatism might accept that there are political problems whose problematic character is independent of ideological affiliation, and thereby concede that ideological conceptions and programmes are not essential in the determination of political ends, because contingent circumstances are sufficient in themselves to supply such ends (in the form of inescapable problems). But they are likely to insist that ideology is essential in the formulation of solutions to those problems. This is a suggestion in keeping with the popular perception of political parties and ideologies, which sees them as groupings around different solutions to common problems – state ownership versus the free market, for instance – rather than rival theories about what the problems are; there is no denying that political rivalries are often presented by politicians in this way.

Nevertheless, even if this common perception is correct, it does nothing to show that any suggested solution to a political problem must be ideologically conceived, or even that disputes about such suggested solutions must be ideological disputes. This is because there is available to the question 'What is to be done?' a purely pragmatic answer: 'Do whatever is most likely to succeed. Choose the policy that works best.' Moreover, this, unlike its ideological rivals, is an answer which enjoys universal authority for all rational agents, since its appeal is to a fundamental principle of practical reason, namely the rationality of desiring the better to the worse. As such, it can hardly be contested.

Of course, those who believe that political action cannot escape ideological commitment will not be inclined to argue that the pragmatic alternative is false, so much as empty. How can we tell what works best, unless we have already settled the question of what we are aiming at? This is true of any practical task. To say that a farmer should use whatever fertilizer works best is to give concrete advice only if we assume some criteria of success – increased yields for instance – by which all fertilizers may be judged, for if we do not make some assumption of this sort, it will be impossible to identify the *best* fertilizer. Similarly, in offering the maxim 'Do whatever works best' as a general political principle, either we are assuming some standard of political success, which is to say that the principle does not really stand alone,

or we are assuming nothing, in which case the principle alone cannot tell us what to do. In other words, we first need some conception of what result would be desirable before we can applaud the steps that would have that result. And this brings us back to the earlier claim that without ideologically-determined ends, political action is impossible.

In response to that claim, I argued that political ends can be *given*, as well as chosen. But, if true, this must carry the implication that the criteria of political success can also be given. If we find ourselves with problems, we already have the knowledge, not of how to solve them but of what would count as their solution. Consider any simple difficulty. If the reception on my radio is so poor that I miss the larger part of most of the broadcasts I try to listen to, we need no further investigation to determine the criteria which any proposed solution must satisfy – any steps which do not produce clarity of reception, however convinced I may be of their efficacy, must be considered a failure. Similarly, where political agents find themselves fighting a war, the criteria of political success are plain – such steps as will bring the war to an end are those that should be taken. Of course, just what these steps *are* may itself be a matter of considerable uncertainty and dispute, but this fact alone does not show that the disputes are ideological, any more than the fact that radio engineers may dispute about what the best solution to poor reception is shows engineering to be inescapably ideological. And we can see this by seeing that most political disputes, even those which are thought to mark deep ideological differences, are about means to ends rather than ends. Those, for instance, who strive to create and sustain bonds of community and fraternity, as opposed to the individualistic pursuit of personal satisfaction, most often commend their ideal on the basis of its ability to realize certain universal and permanent goods – peace, prosperity, reduction of crime and personal fulfilment on the part of citizens – precisely the goals, in fact, which liberal individualism also seeks. Of course, as in every other context, just *which* solutions will be successful is a matter of fact which is often not easy to assess, so that to argue for the adequacy of political pragmatism is not to have put an end to political differences, but only to differences of a recognizably ideological sort.

III

The commonest arguments against pure pragmatism in politics
appear, then, to be inadequate. A pragmatic approach to political
action is possible because we can have political ends in the shape
of problems and formulate solutions to them without recourse to
ideology. The cogency of the last of the arguments considered,
however, is likely to be called into question by raising afresh the
second of the difficulties considered at the start. The adequacy of
the principle 'Do whatever will work best' might be thought to
have indeed been established, but in such a way that the sort of
belief and argument everyone thinks of as ideological – differences
of belief about community and the individual, for instance –
remain a part of political debate. But if so, it is only in a highly
misleading sense that what is left can be called purely pragmatic
and only an odd sort of ideology that has been excluded.

In reply, it is important to stress that the crucial point is not
whether disputes about fundamental strategies ever arise, but how
they enter into the debate. Take, as an example, state versus
private ownership of the means of production. This is commonly
thought of as lying at the heart of ideological differences between
East and West, and so to an extent it does. But we cannot take
the mere dispute over the desirability of one or the other to be
an adequate characterization of these ideological differences. This
is because liberal/conservative governments have often taken control of parts of their country's manufacturing industry in order to
remedy some short-term problem or to protect supplies in times
of emergency, and conversely communist countries have often
employed private capital at home and abroad for similar purposes.
What this shows is that arguments can be made for the wisdom
of both state and private ownership sufficient to convince governments of quite different ideological persuasions. But, in its turn,
this shows that economic policies may be supported independently
of the ideological beliefs that normally underlie them. Thus, the
difference between ideological commitment and pragmatism is
not to be located merely in the remedies or devices that each
recommends, but in the relation between practical recommen-
dations and other beliefs. From this it follows that there *is* an
important difference between the ideological and the pragmatic

approach to politics, even though ideological beliefs may generate policies which pragmatism can commend.

Exploration of the same example will illustrate this important difference further. Marx thought that private ownership of the means of production must come to an end because it was part and parcel of a system that would run further and further into economic difficulty until it was ultimately quite unable to satisfy the material needs of the people within it. Now we will all agree that the sorts of thing which Marx identified as signalling the collapse of capitalism – mass unemployment, chronic deflation, increasing social strife – are indeed political problems with which any serious political agent must be concerned. But whether the principal remedy which his analysis may be thought to support – namely public ownership of the means of production in a classless society – is actually a remedy in any given society is, for pragmatists, a matter of fact into which we ought to inquire. For theoretical or ideological Marxists, however, this is too simple an approach to the question. Their support for the end to private ownership rests not so much on an investigation into its practical defects as a whole conception of history and a vision of the future. And since it is these rather grander beliefs which inform and inspire their political aspirations and policies, those policies are not to be abandoned by more elementary investigations into their efficacy. This does not mean however that such low-level inquiry can play no part in the Marxists' political deliberations. They can acknowledge a temporary necessity for the state's support of capitalism, just as free-marketeers can acknowledge a need for state takeovers of industry on occasion, and this may in fact involve them in employing political strategies not significantly different to those which the pragmatist would support. But the crucial difference is that these are perceived as *temporary*, short-term deviations from a long-term goal, adopted only because of their necessity for the continued pursuit of that goal.

By contrast, the pragmatist's policy, whether it be for or against state ownership, is neither short-term nor long-term. It is simply what is needed for the moment, and the precise length of this 'moment' is something to be determined by contingent circumstances. For this reason, the policies of pragmatism will be highly sensitive to changes in circumstances (the sort of sensitivity that leads to the accusation that pragmatism is opportunist and

unprincipled), because they are in fact sensitive to these alone. The pragmatist operates with no conception of history or vision of the future.

The celebrated image of the 'ship of state' may be used to illustrate this difference between the pragmatic and the ideological. Whereas ideological conceptions of society generally offer some account of where the ship of state has come from and where it must be made to go, pragmatism restricts itself to the belief that it must be kept afloat. In this, as I remarked earlier, it may be contrasted with the more substantial beliefs of a conservatism which holds not just that the proper business of politics is to keep the ship afloat, but that this is so because there is nowhere for the ship of state to have come from and nowhere for it to go.[2] The pure pragmatist, on my account, asserts only that we can do without such visions, not that they are impossible or destructive.

IV

Given my initial contention about the burden of proof, I conclude that since we have seen no good reason to think that ideological beliefs are indispensable to the very business of acting politically, we are free to believe that pure pragmatism in politics is possible. This conclusion, however, although important in the theory of politics, has less practical substance than might at first appear, because it does not follow from the theoretical possibility of ideology-free politics, that such politics is a practical possibility in the modern world. This is because, in many parts of the modern world, the exercise of power is dependent upon popular public appeal and such an appeal can only, *as a matter of contingent fact*, be made successfully in ideological terms. A hereditary and absolute ruler, dependent upon no-one for his continuance in power, might adopt a policy of choosing all and only those measures which could be shown to work best for the problems to which they were intended as solutions, but it is unlikely that a ruler whose power depends upon electoral success and continuing public recognition and support could attract much support for a policy based not upon a sense of history, a conception of society and a vision of the future, but upon the pragmatic if austere commitment to do only whatever needs to be done.

Part of the problem is that such a purely pragmatic stance conflicts, superficially at least, with the theory of democracy and in particular with the idea of a mandate, the idea that politicians should carry out proposals according to the choices of the electorate. But if, at the same time, those elected are to retain their role as representatives, these choices cannot be presented as decisions between day-to-day policies, but between rather more general orientations in politics. What is apparently required, if electoral choice is to function, is a conception around which electors and elected can group, in order that there can be effective exercise of power. For without such general groupings, accession to power in a democracy is virtually impossible. What this means is that general ideological beliefs do have a function in a modern political system and, although it is a function other than the determination of policy, it is a function which the conditions actually prevailing have made no less essential to effective political action. This is true not only of formal constitutional democracies, but of any system in which continued rule depends upon popular support, in however tenuous a way.

If this is correct, there *is* a sense in which some ideological commitment is indispensable to political action, not logically but in practice. This, however, is not the sense in which it is so often thought to be indispensable. Moreover, if ideology is indispensable only in this way, we can coherently hope for a world in which this is no longer the case, however far-fetched that hope may appear to be. We might ask, of course, whether this is something we ought to hope for, and this brings into question another aspect in which a purely pragmatic conception of politics might be thought deficient.

I have argued that there is nothing about the nature of political action which prevents it from being informed by deliberative reason alone. Political action is perfectly possible without recourse to any grand conceptions of history and society. But this is so only insofar as we are content to think of politics as primarily a matter of securing results, and not everything that politicians have attempted, or been urged, to attempt can be construed in this way. Take one very simple example. Many countries have systems of honours which, in principle at any rate, are intended as a means of recognizing the merit of individual citizens. The introduction and maintenance of such systems, however, cannot be construed

in the way that economic policies can. They are not intended to achieve anything, but to express something. To determine how they should be structured or amended, therefore, is not a matter of deciding how they can achieve some result better, but what they should express, and rather obviously this is not something that purely pragmatic reasoning could settle. This example is only one of many (victory celebrations and political anniversaries being among the more obvious) and what this suggests is that pragmatism is not the modest view of political reasoning that it may appear to be, but a theory which inevitably carries with it a radical view of the state as a mere instrument for certain limited purposes. To decide fully upon its merits therefore, we would have to look into the acceptability of the total view of politics which it implies.

Such a conclusion, it might be thought, amounts to a confession that pragmatism is after all ideological. But we do not have to regard the matter in this way. Certainly pragmatism is plausible only in connection with a conception of the limited state; it cannot generate principles of decision-making for a wide variety of actions which states typically engage in. This may be a good or a bad thing, but pragmatism does not need to commend the conception of the state to which it applies; as a philosophical theory of political action it can rest content with observing that there is a possible world in which political action can be based upon purely deliberative reasoning, and this is sufficient to refute the common assumption that politics without ideology is impossible.

There is, however, an interesting rational strategy here that may be made to work in reverse. One of the reasons for preferring a pragmatic to an ideological approach to political action lies in the fact that ideological commitments seem to generate irresolvable political disagreements, and hence lead to political instability. The advantage to pragmatism is that it relies only upon the common ground which all political agents must share. For this reason it may be held preferable. But if a purely pragmatic approach to politics is applicable only to a limited state, the fact that it is preferable to any of its ideological rivals is itself a reason in favour of the limited conception of the state which it implies. In this way, arguments about the nature of political reasoning, such as we have been considering, may be more important than is suggested by the limited scope they have been given here, for they may provide

a telling way of resolving other more deep-seated political disputes.

NOTES

1. One of my purposes in this paper is to expand and improve upon my treatment of pragmatism in the chapter on conservatism in my book *Politics in its Place* (Oxford: Clarendon Press, 1986).
2. Cf. Michael Oakeshott, *Rationalism in Politics* (London: Methuen, 1962) p. 133.

8. The Politics of Ideology

Noel O'Sullivan

Despite the elaborate refinements which have been made in the theory of ideology during the decades since the Second World War, there is still no agreement about one of the most fundamental problems presented by this area of political philosophy. This is the question of whether all politics involve ideology, or whether it is possible to envisage (in principle at least) a non-ideological kind of politics. The present consensus of opinion seems to favour the former position, treating all politics as intrinsically ideological. Such a position, which may be termed the inclusive theory of ideology, is generally characterized by a thorough-going relativism, the chief merit of which is said to be that it avoids the process of ontological upgrading and downgrading of different perceptions of political reality which characterizes ideological thinking. It was on this ground that Paul Ricoeur, for example, recently claimed the support of Aristotle for the inclusive approach. Aristotle's principal criticism of Plato, Ricoeur observed, as that Plato's political philosophy dismissed the opinions of his opponents as distortions of the truth, demoting them in the process to the status of mere cave-dwellers who live in a condition of false consciousness which renders them incapable of anything more than *doxa*. It was to this high-handed Platonic procedure, Ricoeur notes, that Aristotle opposed a view which stressed the 'pluralism of methods and degrees of rigour and truth'.[1]

In opposition to the inclusive approach to politics and ideology stands what may be termed the restrictive position, according to which the concept of ideology is only of analytic value when it is confined to a limited range of political styles. Ignoring, for the present, the disagreement which exists about how these styles are to be characterized, the main problem presented by restrictive

theory is that it appears to presuppose the possibility of locating a completely neutral and objective standpoint outside the political arena as a necessary condition for escaping from ideology. Some of the attempts to indicate what such a position involves will be examined in due course, but it may be said immediately that none has been wholly convincing. In the present essay, a restrictive theory of ideology will be defended, but in a way which does not involve the above-mentioned difficulty. It will be argued that the concept of ideology always presupposes what may be termed a programmatic style of politics and is unintelligible when it is extended beyond that context. The meaning of the term 'programmatic' will be explained in detail later, but for the moment it suffices to say that in programmatic politics there is always some sort of aim or purpose. This aim may be a relatively modest affair, as it is in democratic interest group theory, for example; or the aim may be far more ambitious, as it is in communism and fascism, for example, where it involves changing not only the whole social order, but human nature itself. The alternative to a programmatic style of politics is a formal one. Unlike programmatic politics, the latter style is not concerned with policies, interests, aims or purposes at all, but only with the maintenance of procedural conditions (especially laws) which must be observed by citizens in the course of pursuing whatever aims they may choose to pursue. The concept of ideology is meaningless when applied to formal politics.

With the distinction between programmatic and formal politics in mind, it will be useful to restate the argument in a way which highlights the principal defect of both inclusive and restrictive theories of ideology. This is that neither kind of theory has dealt with the problem of ideology in a way which adequately relates it to the ambiguous nature of the political relationship itself. Specifically, proponents of both the inclusive and the restrictive approaches have tacitly tended to assume that all politics are essentially programmatic. In order to establish that not all politics are ideological, it is therefore only necessary to show that a formal, non-programmatic style of politics is perfectly conceivable, and that the concept of ideology cannot intelligibly be extended from the programmatic style to the formal one. The kind of restrictive approach proposed, then, does not entail the quest for an Archimedean point which has generally vitiated restrictive theories; instead, it requires only that the problem of ideology

should be treated in a way which relates it more closely than is usually done to a fundamental ambiguity in the nature of the political relationship itself.

In order to avoid a possible misunderstanding, it is necessary to add a further word about the relationship between programmatic politics and the concept of ideology. All that is asserted here is that the concept of ideology always presupposes a programmatic style of politics, and not that programmatic politics are *ipso facto* always ideological. Although this qualification is not essential for the present purpose, it is nevertheless worth pausing briefly to recall the precise circumstance in which programmatic politics – which may be traced back at least as far as Plato – became ideological, in the recognizably modern sense of the term which first appeared with de Tracy and the Idéologues. This circumstance was the appearance of a new theory of evil which only emerged in Europe during the eighteenth century, and according to which the causes of human unhappiness are not inherent in the human condition itself but are attributable to the structure of society.

The origin of this theory lies in the epistemology developed by empiricist philosophers from the seventeenth century onwards. According to that epistemology, all ideas enter the mind through the senses, from which it follows that human nature itself may be altered by manipulating the environmental stimuli to which the senses are exposed. Although the radical social and political implications of such a theory might seem obvious enough, they were not made fully explicit until Rousseau made them the basis of Emile's education and, more generally, of his political theory. What this theory implied was that all evil might be banished from the human condition, in principle at least, by appropriate political and social reforms. It was the injection of this component into programmatic politics that converted what had previously been mere Utopian speculation, of the kind familiar from Plato to Sir Thomas More, into modern ideological politics as first envisaged by de Tracy.

Once programmatic politics were combined with the new theory of evil, there was no longer any serious intellectual obstacle to the goal which lies at the heart of ideology. This is nothing less than the complete abolition of the political relationship itself. It must be emphasized in this connection that the ideological dream

of a 'withering away of the state' is not peculiar to Marxism. As David Levy stressed recently, in an acute critique of the 'post-political' social order envisaged by ideological politics, 'not only revolutionary socialism but liberalism too offers men the promise of a world from which rulership and the state have been effectively banished'.[2] It is in this respect, then, that ideological politics differ from programmatic politics at large: whereas all programmatic politics have a purpose, only the ideological variant takes as its purpose the abolition of politics as such.

There are of course serious difficulties presented by the distinction between programmatic and formal politics, but consideration of these must be postponed until later; what is necessary at present is to look more closely at the most influential versions of inclusive and restrictive theories of ideology, in order to determine more exactly why none is satisfactory. We will begin with the restrictive ones, since it was in a restrictive sense that the concept of ideology was first developed.

RESTRICTIVE THEORIES OF IDEOLOGY

The restrictive theory of ideology effectively begins with Marx's doctrine, formulated in the 'Preface' to a *Contribution to the Critique of Political Economy*, that 'It is not the consciousness of men that determines their existence, but on the contrary, their social existence that determines their consciousness'. Whatever revelatory power that proposition might at first sight seem to possess, Marx's own explanation of what it really means left so much to be desired that he has been accused (by John Plamenatz) of doing no more than establish a 'tradition of careless usage' of the concept of ideology that has persisted down to the present day.[3] This careless usage is nowhere more clearly exemplified than in the distinction made by Marx between the material base which is the causal force behind social change and the ideological super-structure which is said to reflect it. Since Marx's own work sheds little light on this relationship, it will be best to concentrate instead upon the subsequent attempts to refine upon it made by thinkers with a deeper awareness of the theoretical difficulties involved.

The initial crudities of Marxist theory arose from what is now universally rejected as vulgar 'economism', by which is meant that

the early Marxist theory of the relation between ideas and their socioeconomic causes relied on a simplistic, quasi-mechanical concept of one-way causation. The refinements made during the past half-century have proceeded in two directions. On the one hand, they have consisted of conferring upon the political and cultural superstructure a degree of relative autonomy from direct determination by the economic base. On the other, they have consisted of conferring a limited causal efficacy upon the superstructure itself, instead of the purely passive role which was previously assigned to it. These revisions received their most influential expression in Althusser's theory of 'overdetermination'. Ironically, however, the revisions did at least as much to effect the final subversion of the traditional Marxist concept of ideology as to revivify it.

The subversion occurred because the revised doctrine entailed a form of structuralism which destroyed the very possibility of distinguishing clearly between the superstructure of 'consciousness' and the infrastructure of 'social existence'. The crucial link between Althusser's structuralism and traditional Marxism was his insistence that the superstructure of consciousness was determined *in the last instance* by the economic base. Unfortunately, Althusser was unable to explain why economic factors should be assigned this special position in the process of social change. He had no convincing reply when, for example, Maurice Godelier declared that the ultimate determining role of the 'last instance' might logically be performed just as well by non-economic elements, located in the religious or political sphere, as by the economic ones stressed by Althusser himself.[4]

Acutely aware of the intellectual chaos by which Marxism was threatened, a leading British Marxist scholar made a valiant attempt to salvage the distinction between base and superstructure. In *Karl Marx's Theory of History: A Defence*,[5] G. A. Cohen sought to provide 'a method of conceiving the economic structure which excludes from it the legal, moral, and political relationships of men'.[6] Cohen endeavoured to show in particular how the concept of property, which entails the legal concept of ownership and might therefore be seen as logically inseparable from the normative sphere of the ideological 'superstructure', can in fact be conceived in non-legal terms. This can be done, Cohen maintained, by a non-normative (or *rechtsfrei*) description of pro-

duction relationships which 'matches' the order of the legal relationships. In other words, Cohen resorts to a form of behaviourism according to which it is logically possible to translate *de jure* propositions about rights into *de facto* propositions about non-normative powers possessed by individuals without any loss of meaning. Unfortunately, Cohen's analysis has been unable to escape the charge of logical reductionism to which all behavioural translations of ethical concepts are exposed. A scholar who is himself sympathetic to Marxism, Steven Lukes, has eloquently identified the precise nature of Cohen's difficulty in this respect. Cohen's quest for a *rechtsfrei* translation is impossible, Lukes has argued, because the concepts embodied in norm-governed economic relationships cannot be identified independently of the norms which govern them. Thus in the case of contract, for example, 'the forms that define the practice of contracting enter into the description of the activities involved in that practice'.[7] In other words, 'The performance of contractual obligation is normally described in a vocabulary (paying wages, supplying services, buying and selling, honouring debts) which already presupposes the institution of contract and its regulatory norms'.[8] In the light of this breakdown of Cohen's sophisticated theory, Lukes concludes, the whole base–superstructure terminology should now be completely abandoned, as 'a dead, static, architectural metaphor, whose potential for illumination was never very great and which has for far too long cast nothing but shadows over Marxist theory and Marxist practice'.[9]

Failure to formulate a coherent theory of economic determinism has not, however, meant the end of the Marxist quest for a non-ideological vantage-point from which to develop a restrictive theory of ideology. Under the influence of philosophers like Husserl and Heidegger, such a vantage-point has been pursued in so-called Critical Theory, amongst whose proponents the most striking contemporary representative is Jürgen Habermas. So far as the theory of ideology is concerned, what is novel about Habermas's version of Critical Theory is the new logical basis that he has sought to provide for the concept of distortion. In Habermas's case, this logical basis initially emerges in the course of a wholesale rejection of Western philosophy as it has been practised during the past two thousand years. Ever since Plato, Habermas maintains, philosophers have tried to clarify the ultimate meaning of exist-

ence by trying to visualize the universe from a position of god-
like detachment. Different philosophers have of course described
this vantage-point in different ways, with metaphysics characteriz-
ing the ancient view, theology the medieval one, and positivism
predominating in the modern period; but these differences must
not conceal the fact that what thinkers as diverse as Plato and
Marx ultimately have in common is an ideal of disinterested
knowledge which is defined in terms that disconnect knowledge
from desire. It is against the yardstick provided by this abstract
knowledge that they have attempted to determine which of our
moral and political ideals are distorted.

For Habermas, by contrast, the ideal of absolutely disinterested
knowledge is absurd. It is absurd for the reason just indicated,
which was that that ideal attempts to make an impossible separation between knowledge, on the one hand, and human desires
or interests on the other. In fact, knowledge and desire are
inseparable since, if knowledge is to exist at all, it must always
be directed and ordered by an interest of some kind. The ideal
of absolute and disinterested knowledge, consequently, is a logical
impossibility, since it is a desire for undirected or unfocused
knowledge, which is no knowledge at all. The detail of Habermas's
account of the relationship between knowledge and interests is
not relevant here;[10] what matters is its general implication for the
theory of ideology. This is that the unbreakable link between
knowledge and interests makes an escape from ideology impossible, since all knowledge must inevitably be eternally distorted by
the interests which direct and order it. Distortion is built into
knowledge itself.

And yet, in spite of this, Habermas nevertheless frequently
writes in a way which appears to envisage at least the possibility
of an ultimate escape from ideology. Such a possibility emerges
most clearly in his vision of the ideal society as one based on
equal and voluntary participation by all its members in a process
of 'rational communication', the outcome of which would be a
perfect consensus embodied in a collective 'rational will'.[11] The
intellectual pedigree of the concept of rational will points back to
Rousseau's *volonté générale* and Kant's ideal of a kingdom whose
subjects are all ends in themselves rather than to the materialism
of Marxist doctrine; but the main point at present is that it enables
Habermas to reformulate the Marxist distinction between true

and false consciousness in terms of a distinction between rational 'insight' on the one hand, and ideological 'delusion' on the other.[12]

This reformulation is in terms of what Habermas terms a 'depth-hermeneutic', which is the method used by Critical Theory for unmasking 'remaining natural–historical traces of distorted communication which are still contained even within fundamental arguments and recognized legitimations.'[13] Rejecting positivist pretensions, the method nevertheless claims to be an objective one, to the extent that it is based upon the rationality (or 'regulating principle') immanent in all communication. The problem, however, is to determine what the nature of this immanent rationality is, and in particular to allay the suspicion that it opens up the Rousseauian prospect of 'forcing men to be free', should they be deemed to have failed to grasp what the 'true' rationality supposed to be immanent in their distorted communication entails. Anxious to strike a liberal note, Habermas insists that no individual or group may invoke hermeneutic theory as a device for identifying some particular interest with the rational needs of society at large, declaring that: 'There is no validation of depth-hermeneutical interpretation outside of the self-reflection of all participants that is successfully achieved in dialogue'.[14] This suggests that any appeal to immanent rationality must conform with the conscious self-interpretation of the participants in a dialogue, and that Habermas is therefore content to build his politics upon what individuals actually think and say they want; but that view is at odds with the hermeneutic conception of rationality as an impersonal, supra-individual logic immanent in all communication. Torn between the individual's 'actual will' and his impersonal 'real will' – to use Rousseau's language – Habermas ultimately follows Rousseau and opts for an appeal to the real will. Thus he maintains, for example, that hermeneutic 'insight' into ideological distortion must not 'paralyse the determination to take up the struggle against the stabilization of a nature-like social system [that is, one in which men are not fully conscious of the reality of domination] *over* the heads of its citizens, that is, at the price of – so be it! – old European human dignity'.[15]

The moral to be learnt from the hermeneutic revision of Marxism is not difficult to state. It is that the old foundation for a restrictive theory of ideology, which was the distinction between base and superstructure, has been discarded only to make room

for an ideal of perfectly rational communication which revives all the difficulties formerly associated with Rousseau's distinction between the 'actual' and the 'real' will, along with all the related problems of deciding what the relationship between them is and the lingering suspicion that, even if one is not actually forced to be free, one enjoys one's freedom only on sufferance from the possessors of hermeneutic insight.

The intellectual difficulties which have emerged in the course of Marxist attempts to formulate a restrictive theory of ideology are not in fact peculiar to the Marxist tradition, but re-emerge in an equivalent form in every restrictive theory. To examine alternative restrictive theories in detail would, however, add nothing of significance to what has gone before, since in each case the objection is the same: it is that every such theory involves an implicit claim to transcend ideology without making clear how this transcendence is to be achieved.

Nevertheless, one such theory deserves mention, mainly because it seems at first to be a notable exception to the claim that restrictive theories have generally presupposed the framework of a programmatic conception of politics – the liberal version developed by Hannah Arendt in *The Origins of Totalitarianism*.[16] Here, ideology is identified as a flight from the complexities and uncertainties of reality into a world of myth which provides the meaning of life, but only at the expense of gross oversimplification. The institutional embodiment of ideology is the totalitarian system of government which Arendt attributes to the rise of contemporary mass society. Mass society she defines as 'a society of men who, without a common world which would at once relate and separate them, either live in desperate lonely separation or are pressed together into a mass'.[17] The means by which Arendt believes totalitarian regimes insulate believers in the ideology from the pressure of reality are not relevant here, and the difficulties presented by her use of the concept of mass society to explain the historical origin of totalitarianism may also be passed over; what is important is her fundamental distinction between the real world, on the one hand, and a fictitious world of ideology on the other. The problem is that her criterion for determining what constitutes 'normal' or 'non-ideological' reality ultimately proves to be a highly idiosyncratic one, involving the arbitrary elevation of ancient Greek participatory politics into a paradigm for all genu-

inely human and authentically free action. Arendt's esteem for Greek experience is illuminating in many contexts, but it provides no philosophical foundation for her restriction of the concept of ideology to Nazism and Stalinism. In the last resort, this restrictive use owes more to liberal prejudice than to any clearly developed philosophical position. It might seem, nevertheless, that Arendt's version of restrictive theory is an important exception to the claim that restrictive theories at large have been dominated by a programmatic conception of politics. Rather than being about interests, aims, or purposes, her view of politics seems to be dominated by a latter-day Hellenism which stresses the intrinsic value of political participation and heroic action.

A moment's reflection, however, indicates that her view is nevertheless programmatic since politics, as she understands them, have a very definite aim – namely to permit the achievement of personal immortality through dramatic self-expression in the presence of one's peers. To this aim everything in the political sphere is subordinated. She has, for example, no sympathy for freedom as secured by the formal ideal of the rule of law; no sympathy for representation as a means of checking power and ensuring political accountability; and no sympathy, indeed, for institutions of any sort, insofar as their existence limits the scope for individual self-definition through action. What distinguishes Arendt's version of programmatic politics is its non-hedonistic, highly romantic character but, despite that, hers remains a programmatic ideal.

INCLUSIVE THEORIES OF IDEOLOGY

It was Karl Mannheim who first abandoned the search for a restrictive theory of ideology and insisted upon the need for an inclusive or, as he himself termed it, a 'total' one. As soon as *all* parties subject the ideas of their opponents to analysis in ideological terms, Mannheim wrote,[18] a new situation develops. Although the apparently most obvious interpretation of this new situation might be that it makes the concept of ideology worthless, that was not the conclusion that Mannheim himself drew. For him, the framework of universal relativism which now threatened to emerge provided the basis for a new discipline which he described

as the sociology of knowledge. Within this discipline, ideology
was transformed from a largely rhetorical device for debunking
political opponents 'into a method of research in social and intellectual history generally'. What excited Mannheim about the new
sociology of knowledge was that it appeared to provide a solution
to the great task of modern political science as formulated by Max
Weber – that is, the task of placing the study of politics on a truly
objective foundation by offering 'a specifically non-evaluative
investigation of ideas'.[19] Mannheim encountered an insuperable
difficulty, however, when he attempted to explain exactly what
he meant by a value-free study of ideas. This referred, he wrote,
to 'a political science which will not be merely a party science,
but a science of the whole'.[20] But how were individuals to escape
from what he called the inevitable 'narrowness' of their particular
viewpoint?[21] The answer he gave was that the investigator must
adopt a 'dynamic relationism'. This meant that 'instead of at once
taking a definite position, he will incorporate into his vision each
contradictory and conflicting element', so that his thought 'will be
flexible and dialectical, rather than rigid and dogmatic'.[22] Notoriously, Mannheim believed that 'free-floating' intellectuals who
had detached themselves from class perspectives might rise to this
'dynamic relationism'. Ultimately, however, it was impossible to
explain how all thought could be conditioned, whilst simultaneously holding that intellectuals could rise above the conditioning process.

After Mannheim, no further significant theoretical work on
ideology took place for several decades. The next step was taken
only after a radical change had occurred in the intellectual climate
of post-war political and social theory, namely the critique of
positivism (or scientism) mounted by such scholars as Kuhn,
Gadamer and Feyerabend.[23] The outcome of this critique was that
the natural science model of explanation which was vital for Marx,
and still important for Mannheim, now finally ceased to be available as a paradigm of objective or 'non-ideological' explanation.
Against this background, two works which attempted to advance
upon Mannheim's inclusive concept of ideology are of special
interest. One is John Plamenatz's study, *Ideology* (1970); the
other is Martin Seliger's *Ideology and Politics* (1975). Whilst both
scholars follow Mannheim in adopting a 'total' concept of ideology, both qualify in different ways Mannheim's belief in the possi-

bility of transcending the sociological conditioning process to which he considered all ideas to be subject.

In 1970, Plamenatz published a short but searching study, *Ideology*.[24] His starting-point was an inclusive definition of ideology as 'the ideas and attitudes characteristic of a group or community'.[25] The sociological element in this definition, it is apparent, has now been diluted to the point where it is almost non-existent: ideas are no longer 'determined' or 'conditioned' by social existence, but are merely 'characteristic' of it. Plamenatz is emphatic that 'we ought not, as social theorists sometimes do, speak of these ideological beliefs as if they were determined by the group's interests'. The most we can do is to assert a correlation, by using the term 'reflect' to indicate the relation between ideas and group interests.[26] The difficulty now, however, is to see why Plamenatz continues to use the term 'ideology' at all, since the removal of the idea of sociological conditioning, as well as that of distortion, seems to strip it of all explanatory value. He himself suggests that, at first sight, one possible reason for retaining it would seem to be the claim that, although ideas and beliefs are not conditioned by social existence, they are nevertheless in some way relative to the social situations or points of view of the people who have them. Plamenatz, however, emphatically rejects this redefinition of ideology in terms of epistemological relativism, on the ground that we are not in fact intellectually imprisoned by our own social situations in the way the relativist theory of ideology supposes. On the contrary, men who come from radically different civilizations and cultures can understand *why* they see things differently, and can even understand the other civilization better than their own, as is frequently the case with outstanding historians.[27] But in that case, the above-mentioned problem still remains acute: if Plamenatz rejects both the sociological theory of ideology and the relativist one, why does he need the concept at all? What is there left for the word to designate?

In order to deal with this problem, Plamenatz steers the concept of ideology in an entirely different direction from those pursued by Marxism and by Mannheim. The novel element in his analysis is his introduction of Sorel's theory of myth. By restating the theory of ideology with the aid of this concept, Plamenatz feels able, in particular, to explain the sense in which ideological thinking is in some way limited, yet is not conditioned or distorted.

Unlike Marxism, Sorel's theory does not require that ideas should be shown to derive ultimately from an 'objective' order of 'true interests', since Sorel rejects the whole materialist conception of human nature which inspires this view, replacing it instead with a view of man which stresses an almost existential ideal of self-assertion, or self-definition, as the mainspring of political action. Sorel's chief appeal for Plamenatz, however, is his theory of social and political myths as deriving their power, not from their truth, but from the emotional inspiration by which they justify and structure action.[28] In a similar way, Pareto regards 'derivations' not as a means of promoting interests, but as the medium which defines group identity itself, serving 'to bring and hold together people who have similar ambitions, impulses and attitudes'.[29] For both thinkers, the ideological dimension relates not to aims, desires, or interests, but (in the first instance, anyway) to the constitutive structures of social relations.

Plamenatz thus uses Sorel and Pareto to make two major revisions in the concept of ideology. On the one hand, the Marxist concept of the social conditioning of ideas by class or group 'interests' which Mannheim had retained is now dropped. On the other hand, the inclusive or 'total' concept of ideology is retained, but in a form far different from that which Mannheim gave to it. In the revised concept of ideology proposed by Plamenatz, *all* beliefs, attitudes and ideas may be treated as ideological, *but* only when seen in a certain perspective – they are not 'absolutely' or 'intrinsically' ideological. This perspective, as was just seen, is a functional one: what makes a set of beliefs 'ideological' is neither its truth nor falsity, nor its 'limited' or 'distorted' character, but the fact that it may be seen as serving 'to hold a group together or to justify its activities and to promote its interests'.[30]

It is the functional approach, then, that is the main feature of Plamenatz's work. Unfortunately, however, this revision of the theory of ideology presents a major difficulty, which is that functionalism is ethically indifferent; in other words, all ideologies are equally good provided that they hold a group together, justify its ideals, and promote its interests. Yet Plamenatz is reluctant to entertain this result. In order to reject it, however, he must be able to identify a perspective which has absolute validity and, for this, he needs a criterion which his functionalist approach cannot itself provide. But where is such a criterion to be found? Here,

Plamenatz falls back on a well-worn distinction between 'descriptive' and 'prescriptive' utterances. In the political context, he writes, this distinction becomes one between 'instruction' and 'indoctrination'.[31] Instruction is permissible, but indoctrination is what ideology is about, and is therefore unacceptable. The problem, of course, is how to distinguish between them.

Instruction, Plamenatz maintains, is in some sense factual, detached, and non-functional in approach, since it 'aims at preparing people for the roles, occupations and opportunities that fall to their lot or that they choose'. Indoctrination, by contrast, exploits the functional aspect of ideas and beliefs, since it aims 'at getting [people] to think or feel or act in ways that the teacher thinks good or favourable to this purpose'.[32] However, the trouble is that instruction and indoctrination cannot be clearly distinguished in this way, since whether we speak of instruction or indoctrination depends on whether we approve of the teacher's purpose; and this depends, in turn, upon whether we happen to be liberals, Marxists, and so on. Plamenatz attempts to escape from this dilemma by identifying the essence of ideology with the quality of one's motives: to have an ulterior motive of any sort, he maintains, is to lapse into ideology. Thus if anyone attempts, he writes, 'to get people to accept beliefs (or to seem to do so) for some p. .pose which he does not disclose to them, even one that they later come to approve, he is an exploiter of beliefs. . . . It is he having this ulterior motive that makes him an exploiter'.[33] But if that is so, then exploitation may, in some circumstances, become a most admirable thing since there are obviously many situations where failure to disclose a purpose might be considered wise and prudent. All that saves Plamenatz's theory of ideology from patently collapsing into the subjectivism opened up by the introduction of motives into this definition is the fact that the liberal prejudices which inspire his position command widespread sympathy, and are endowed with intrinsic or absolute value by Plamenatz. The fact that his own motives may be admirable must not, however, be allowed to conceal the ultimate theoretical flimsiness of his restatement of the case for an inclusive concept of ideology.

Plamenatz's main problem arose from the attempt to combine an inclusive definition of ideology, on the one hand, with a distinction between ideology and instruction on the other. In a sub-

sequent study, Martin Seliger took a decisive step when he embraced an unreservedly inclusive theory, based on the claim that all politics are necessarily and inescapably ideological. In the event, this approach is even less satisfactory than Plamenatz's. It is instructive, nevertheless, to consider precisely why it fails.

Seliger's starting-point in *Ideology and Politics* (1976) is the conviction that no previous thinker has consistently adopted a 'total' or 'inclusive' concept of ideology, with the result that incoherence has inevitably bedevilled all previous work on the subject. Even those thinkers who have overtly adopted an inclusive definition, he rightly observes, have ended by adding restrictive qualifications, in order to exempt their own (usually liberal or conservative) political prejudices from the charge of being ideological. The principal merit of his own work, Seliger claims, is that he is the first to go the whole hog and defend an unreservedly inclusive definition, based on the nature of political activity itself.

According to Seliger, 'in so far as politics implies the pursuit of policy – i.e. a somehow interconnected sequence of projects of action – there is no politics without ideology'. This, he maintains, 'must be so because there are no policies which are conceived and executed without some relations to ideals that embody moral judgements in favour of the justification, emendation or condemnation of a given order'.[34] In practice, however, Seliger does not consistently apply his own inclusive concept of ideology. At the end of his book, for example, he speaks of evading 'the fetters of ideology' in a way which implies that it is somehow possible to get beyond ideological politics.[35] Elsewhere he refers to the possibility of creating what he calls 'responsible' ideology, and seems to echo Mannheim's belief in the ability of intellectuals to create a value-free political doctrine when he writes that 'to neutralize the ideological elements in the scholar's interpretation of politics and thereby clear the way for the production of responsible ideology, one must distinguish tested and testable empirical claims from claims that are neither'.[36] Specifically, the task of intellectuals is to use philosophy and scientific theory to create 'an ideal or model' which will 'serve as the foundation of intellectual and moral appeal against the excess and shortcomings of ideology'. The sense in which such a model can transcend ideology, however, is hard to determine, since any attempt to apply it to politics must mean that it would immediately be 'transposed

by ideology so as to meet the requirements of action'.[37] No explanation is given about how this transposition is to be avoided: Seliger merely reasserts the possibility of an objective 'critique of ideology',[38] and simultaneously insists that 'strictly speaking, politics can become entirely unideological only if they become completely incoherent'.[39]

Seliger's work constitutes the most ambitious and sustained advocacy of the inclusive theory of ideology that has yet appeared. Nevertheless it has been seen that even he does not manage to present a coherent version of that position. He assumes, in particular, not only that a coherent style of politics is necessarily a programmatic one, but that all programmatic politics are *ipso facto* ideological. In general terms, Seliger's work suggests that the quest for an inclusive theory of ideology leads into a blind alley. In such a situation the only one way out is to retrace one's steps, which, in the present case, means returning to a restrictive theory. It has already been indicated that such a theory can only be satisfactory if it is based upon a formal concept of politics.

So far, however, the implications of a formal style of politics have only been touched upon in general terms. In order to shed more light upon those implications, it will be useful to consider them as they were developed in the course of the most thorough exploration of a formal interpretation of politics to be found in Western political theory. This occurs in the classical theory of civil society, as exemplified above all by Hobbes' *Leviathan*. By drawing on the classical ideal, it is possible to highlight the nature of formal politics, through a contrast with the programmatic conception of politics upon which ideology relies.

FORMAL AND PROGRAMMATIC POLITICS

The contrast between formal and programmatic politics has five related aspects. In the first place, the central concern of formal politics is with the concept of legitimacy, whereas the central concern of programmatic politics is with the effective implementation of an end or purpose. The term 'legitimacy' in this context requires a word of explanation because it is now the subject of a major confusion. Unfortunately, it is commonly used – in phrases like 'legitimation crisis' – to refer to a state of affairs

in which power is not being used in approved ways. But legitimacy does not refer to the ways in which power is used, because it does not refer to power at all but, rather, to the procedural conditions for distinguishing between authority and power. It is these conditions, then, that are the central concern of formal politics, in contrast to programmatic politics which are concerned solely with power.

It was in the course of developing the classical theory of civil society that Hobbes provided formal politics with a vocabulary for theorizing the difference between authority and power. The key concept in this vocabulary is not the idea of covenant or consent, but rather a distinction between 'natural' and 'artificial' personality which Hobbes took from Roman law, and to which he attached so much importance that he placed nearly the whole of the first sentence of Chapter 16 of the *Leviathan*, in which these concepts are defined, in italics for special emphasis. 'A Person', he wrote, is he 'whose words or actions are considered, either as his own, or as representing the words or actions of an other man, or any other thing to whom they are attributed, whether Truly or by Fiction.' When these words or actions are considered as his own, Hobbes continued, 'then he is called a *Naturall Person*. And when they are considered as representing the words and actions of an other, then is he a *Feigned* or *Artificial* person.' In Hobbes' language, Mrs Thatcher is a 'natural' person, whereas the prime minister is an 'artificial' person. It is clear that what Hobbes means by an artificial person is what we would call an office, and what he means by a natural person is the office-holder considered in a purely private capacity. The point behind the distinction is that a natural person, as such, can possess only power, not authority. But how is the artificial *persona*, which confers authority, created? It is at this secondary level that consent comes in, in the form of the covenant. The nature and function of this covenant, however, must not be misunderstood. On Hobbes' view, civil obligation to the sovereign arises entirely from the citizens' acknowledgement of his authority (that is, his artificial personality). Their obligation is therefore logically independent of their approval or disapproval of the sovereign's specific acts – although their consent is, of course, unlikely to last long in practice if the sovereign rules badly. In a formal style of politics, then, what unites citizens is neither an agreed end, nor personal approval of

the rule and his actions, but acknowledgement of the procedural considerations which confer authority. And such a style of politics cannot intelligibly be called ideological, since the concern with interests, aims and purposes which is the focal point of ideology is absent.

In programmatic politics, by contrast, authority can never be clearly distinguished from power. To make a clear theoretical distinction between authority and power is indeed irrelevant in programmatic politics, since the programmatic concern is solely with the expertise, technical competence, or other special qualities which are assumed to be vital for implementing the programmatic aim. In this respect Marxism, for example, is typical of programmatic politics at large in its complete indifference to the problem of legitimacy. The forms which are fundamental to legitimacy are dismissed, in Claus Offe's words, in order to stress 'state functions, their consequences and the contending interests within the state'.[40] To theorize the nature of authority is simply irrelevant, since it is assumed that there is one group of people – viz. the proletariat – whose special qualities entitle them to be entrusted with absolute power, in the naive faith that those qualities automatically guarantee that they will never abuse it.

The second difference between formal and programmatic politics is closely related to the first, being concerned with the two different attitudes towards power found in the two kinds of politics. In formal politics, the existence of power is regarded as inevitable and ineradicable, and the possibility that power will be abused is also regarded as an inevitable and ineradicable feature of political existence. In formal politics, power is therefore always an object of suspicion, regardless of who exercises it and of the excellence of the ends for which it is used. Great stress is consequently placed upon creating institutions whose purpose is not to ensure the efficient use of power, nor its location in some specific quarter, but to ensure instead that those who exercise it can always be called to account, regardless of who they are and how they use it. In programmatic politics, by contrast, there is never any suspicion of power simply as such, regardless of who exercises it, or for what ends; attention is focused, rather, on who is best qualified to exercise power, and for what purpose. A programmatic interpretation of politics therefore provides the essential precondition for the naive framework within which all ideological debates

about the nature of power takes place. Within this framework discussion is confined to creating an ideal community where power will either be eliminated from human existence altogether, or else, if that cannot be done, will at least be transferred into hands that will never be capable of abusing it. In democratic theory, this means the hands of the sovereign people; in socialist theory, those of the workers; in liberal theory, those of the middle class; and in fascist doctrine, those of the Führer or Duce.

The attitude towards power found in formal politics, then, cannot intelligibly be described as ideological since the primary concern there is neither with the aims or interests to be served by power, nor with the group or class which is to benefit from it; the primary concern, as expressed in the classical theory of the separation of powers, is with the limitation and scrutiny of power as such, to be secured above all by representative institutions and an independent judiciary. It follows that, just as the Marxist dismissal of the concept of authority in formal politics as a mask for the defence of capitalism is a travesty, so too is the dismissal of the concept of power in formal politics as nothing more than a restatement of the old *laissez-faire* ideal of the minimal state. The concern of formal politics is not with the minimal, but with the procedural, state.

The third feature of formal politics developed in classical political thought consists of the crucial significance assigned to the rule of law. This ideal is intimately related to the first, since not only is the 'artificial personality' of the sovereign constituted by legal rules, but the activity of ruling conducted by the sovereign itself also consists in making rules or laws. It is vital to stress that, in classical theory, laws are not commands or orders specifying particular actions; they are, rather, rules which specify *conditions* that must be observed by citizens in doing whatever actions may be chosen by the citizens themselves. Hobbes' description of the classical ideal of law as 'hedges' conveys this concept of law in a graphic image:

> For the use of laws, (which are but rules authorized), is . . . but to direct and keep them [the people] in such a motion as not to hurt themselves by their impetuous desires, rashness or indiscretion; as hedges are set, not to stop travellers, but to keep them in their way.[41]

It follows from the 'hedge-like' character of law in civil society

that the rule of law cannot intelligently be described as ideological, since it serves no substantive purpose, promotes no interests, and maintains no specific type of social organization. This, at least, is its ideal character, and it is in relation to this character, rather than to the distortion of the ideal which may of course occur in practice, that the formal conception of politics must be judged.

In programmatic politics, by contrast, the bond of society is not law but a common aim or purpose, which is characteristically expressed in administrative decrees, orders and commands, rather than in laws. Law may indeed play a part in programmatic politics, but when it does so it is only as one instrument amongst others for facilitating the pursuit of the common aim or purpose. Reduced in this way to an instrumental device, the rule of law loses the intrinsic moral value it possesses in formal politics where its existence is synonymous with liberty. Thus, whereas law in programmatic politics is in the service of a purpose and is therefore open to the charge of being ideological, the formal nature of law in classical politics makes the charge inappropriate.

The fourth characteristic of formal politics is a division between public and private life, or between state and society. This division is entailed by the fact that the formal conception of law is an essentially impersonal one, touching on the lives of men only in their public capacity as citizens, and not in their private relationships. In programmatic politics, by contrast, there is no distinction, in principle at least, between state and society; whatever sphere may be left to the individual is so only because intrusion upon it seems, for the time being, to be irrelevant to the implementation of the rulers' programme. This distinction between formal and programmatic politics may be restated in a way which makes its relevance for the theory of ideology more obvious. All ideological politics are marked by a simple division of the political arena into an in-group and an out-group. Thus in the democratic theory of the French revolutionaries, for example, the in-group was 'the people', which was defined as the community minus king, priests and aristocrats, who together constituted the out-group. In Marxist theory, the in-group is the proletariat and the out-group is the bourgeoisie. And so on. In formal politics, this ruinous polarization of the public realm is excluded, since the formal ideal of the impersonal rule of law is indifferent to the particularity of human interests and purposes upon which ideology seizes. Programmatic

politics, however, always contain the seeds of the ideological division of society into an in-group and out-group, since the impossibility of securing universal consent means that the political arena is automatically divided into those who support the aim or purpose of the rulers, on the one hand, and those who oppose it on the other. in the mild ethos of Western social democracies, where the programmatic purposes are prosperity, full employment, and 'social justice', the programmatic division of a community into supporters and opponents is easily passed over as of relatively little consequence, since the opponents generally suffer little more than the stigma of being regarded as 'uncaring', or socially irresponsible; but in more intransigent regimes, such as those which subscribe to Nazism or communism, the out-group does not escape so lightly. Putting a sharper point on the matter: the division between state and society which characterizes formal politics is not an indication of an underlying commitment to liberal ideology, but is a product of the absence of the programmatic political structure upon which ideology feeds.

The fifth and final difference between formal and programmatic politics involves two entirely different understandings of the meaning and place of rationality in political life. In formal politics, rationality has no content. It consists, that is, solely in the acknowledgement of formal procedures for the resolution of conflicts. From the standpoint of classical political thought, Hobbes sindicated the theory of rationality appropriate to formal politics when he dismissed the search for a non-existent 'right reason' which would be able to provide objective answers in cases of moral and political dispute. The possibility of an 'answer' only begins to emerge in such cases, Hobbes wrote, when men accept that:

> . . . as when there is a controversy in an account, the parties must by their own accord, set up, for right reason, the reason of some arbitrator, or judge, to whose sentence they will both stand, or their controversy must either come to blows, or be undecided, for want of a right reason constituted by nature; so it is also in all debates of what kind soever.[42]

The fact that the concept of rationality found in formal politics has no content means that it is easily travestied as a device for adopting a wholly uncritical attitude towards the existing social

order. Nevertheless, formal rationality does secure an equal respect for the diversity of human opinions about the good. In programmatic politics, by contrast, diversity as such is never respected, since those who define the programme generally under-pin their preferred ends with a substantive theory of rationality that privileges those ends, while downgrading the rival ends pro-posed by those who disagree with them. In its most dramatic form, the conception of rationality found in programmatic politics involves a radical distinction between appearance and reality which is quite alien to formal politics. There is indeed no logical necessity why such a distinction need be made, but in practice it tends to be, insofar as those who define the programme are prone to succumb to the conviction that they are upholding absolute truths of some kind. Like all true believers, they then dismiss any disagreement with their position as at best a form of misunder-standing or 'false consciousness', and at worst as wilful blindness. This belief in absolutes is expressed, in theoretical terms, as the claim to possess a 'deep' form of rationality, in the form of a scientific knowledge of the dialectical laws which govern historic change, for example, or in the racial basis of all civilization, and so on. Programmatic politics thus open the way to the most strik-ing feature of ideology, which is a wholesale rejection of the existing order, not on the ground that it causes actual human misery or dissatisfaction, but on the entirely *a priori* ground that it masks the 'true' nature of man, defined of course in terms of the ideology's own concept of rationality. In formal politics, by contrast, the fact that rationality has no content means that there is no place for any appeal to a supposedly 'deep' objective or scientific conception of rationality, since such a conception of rationality always claims to reveal a specific type of society, or a particular kind of human being, or a certain sort of policy, as the most rational.

BEYOND IDEOLOGY: THE POLITICAL AND THE IDEOLOGICAL

Far from being a fundamentally homogeneous activity, then, as theorizing about ideology has generally assumed, the concept of the political is susceptible to two entirely different interpretations.

And because ideology always presupposes a programmatic vision of what men are really like, and of how society should accordingly be organized, the only kind of politics which can intelligibly be described as ideological is programmatic politics. The precise relationship between formal and programmatic politics, however, is a matter which still requires brief consideration.

The relationship between formal and programmatic politics may initially be characterized by means of an important caveat. Although the two styles of politics may be considered in terms of two distinct ideal-types for purposes of analysis, as they have been above, it is not maintained that they can in practice exist in separation from one another. In reality, all politics have both a formal and a programmatic dimension. That is, every government will inevitably have some aims and purposes, no matter how profound its regard for forms; and every government, no matter how profound its programmatic commitment, will display some regard for forms. The different emphasis is, however, crucial. The basis of formal politics consists of the primary emphasis placed on legitimacy, the suspicion of power, the intrinsic value of the rule of law, a division between state and society, and acceptance of the diversity of human opinions about the good. Taken together, these formal concerns constitute the political embodiment of the moral injunction to treat men as ends and never as means. The basis of programmatic politics, by contrast, is concern for the creation of a particular kind of social order, or for the carrying out of particular policies. In the programmatic context, there may indeed be a concern for forms, but these have no intrinsic moral significance, being valued only insofar as they play an instrumental role in realizing the ends in question.

If what has just been said about the coexistence of two dimensions within the political arena is now related to Western liberal democratic states, it follows that the system of limited politics, which is their hallmark, is essentially a politics of tension. This tension, it should now be clear, is not merely the specific tension, diagnosed by de Tocqueville and J. S. Mill amongst others, between the liberal concern with freedom and democratic concern for equality; it is also the deeper tension between the formal and the programmatic dimensions of politics. So far as the preservation of the Western constitutional tradition is concerned, the tension between the formal and programmatic dimensions of the political

realm can never be resolved, but priority must always be given to the formal dimension, since it is this which provides the ultimate political framework for Western moral values. The pressure created by the programmatic pole of the tension upon the formal one becomes well-nigh irresistible, however, once programmatic politics are infused with the new theory of evil that is now the orthodoxy of radical and progressive thought. In the absence of that theory of evil, programmatic politics may remain a more or less piecemeal and pragmatic affair. In other words, the ideological propensity, which is always inherent in programmatic politics, remains latent. Once the new theory of evil infuses programmatic politics, however, all that remains is to observe the resultant varying degrees of ideological intransigence, together with the corresponding degrees of contempt thereby engendered for the forms which are the sole safeguard of limited politics. Unfortunately, the inclusive approach to ideology obscures the nature of the tension to which limited politics are exposed, while the various restrictive approaches generally adopted also fail to make it explicit. The aim of this chapter has been to modify the basis of the restrictive theory of ideology in a way which will facilitate recognition of the tension between the two dimensions of politics by confining the theory of ideology to programmatic politics, and exempting the formal dimension from the charge of being ideological, so long as the latter dimension is regarded as of primary and intrinsic value.

NOTES

1. Paul Ricoeur (ed. J. B. Thompson), *Hermeneutics and the Human Sciences* (Cambridge: Cambridge University Press, 1981), p. 224.
2. David Levy, 'Conservatism and Ideology', *The Salisbury Review*, vol. 3, no. 3 (April 1985) p. 15.
3. John Plamenatz, *Ideology* (London: Macmillan, 1970), p. 20.
4. Quoted by Jean-Marie Benoist, *The Structural Revolution* (London: Weidenfeld and Nicolson, 1978), p. 56.
5. G. A. Cohen, *Karl Marx's Theory of History: A Defence* (Oxford: Clarendon Press, 1978).
6. Quoted by Steven Lukes, 'Base and Superstructure' in D. Miller and L. Siedentop (eds), *The Nature of Political Theory* (Oxford: Oxford University Press, 1983).
7. Lukes, op. cit., p. 115.
8. Loc. cit.

9. Loc. cit.
10. See Jürgen Habermas, *Knowledge and Human Interests* (Oxford: Polity Press, 1987).
11. Jürgen Habermas, 'On the logic of legitimation problems' in *Legitimation Crisis* (London: Heinemann, 1976), p. 143.
12. Jürgen Habermas, 'The Hermeneutic Claim to Universality' in Michael T. Gibbons (ed.) *Interpreting Politics* (London: Blackwell, 1987), p. 197.
13. Loc. cit., p. 200.
14. Ibid., p. 201.
15. Habermas, 'On the logic of legitimation problems', op. cit., p. 143.
16. H. Arendt, *The Origins of Totalitarianism*, (1st edn.) (London: George Allen and Unwin, 1958).
17. H. Arendt, *Between Past and Future* (London, 1961), p. 90.
18. Karl Mannheim, *Ideology and Utopia* (New York: Harvester Press, 1936), p. 78.
19. Loc. cit.
20. Ibid., p. 149.
21. Ibid., p. 81.
22. Ibid., p. 99, fn. 32.
23. T. Kuhn, *The Structure of Scientific Revolution* (Chicago: University of Chicago Press, 1970); H-G. Gadamer, *Truth and Method* (New York: Seabury Press, 1976); P. Feyerabend, *Against Method* (London: New Left Bookclub, 1975).
24. Plamenatz, op. cit.
25. Ibid., p. 20.
26. Ibid., p. 98.
27. Ibid., p. 68.
28. Ibid., p. 25.
29. Ibid.
30. Ibid., p. 31.
31. Ibid., p. 134.
32. Ibid., p. 135.
33. Ibid., p. 135.
34. M. Seliger, *Ideology and Politics* (London: Allen & Unwin, 1976), p. 99.
35. Ibid., p. 277.
36. Ibid., p. 104.
37. Ibid., p. 117.
38. Ibid.
39. Ibid., pp. 103–4.
40. Claus Offe, *Contradictions of the Welfare State*, ed. J. Keane (London: Hutchinson, 1984), pp. 88–9.
41. T. Hobbes, *Leviathan* (Oxford: Blackwell, 1947), ch. 30, p. 268.
42. Hobbes, *Leviathan*, op. cit., ch. 5.

Index

213